D0852540

NEW PERSPECTIVES ON NARCISSISM

Number 13

Judith H. Gold, M.D., F.R.C.P.(C)
Series Editor

NEW PERSPECTIVES ON NARCISSISM

Edited by

ERIC M. PLAKUN, M.D.

Director of Admissions and member of the senior staff, Austen Riggs Center, Stockbridge; and Clinical Instructor in Psychiatry, Harvard Medical School, Cambridge, Massachusetts

1400 K Street, N.W.
Washington, DC 20005

Note: The authors have worked to ensure that all information in this book concerning drug dosages, schedules, and routes of administration is accurate as of the time of publication and consistent with standards set by the U.S. Food and Drug Administration and the general medical community. As medical research and practice advance, however, therapeutic standards may change. For this reason and because human and mechanical errors sometimes occur, we recommend that readers follow the advice of a physician who is directly involved in their care or the care of a member of their family.

Manufactured in the United States of America
First Edition

93 92 91 90 4 3 2 1

The paper used in this publication meets the minimum requirements of the American National Standard for Information Sciences—Permanence of Paper for Printed Library Materials, ANSI Z39.48-1984. ∞

Library of Congress Cataloging-in-Publication Data

New perspectives on narcissism/edited by Eric M. Plakun.—1st ed.
p. cm.—(Clinical practice; no. 13)
Includes bibliographical references.
ISBN 0-88048-178-1 (alk. paper)
1. Narcissism. 2. Borderline personality disorder.
3. Psychoanalysis. 4. Borderline personality disorder—Case studies. I. Plakun, Eric M., 1947– . II. Series.
[DNLM: 1. Narcissism. 2. Personality Disorders.
3. Personality Disorders—therapy—case studies. W1 CL767J no. 13/WM 460.5.E3 N532]
RC553.N36N48 1990
616.85′85—dc20
DNLM/DLC 89–17973
for Library of Congress CIP

Contents

Contributors

Joseph A. Flaherty, M.D.
Professor of Psychiatry, Department of Psychiatry, University of Illinois at Chicago

Otto F. Kernberg, M.D.
Associate Chairman and Medical Director, The New York Hospital–Cornell Medical Center, Westchester Division, White Plains; Professor of Psychiatry, Cornell University Medical College; and Training and Supervising Analyst, Columbia University Center for Psychoanalytic Training and Research, New York, New York

Paul H. Ornstein, M.D.
Professor of Psychiatry, University of Cincinnati, Department of Psychiatry; Co-Director, International Center for the Study of Psychoanalytic Self-Psychology; and Training and Supervising Analyst, Cincinnati Psychoanalytic Institute, Cincinnati, Ohio

Eric M. Plakun, M.D.
Director of Admissions and member of the senior staff, Austen Riggs Center, Stockbridge; and Clinical Instructor in Psychiatry, Harvard Medical School, Cambridge, Massachusetts

Judith A. Richman, Ph.D.
Associate Professor of Epidemiology in Psychiatry, Department of Psychiatry, University of Illinois at Chicago

James L. Sacksteder, M.D.
Associate Medical Director and member of the senior staff, Austen Riggs Center, Stockbridge; and Clinical Instructor in Psychiatry, Harvard Medical School, Cambridge, Massachusetts

Introduction

to the Clinical Practice Series

Over the years of its existence the series of monographs entitled *Clinical Insights* gradually became focused on providing current, factual, and theoretical material of interest to the clinician working outside of a hospital setting. To reflect this orientation, the name of the Series has been changed to *Clinical Practice.*

The Clinical Practice Series will provide readers with books that give the mental health clinician a practical clinical approach to a variety of psychiatric problems. These books will provide up-to-date literature reviews and emphasize the most recent treatment methods. Thus, the publications in the Series will interest clinicians working both in psychiatry and in the other mental health professions.

Each year a number of books will be published dealing with all aspects of clinical practice. In addition, from time to time when appropriate, the publications may be revised and updated. Thus, the Series will provide quick access to relevant and important areas of psychiatric practice. Some books in the Series will be authored by a person considered to be an expert in that particular area; others will be edited by such an expert who will also draw together other knowledgeable authors to produce a comprehensive overview of that topic.

Some of the books in the Clinical Practice Series will have their foundation in presentations at an annual meeting of the American Psychiatric Association. All will contain the most recently available information on the subjects discussed. Theoretical and scientific data will be applied to clinical situations, and case illustrations will be utilized in order to make the material even more relevant for the practitioner. Thus, the Clinical Practice Series should provide educational reading in a compact format especially written for the mental health clinician–psychiatrist.

Judith H. Gold, M.D., F.R.C.P.(C)
Series Editor,
Clinical Practice Series

Clinical Practice Series Titles

Treating Chronically Mentally Ill Women (#1)
Edited by Leona L. Bachrach, Ph.D., and Carol C. Nadelson, M.D.

Divorce as a Developmental Process (#2)
Edited by Judith H. Gold, M.D., F.R.C.P.(C)

Family Violence: Emerging Issues of a National Crisis (#3)
Edited by Leah J. Dickstein, M.D., and Carol C. Nadelson, M.D.

Anxiety and Depressive Disorders in the Medical Patient (#4)
By Leonard R. Derogatis, Ph.D., and Thomas N. Wise, M.D.

Anxiety: New Findings for the Clinician (#5)
Edited by Peter Roy-Byrne, M.D.

The Neuroleptic Malignant Syndrome and Related Conditions (#6)
By Arthur Lazarus, M.D., Stephan C. Mann, M.D., and Stanley N. Caroff, M.D.

Juvenile Homicide (#7)
Edited by Elissa P. Benedek, M.D., and Dewey G. Cornell, Ph.D.

Measuring Mental Illness: Psychometric Assessment for Clinicians (#8)
Edited by Scott Wetzler, Ph.D.

Family Involvement in Treatment of the Frail Elderly (#9)
Edited by Marion Zucker Goldstein, M.D.

Psychiatric Care of Migrants: A Clinical Guide (#10)
By Joseph J. Westermeyer, M.D., M.P.H., Ph.D.

Office Treatment of Schizophrenia (#11)
Edited by Mary V. Seeman, M.D., F.R.C.P.(C), and Stanley E. Greben, M.D., F.R.C.P.(C)

The Psychosocial Impact of Job Loss (#12)
By Nick Kates, M.B.B.S., F.R.C.P.(C), Barrie S. Greiff, M.D., and Duane Q. Hagen, M.D.

New Perspectives on Narcissism (#13)
Edited by Eric M. Plakun, M.D.

Introduction

The ancient Greeks tell us that Narcissus, having been wounded in an affair of the heart, fell in love with the reflection of his own image in a pool, remaining transfixed and immobile until through some magical transformation wrought by the gods he became a flower which blooms eternally as winter gives way to spring. If we assume that Narcissus's fate was a bad outcome, we are led to conclude that his fault lay in having fallen in love with the image of himself, sacrificing his ties to the world in favor of the relief from emotional pain offered by loving the one lover who never leaves. In the many succeeding centuries since the tale of Narcissus was first told in ancient Balkan amphitheaters, his fault has not been without replication, but it is only within the last century that his name has become associated with a kind of psychopathology.

It is not only patients to whom the term *narcissism* has been applied, though. We are told we live in an age of narcissism, and have been raising the "me" generation. Indeed, the mental health fields, psychiatry and psychoanalysis among them, have sometimes engaged in behavior not unlike Narcissus, gazing lovingly at his reflection with self-adoration brimming forth. Many feel that for too long psychoanalysis stood transfixed in omnipotent adoration of its own image, promising too much while delivering too little and having long forgotten its origins in neurology and the neurosciences, Freud's first love. Perhaps in the same way, empirical psychiatry and psychobiology have ignored the wisdom learned from listening to patients that has become part of psychoanalysis and have swung too far toward believing that a biogenic amine analysis of a synapse really explains something about human sadness or love.

My hope for this humble volume is that it will be a small step toward bridging the gulf between psychoanalytic conceptualizations and empirical psychiatry, with those interested in each subject finding something of value, but also an opportunity to learn something from the other's point of view. This may be an especially relevant approach to narcissistic personality disorder, which has long been included in psychoanalytic theory, but which has just begun to find its way into the psychiatric lexicon. This collaborative volume is not intended to become the definitive text on narcissism, but rather a compendium of the leading psychoanalytic conceptualizations of narcissistic personality disorder, with special emphasis on its relationship to borderline personality disorder, coupled with a presentation of empirical psychiatry's recent contributions. The volume has been written with general psychiatrists, psychologists, social workers, psychiatric residents, medical students, and other practitioners and trainees in mind.

Chapter 1 is a summary of psychoanalytic conceptualizations of narcissism from Freud to Kohut and Kernberg. In this chapter, Dr. Sacksteder has highlighted the contributions of Melanie Klein, Edith Jacobson, Michael Balint, W.R.D. Fairbairn, and others, searching for the common threads of the two leading but contrasting views of narcissism today—the ego psychology–object-relations perspective of Otto Kernberg and the self psychology viewpoint of Heinz Kohut, often associated today with the psychoanalytic writings of Paul and Anna Ornstein. Dr. Sacksteder's thoughtful summary is thorough, detailed, and in many ways an important contribution to the understanding of these disorders.

In Chapter 2, Drs. Richman and Flaherty offer the book's first empirical data, examining gender differences in the prevalence of narcissistic traits and summarizing some of the sociological literature of the late twentieth century's age of narcissism. Although the results are preliminary, this chapter raises interesting and exciting questions about the role of gender bias in psychiatric diagnosis.

In the next chapter, I have attempted a summary of the empirical data currently available on narcissistic personality disorder. Only since the introduction of DSM-III, with its uniform diagnostic criteria, and the availability of semistructured diagnostic interviews has it been practical to obtain longitudinal course and outcome data on narcissistic and borderline personality disorders. The picture of narcissistic personality disorder that emerges suggests that, at least in a subset of these patients whose difficulties led to inpatient treatment, there is evidence of its validity as a sometimes severe form of psychopathology comparable to borderline personality disorder but distinct from it in several ways.

In Chapter 4, we begin to move beyond numerical description of the longitudinal course and outcome of narcissistic and borderline personality disorders. Detailed case histories present the lives of four troubled individuals: two narcissistic personality disorder patients, one with a good and one with a poor long-term outcome, and two borderline personality disorder patients, one with a good and one with a poor outcome.

In the final two chapters of the book, the four case histories are discussed by two leading psychoanalysts who represent two contrasting points of view about the treatment of narcissistic personality disorders. Dr. Kernberg offers his ego psychology–object-relations perspective on the treatment of narcissism in Chapter 5. In Chapter 6, Dr. Ornstein offers a similar commentary from his viewpoint, most often associated with the work of the late Heinz Kohut and other self psychologists. It is hoped that the reader will benefit from this opportunity to understand the similarities and differences between these two leading psychoanalytic theories on the treatment of narcissistic personality disorder, using identical case material and within the context of empirical data already presented.

I would like to express my personal gratitude to my collaborators on this volume, without whose patient and diligent effort it could not have come into print. In addition, I would also like to thank Daniel Schwartz, M.D., Albert Rothenberg, M.D., and John Muller, Ph.D., of the Austen Riggs Center for their moral and material support and John Gunderson, M.D., for giving us the initial push in the direction of exploring narcissistic personality disorder. The patience and tolerance of my wife, Catherine, and my sons, Noah and Caleb, are also gratefully acknowledged. Special thanks are also owed to Barbara Conway, M.S., of the Yale University computer center for conducting statistical analyses and to my assistant, Barbara O'Neil, for her energy, devotion, and hard work.

Eric M. Plakun, M.D.

Chapter 1

Psychoanalytic Conceptualizations of Narcissism From Freud to Kernberg and Kohut

JAMES L. SACKSTEDER, M.D.

Editor's Note

By the time narcissistic personality disorder had been included as a diagnostic entity in DSM-III, the concept of narcissism already had a lengthy and important history in psychoanalysis. Used differently, narcissism can refer to an important line of development for every individual, a personality type, or a specific pathological personality disorder. Dr. Sacksteder's chapter begins this book with an analysis of the history of psychoanalytic conceptualizations of narcissism from Sigmund Freud to Heinz Kohut and Otto Kernberg. Along the way, he shows how such post-Freudian European analytic contributors as Klein, Fairbairn, and others contributed to the development of the concept of narcissism, foreshadowing the contrasting points of view espoused by Kernberg and Kohut in modern psychoanalytic conceptualizations of narcissism.

Chapter 1

Psychoanalytic Conceptualizations of Narcissism From Freud to Kernberg and Kohut

Psychoanalytic investigators beginning with Freud have contributed to psychiatry the progressive delineation of specific types of character pathology and the formulation of recommendations with regard to their treatment predicated on the genetic, dynamic, and structural characteristics defining them. The ongoing nature of this work and its importance for clinical practice are highlighted by comparing DSM-III (American Psychiatric Association 1980) with DSM-II (American Psychiatric Association 1968). DSM-III includes several personality disorders not included in DSM-II, and at least some of these "new" personality disorders were originally "discovered" and systematically investigated by psychoanalytic investigators. The category of narcissistic personality disorder is unquestionably one of these. However, despite the inclusion of narcissistic personality disorder in DSM-III, largely because of consensus about the descriptive characteristics of individuals with this disorder, there nonetheless remains intense disagreement and controversy about the dynamic, genetic, and structural characteristics of these individuals, and thus about their treatment.

Many investigators have made important contributions to clarifying narcissistic personality disorder as a subtype of character pathology. But to an unusual extent, the controversies with regard to the nature and treatment of narcissistic disorders can be captured by comparing and contrasting the work of two contemporary psychoanalysts: Otto Kernberg and the late Heinz Kohut.

Kernberg's highly original contributions to understanding the nature of normal and pathological narcissism are predicated on his unique synthesis and integration of contemporary ego psychology with aspects of various different object-relations theories, including most importantly those of Melanie Klein and W.R.D. Fairbairn.

Kohut, by contrast, after first attempting to integrate his findings into classical ego psychology theory, eventually repudiated ego psychology and founded a new "school" of psychoanalysis—self psychology. This new school, of course, was not created in a vacuum. It reflects aspects of ego psychological thought as well as the work of various object-relations theoreticians, including Sandor Ferenczi, Michael Balint, and W.R.D. Fairbairn. Fairbairn's work seems an especially important precursor to and influence on self psychology. Anticipating Kohut, Fairbairn came to repudiate classical drive theory after first embracing it, replacing it with an object-relations theory of personality that placed the establishment and maintenance of ongoing good relationships with others at the center of his theory of motivation, development, structure formation, and therapy.

Both Kernberg and Kohut have written extensively about working analytically with adults with narcissistic pathology. One point of agreement between them is with regard to the general descriptive characteristics of individuals with narcissistic personality disorders, but that is basically all they agree about. They have very different points of view about 1) the nature of normal and pathological narcissism; 2) the nature of development from normal infantile narcissism to mature, healthy forms of narcissism; 3) the relationship between pathological narcissism and normal infantile forms of narcissism; 4) the nature, origin, and development of the intrapsychic structures associated with normal and pathological narcissism; 5) the nature of the conflicts, varieties of anxiety, and defenses operative in the narcissistic personality disorders; 6) the relative contribution of intrapersonal and interpersonal factors in determining the nature of the anxieties, conflicts, defenses, and structures involved in normal and pathological narcissism; and 7) the treatment interventions required to achieve transformative, therapeutic change in individuals with narcissistic disorders.

It is my intent in this chapter to contribute to an understanding of how Kernberg and Kohut came to have their very different points of view by sketching out a brief history of the evolution of psychoanalytic thinking about the nature of normal and pathological narcissism. The current controversies can best be understood by placing them in a historical context, thereby clarifying the lines of development in psychoanalytic thinking about narcissism in different psychoanalytic schools. In this context, I will briefly review the work of Klein, Fairbairn, and members of the Hungarian school. I will attempt to underscore, in particular, the relationship of the views of Kernberg and Kohut to the views of those preceding and influencing them.

Contributions of Freud

Unquestionably, the first important psychoanalytic contributions with regard to normal and pathological narcissism were those made by Freud (1905, 1910, 1911, 1912–1913, 1914, 1916–1917). Unfortunately, all of these contributions occurred before Freud wrote the series of articles that transformed psychoanalysis from an "id psychology" to "ego psychology." Thus, they were written before he formulated his structural hypothesis of the mind as constituted by the id, the ego, and the superego, before he revised his theory of anxiety and outlined a developmental sequence of situations of anxiety, and before he had proposed aggression as a drive as important as the sexual drive in determining the course of development. It was not until the work of Hartmann and Jacobson that a more contemporary ego psychological approach to the study of narcissism was undertaken. Nevertheless, Freud's work has been enduringly influential, and aspects of it remain clinically relevant to this day.

Freud's contributions included

1. Introducing the term and the concept of narcissism to psychoanalysis and exploring its contribution to normal and pathological phenomena.
2. Establishing that narcissism has its own unique developmental line from infantile to mature forms that contributes importantly to intrapsychic structure formation.
3. Noting that narcissistic development can go awry with the consequence that specific forms of narcissistic psychopathology can develop.
4. Discovering that narcissism determines specific types of object relations involving "narcissistic" object choice (as opposed to "anaclitic" object choice) that are important in both normal and pathological development.
5. Exploring the contributions that the developmental line of narcissism makes to one's experience of oneself and of one's feelings about oneself—especially its contributions to self-regard and self-esteem regulation.

In this brief review of Freud's work, I can only touch on the phenomena that these contributions were based on.

Narcissism as a Determinant of Specific Forms of Psychopathology

As was typical of Freud, he discovered normal narcissism by first finding evidence for narcissism in pathological phenomena. Psychopathology that he felt was uniquely narcissistic included two types of sexual perversion and schizophrenia. It was his exploration of schizophrenic psychopathology that led Freud to hypothesize "primary narcissism" as a normal stage in psychosexual development but one to which there could be arrest and/or later regression which in turn led to serious psychopathology. This, in turn, led Freud to differentiate between "narcissistic neuroses" and "transference neuroses."

Freud felt that an individual formed relationships with others and with the world by cathecting mental representations of others and the world with libido. If that cathexis was withdrawn, others and the world quite literally were felt to cease to exist. Freud felt the primary pathological event in a schizophrenic break was the break with reality: "He [the schizophrenic] seems really to have withdrawn his libido from people and things in the external world, without replacing them by others in phantasy" (1914, p. 74). This explained for Freud the loss of interest in the world and in relating to others that had previously been very important to the schizophrenic person. Freud further postulated that the libido withdrawn from external reality was then shifted to the schizophrenic patient's "ego" and his or her body. This explained for him the symptoms of megalomania and hypochondriasis that often accompany a schizophrenic break.

It was Freud's belief that schizophrenic persons withdraw from object relationships in fantasy as well as in reality that led him to be so pessimistic about their ability to potentially profit from psychoanalysis. He felt these patients would be unable to form a transference to their therapist and without a transference there can be no psychoanalysis. Only much later was it demonstrated that schizophrenic patients do, in fact, develop potentially analyzable transferences, and thus, Freud's distinction between the narcissistic neuroses and the transference neuroses on this basis was not valid. Unfortunately, before this became clear, Freud's pessimism about the treatment of schizophrenia as a type of narcissistic disorder had been generalized by many therapists and influenced their judgment about the treatability of all narcissistic disorders. This, in turn, retarded interest in and enthusiasm for engaging in research into the nature and function of narcissistic disorders and their treatment.

Narcissism as a Determinant of Normal and Pathological Relationships With Others

Freud initially arrived at his concept of a specifically narcissistic type of object choice through analysis of the genetic and dynamic determinants of one type of male homosexual object choice.

> . . . future inverts, in the earliest years of their childhood, passed through a phase of very intense but short-lived fixation to a woman (usually their mother), . . . after leaving this behind, they identify themselves with a woman and take themselves as their sexual object. That is to say, they proceed from a narcissistic basis, and look for a young man who resembles themselves and whom they love as their mother loved them. (Freud 1905, p. 145)

> They are plainly seeking themselves as a love-object, and are exhibiting a type of object-choice which must be termed narcissistic. In this observation we have the strongest of the reasons which have led us to adopt the hypothesis of narcissism. (Freud 1914, p. 88)

Note, however, that this is an example par excellence of *secondary* narcissism, not *primary* narcissism. The homosexual in this relationship is not being himself as he loves someone who stands for himself, but rather takes the role of his mother and loves his lover as his mother once loved him, i.e., the homosexual enacts with his lover an eroticized infantile object relationship.

Freud's analysis of the determinants of this type of male homosexual object choice, as well as his investigations into the determinants of different types of autoerotic and heterosexual behavior, and into the nature of a mother's relationship to her children, led him to distinguish between two types of object choice operative in both normal and pathological development: an anaclitic, or attachment, type and a narcissistic type. Thus Freud felt that

> A person may love:
> 1) according to the narcissistic type
>   a) what he himself is (i.e., himself),
>   b) what he himself was,
>   c) what he himself would like to be,
>   d) someone who was once part of himself.
> 2) according to the anaclitic (attachment) type:
>   a) the woman who feeds him,
>   b) the man who protects him,
>
> and the succession of substitutes who take their place. (1914, p. 90)

Freud's clarification of a narcissistic basis for object choice has been especially important and influential.

Narcissism as a Normal Developmental Line Contributing to Acquisition of New Intrapsychic Structure

As mentioned, Freud moved from discovering and understanding the role of narcissism in pathological development to an attempt to understand its role in normal development in a manner that paralleled his earlier discovery of normal infantile sexual development from the analysis of neurotic disorders. Freud's concept of primary narcissism as a normal developmental stage was a theoretical extension of his theory of infantile psychosexual development based largely on his understanding of the psychopathology of schizophrenia and narcissistic perversions. Specifically, in schizophrenia, Freud felt there was a complete rupture in relationship to others and a return to a previously undetected state of primary narcissism in which only the schizophrenic patient's ego was cathected with libido. Freud felt this stage reflected a regression to a normal developmental stage in psychosexual development that had previously been undetected.

The new theory of normal psychosexual development advanced by Freud in his article "On Narcissism" (1914) begins with an autoerotic stage preceding both primary narcissism and the establishment of object relations. Freud (1914) remarked: "we are bound to suppose that a unity comparable to the ego cannot exist in the individual from the start; the ego has to be developed. The auto-erotic instincts, however, are there from the very first. . . ." (pp. 76–77).

The stage of primary narcissism follows the autoerotic stage and reflects the emergence of the ego and its cathexis by all of the individual's libido. Implicit in the theory of an autoerotic stage and then a stage of primary narcissism is the idea that the infant has no relationship to external objects during these periods. Freud commented, though, that after the ego has been cathected by the libido, some libido is subsequently "given off to objects," and thereby an individual comes to have relationships with others. At this point in his theorizing, Freud felt there was a finite amount of libido and that one either cathected one's ego or an other, and anytime an object relation was given up or lost the libido invested in that relationship would revert to the ego. On the other hand, anytime one invested in an other, one necessarily invested less in one's own ego.

Freud's concept of primary narcissism, in which all libido is directed to the ego and no relationship with others exists, and his theory that, to the extent one invests in others, investment in the ego decreases are both aspects of Freud's theories that have been repeatedly criticized. Many feel there is simply no convincing clinical evidence for these theoretical positions. Nonetheless, these ideas have remained powerfully influential for others. For example, many feel these ideas contributed to Margaret Mahler's postulation of an initial autistic phase of development during which the newborn infant is unrelated to the world (Mahler et al. 1975). Only recently have infant researchers like Daniel Stern seriously challenged this view (1985).

Most investigators who have criticized the evidence Freud offered to support his hypothesis of primary narcissism feel that, in retrospect, he offered examples of secondary narcissism. The concept of secondary narcissism, especially as augmented by an object-relations perspective, has proved to be enduringly clinically useful. *Secondary narcissism,* as most analysts use the term, refers to a secondary doing to or for oneself what was initially done to or for one by others. One does this for oneself because the other cannot or will not. Thus, it is the enactment of an object relationship with oneself enacting the role of both self and object.

Intimately related to the concept of narcissism as a developmental line is the concept that development from infantile to mature forms of narcissism contributes to intrapsychic structure formation. This aspect of Freud's work is extremely important as it touches on the processes involved in the acquisition of intrapsychic structure. That is, Freud began to address the questions of why and how children internalize aspects of their interpersonal relationships with others and thereby form enduring intrapsychic structures with varying functions that lead ultimately to individuals being able to rely on intrapsychic agencies to do what they initially required others to do for them. All of these issues are to this day controversial. Kernberg and Kohut are sharply divided in their own theories with regard to these issues, especially as they apply to individuals with narcissistic personality disorders.

Freud postulated that the developmental path from infantile to mature narcissism contributed importantly to the formation of the ego ideal as one important constituent of the superego:

> This ideal ego is now the target of the self-love which was enjoyed in childhood by the actual ego. The subject's narcissism makes its appearance displaced onto this new ideal ego, which, like the infantile ego, finds itself possessed of every perfection that is of value.... [An individual]... is not willing to forego the narcissistic perfection of his childhood; and when, as he grows up, he is disturbed by the admonitions of others and by the awakening of his own critical judgment, so that he can no longer retain that perfection, he seeks to recover it in the new

> form of an ego ideal. What he projects before him as his ideal is the substitute for the lost narcissism of his childhood in which he was his own ideal. (1914, p. 93–94)

As we shall see, the special relation of the ego ideal, its contents, and the nature of its functioning to vicissitudes in the developmental line of narcissism have subsequently been repeatedly affirmed and further explored by ego psychologists, including Kernberg and even Kohut before his break with ego psychology.

Concept That Narcissism Contributes Importantly to Self-esteem Regulation

Freud postulated three determinants of self-regard: 1) love for oneself, 2) being loved by others, and 3) success at achieving whatever ambitions and goals the ego ideal sets for oneself.

With regard to love for oneself, Freud (1914) noted "One part of self-regard is primary—the residue of infantile narcissism" (p. 100). With regard to being loved by others, Freud (1914) wrote: "As we have indicated, the aim and the satisfaction in a narcissistic object choice is to be loved. . . . being loved, having one's love returned, and possessing the loved object, raises [self-esteem]" (p. 98–99). And, finally, Freud (1914) noted: "Everything a person possesses or achieves, every remnant of the primitive feeling of omnipotence which his experience has confirmed, helps to increase his self-regard" (p. 98).

Freud's comments on the relationship of narcissism to self-esteem regulation are rather condensed and simply adumbrate the nature of their interconnectedness. It is this aspect of Freud's theorizing about narcissism that has been most expanded since Freud's time. For self psychologists, it has become absolutely central, as they hold that narcissistic object relations or, as they term them, self-selfobject relationships, have as their central function the establishment and maintenance of a cohesive sense of self associated with an ongoing sense of positive self-regard and self-esteem. Kohut's later writings break completely with Freud about the structures and processes underlying self-esteem regulation, but his early writings clearly reflect Freud's influence on his thinking. Kernberg, in contrast to Kohut, has remained closer to Freud, but his views about self-esteem regulation have been modified and expanded in light of post-Freudian clinical experience and theory contributed by other analytic schools.

Having completed my survey of Freud's contributions to the concept of narcissism, I will turn now to the contributions made by subsequent ego psychologists who have extended Freud's work, focusing on the work of Heinz Hartmann, Edith Jacobson, and Annie Reich.

Ego Psychological Contributions of Heinz Hartmann, Edith Jacobson, and Annie Reich

One problem ego psychologists had to address in the post-Freudian era was Freud's definition of narcissism as reflecting a libidinal attachment to the "ego." Again, it is important to remember that Freud wrote his most important papers on narcissism in his pre–ego psychology era. As Freud's editors noted in their introduction to his paper "On Narcissism" (1914),

> the meaning which Freud attached to "das Ich" (almost invariably translated by the "ego" in this Edition) underwent a gradual modification. At first he used the term without any great precision, as we might speak of the self; but in his latest writings he gave it a very much more definite and narrow meaning. The present paper (On Narcissism) occupies a transitional point in this development. (p. 71)

As we shall see, Hartmann's and Jacobson's clarification of the distinctions between the "ego," the "self," and "self-representations" were critical to furthering subsequent psychoanalytic explorations into the nature and function of normal and pathological narcissism.

I believe it was Heinz Hartmann who first argued for a redefinition of narcissism in terms of the concept of the "self."

He also spearheaded the effort to understand narcissism in terms of post-Freudian ego psychology:

> Many analysts do not find it altogether easy to define the place which the concept of narcissism holds in present analytic theory. This, I think, is mainly due to the fact that this concept has not been explicitly redefined in terms of Freud's later structural psychology. . . .
>
> The equivalence of narcissism and libidinal cathexes of the ego was and still is widely used in psychoanalytic literature, but in some passages Freud also refers to it as "cathexis of one's own person, of the body, or of the self." In analysis a clear distinction between the terms ego, self, and personality is not always made. But a differentiation of these concepts appears essential if we try to look consistently at the problems involved in the light of Freud's structural psychology. But actually, in using the term narcissism, two different sets of opposites often seem to be fused into one. The one refers to the self (one's own person) in contradistinction to the object, the second to the ego (as a psychic system) in contradistinction to other substructures of personality. However, the opposite of object cathexis is not ego cathexis but cathexis of one's own person, that is self-cathexis; in speaking of self-cathexis we do not imply whether this cathexis is situated in the id, in the ego, or in the superego. This formulation takes into account that we actually do find "narcissism" in all three psychic systems; but in all of these cases there is opposition to (and reciprocity with) object cathexis. It therefore will be clarifying if we define narcissism as the libidinal cathexis not of the ego but of the self. (It might also be useful to apply the term self-representation as opposed to object representation.) Often, in speaking of ego libido, what we do mean is not that this form of energy cathects the ego, but that it cathects one's own person rather than an object representation. Also in many cases where we are used to saying "libido has been withdrawn into the ego" or "object cathexis has been replaced by ego cathexis," what we actually should say is "withdrawal on the self" in the first, and either "by self-love" or "by a neutralized form of self-cathexis" in the second case. (Hartmann 1950, pp. 83–85)

Roy Schafer (1976) commented: "Hartmann legitimized the language of representations through his study of narcissism" (p. 77), and this "language of representations" has proved to be one of Hartmann's most important and enduring contributions to psychoanalysis. Subsequent investigations into the nature of narcissism were vastly facilitated by his clarification of the distinction between the "ego," the "self," and "self-representations." Kohut (1971), for example, referred to Hartmann's conceptual separation of the self from the ego as "a deceptively simple but pioneering and decisive advance in psychoanalytic metapsychology" (p. xiii). Hartmann also made pioneering contributions to exploring the processes involved in the gradual differentiation of the self from the object world. These investigations were extended by Edith Jacobson.

Jacobson systematically investigated "the normal developmental processes which build up the cathexes of the self and of the object world with libidinous, aggressive, and neutralized drive energy in the course of structural differentiation" (1954, p. 75). Jacobson began her extraordinarily wide-ranging article "The Self and the Object World" (1954) with an incisive critique of Freud's concepts of primary narcissism and primary masochism:

> We shall first concentrate on the meaning of Freud's concepts of primary narcissism and masochism.... the terms "narcissism" and "masochism" imply that in the primal state the drives are actually turned toward, i.e., aimed at discharge on, the self. To be sure the latter idea is the basis for Freud's conception of the death instinct.... I believe that these conceptions are quite puzzling and deserve more elucidation....
>
> Regarding the more advanced psychic organization *after* structural differentiation and establishment of object representations have taken place, we know, at least practically, fairly well what we mean by the turning of libido or aggression toward the self. People with narcissistic or masochistic sexual or social behavior document clearly enough the tendency to withdraw object cathexis and to make their own person the object either of love, admiration and libidinous gratification or of hate, depreciation and destruction. But what precisely is the meaning of narcissism and masochism in the primitive psychic organization *prior* to the child's discovery of his own self and of the object world? [italics added] (pp. 77–78)

Jacobson postulated that this earliest developmental stage is characterized by a totally undifferentiated state out of which the id, ego, and superego, a sense of self and of others, and the two drives all slowly differentiate and consolidate. Her postulate that *the drives* differentiate out of what is initially an undifferentiated type of psychic energy is a significant alteration in classical theory, one that Kernberg has followed and extended.

To return to the concept of primary narcissism, Jacobson feels this term cannot be applied to this early developmental stage. In a sense, her argument boils down to: Because there is no "self" at the start and because there are no differentiated drives at the start, one cannot speak of the initial state in terms of primary narcissism or primary masochism. One can speak of narcissism or masochism only after the drives have differentiated into the libidinal and the aggressive drives and only after some sense of self, differentiated from the object world, has been established. Only then can one speak sensibly of narcissism and masochism as reflecting self-directed love and hate. This is a line of theory development that Kernberg follows closely.

After advocating abandonment of the concepts of primary narcissism and primary masochism as defined by Freud, Jacobson turned her attention to the concept of secondary narcissism: "the development of secondary narcissism is a complex process closely linked up with the structural differentiation and the constitution of the system ego. . . ." (1954, p. 84). However, "secondary narcissism and masochism are not identical with the libidinous and aggressive cathexis of the system ego; it is the mental representations of the self, constituted in the course of ego formation, which become endowed with libido and aggression and force themselves as objects of love and hate on the Id" (1954, p. 85).

Thus, the concept of the "self" was, for Jacobson, absolutely critical to understanding narcissism. This was, however, still a new, unfamiliar, and somewhat hazy concept for most analysts. Among Jacobson's most important contributions to psychoanalysis were her efforts to achieve a more precise definition of the concept of the self and to clarify the nature of its origin, genetic development, and contribution to normal and pathological phenomena.

With regard to the origin and genetic development of the sense of self, Jacobson (1954) wrote:

> The concept of our self issues from two sources: first from a direct awareness of our inner experiences, of sensations, of emotional and of thought processes, and, second, from indirect self-perception and introspection; i.e., from the perception of our bodily and mental self as an object.
>
> ... the kernels of the early infantile self-images are the memory traces of pleasurable and unpleasurable sensations which under the influence of auto-erotic activities and of playful general body investigation become associated with body images.
>
> Like the primitive object images, our concept of the self is at first not a firm unit ... it is first fused and confused with the object images and is composed of a constantly changing series of self-images which reflect mainly the incessant fluctuations of the primitive mental state.
>
> ... with advancing psychosexual and ego development, with the maturation of physical abilities, of emotional and ideational processes and of reality testing, and with increasing capacity for perception, self-perception and introspection, the images become unified, organized, and integrated into more or less realistic concepts of the object world and of the self. (pp. 86–87)

The following is Jacobson's definition of a realistic concept of the "self":

> By a realistic concept of the self we mean one that mirrors correctly the state and the characteristics, the potentialities and abilities, the assets and the limits of our bodily and mental ego: on the one hand, of our appearance, our anatomy and our physiology; on the other hand, of our conscious and preconscious feelings and thoughts, wishes, impulses and attitudes, of our physical and mental activities.
>
> Whereas all of these single specific features will have corresponding psychic representations, a concept of their sum to-

tal, i.e., of the self as a differentiated but organized entity, will simultaneously develop. (p. 87)

Jacobson then proceeded to explore the interrelationships between the building up of self-representations and object representations and the development of ego functions and sublimations. She explored the advance from primitive preoedipal identifications to ego identifications and the development of the superego from its preoedipal precursors to its postoedipal consolidation. These discussions are wide ranging and touch on virtually every issue of importance in psychoanalytic theory. Especially significant in terms of conceptualizations with regard to narcissism are her discussions of development of the ego ideal and other aspects of superego formation, her thoughts on the processes and motivations underlying idealization and devaluation, shame, self-evaluation, self-esteem regulation, guilt, and the regulation of moods. There is virtually no aspect of the current controversy between Kernberg and Kohut that is not touched on in this wide-ranging article. As one might expect, given Kohut's repudiation of ego psychology, Kernberg's thinking is closer to Jacobson's than is Kohut's. However, it is also clear that Kohut was influenced by her ideas, especially in his early writings before repudiating ego psychology.

This section concludes with a discussion of Annie Reich's contributions to psychoanalytic explorations of narcissism. Two of her articles in particular bear careful reading. These are "Narcissistic Object Choice in Women" (1953) and "Pathologic Forms of Self-esteem Regulation" (1960). In these two important and influential articles, Reich focuses on pathologic forms of self-esteem regulation found in patients with different types of narcissistic pathology. She focuses especially on the dynamic of compensatory narcissistic self-inflation and compensatory narcissistic restitution via identification with a partner's greatness. The partner in these circumstances, however, is important only insofar as he or she serves as an externalized representative of the patient's ego ideal and thus represents a form of narcissistic object choice and relationship. In these articles, Reich argued persuasively to broaden the range of pathology that was related to primarily narcissistic issues. Through vivid clinical vignettes of patients ranging from neurotic to borderline states, Reich sketched out various stable subtypes of narcissistic pathology. Reich linked the narcissistic pathology of her patients to excessively repeated preoedipal and early genital traumas at the hands of characterologically disturbed parents. Explicitly following Edith Jacobson's theoretical formulations, Reich outlined the developmental consequences of these traumas in terms of their pathological effects on her patients' ego, superego, and especially ego-ideal formation and functioning. Her accounts of her therapeutic work with these individuals helped end the therapeutic nihilism previously often associated with narcissistic pathology by convincingly demonstrating the capacity of her patients to develop analyzable transferences.

A critical aspect of Reich's thinking was the central place of the fragility of her patients' sense of their "self" and the fragility of their ability to maintain self-esteem. In this context, Reich noted the way these patients manifested ongoing dependence on others perceived and experienced narcissistically, i.e., in terms of their ability to function as an externalized ego ideal for the maintenance of their sense of self, and of their self-esteem, and the ease with which the intrapsychic regulation of these functions was regressively lost and interpersonal regulation reinstated. Associated with this vulnerability were recurrent oscillations between primitive idealization and overvaluation of the self and/or of others, and corresponding reciprocal oscillations between intense self-contempt and self-devaluation and contempt and devaluation of others. Reich also discussed the specific types of anxiety, particularly annihilation anxiety, severe separation anxiety, and hypochondriacal anxiety; the vulnerability to depression; the shame propensity; and the propensity to states of intense self-consciousness to which these individuals were liable, as well as their tendencies to rage reactions and to regressive sexualized acting out, as secondary consequences of traumatic disruptions in relationships determining their sense of self and self-worth. The important implications of Reich's work for the work of Kernberg and Kohut are obvious.

Kleinian Contributions to the Concept of Narcissism

The work of Melanie Klein and her followers is little known in the United States. Otto Kernberg has become Klein's principal interpreter in the United States. Her influence on his thinking has been profound. One of Kernberg's gifts has been a capacity to extract from the work of Klein and her followers what is clinically and theoretically valuable while remaining critical of aspects of Kleinian theory for which he finds no good clinical evidence. I will now briefly review those aspects of her work that have most influenced Kernberg's views of the genetic, dynamic, and structural features of both narcissistic and borderline personality disorders.

Hanna Segal (1973), one of Klein's most articulate proponents, divides Klein's contributions to psychoanalytic theory and technique into three phases. The first occurred from 1921 until 1932, during which time Klein laid down the foundations of child analysis. The second phase was from 1934 to 1940, during which time Klein formulated the concept of the depressive position and investigated manic defense mechanisms. The third phase was from 1946 to 1957, during which time Klein formulated the concept of the paranoid/schizoid position and explored the nature of the conflicts, anxieties, and object relations characterizing this stage of development.

During the first phase of her work, Klein (1923, 1926, 1928, 1929, 1930) developed the play technique of child analysis, discovering that play was the child's equivalent of free association and quickly coming to understand that a child can symbolically represent anxieties, conflicts, and defenses in the fantasies that underlie play.

She found abundant confirmatory evidence for Freud's theory of infantile sexuality and for the hypothesis that unresolved conflicts associated with different stages of psychosexual development determine different types of neurotic psychopathology. She quickly learned, though, that oedipal desires, conflicts, and anxieties occurred much earlier than Freud had hypothesized and that preoedipal developments, especially weaning and its consequences, played a central role in determining the form and intensity of oedipal conflict, especially the extent to which it was overlaid with aggression. Klein was one of the first analysts to investigate thoroughly the effects of aggression on development, coming to feel that conflicts over aggression had greater impact on development than conflicts over sexual desires, especially early in life.

Klein also learned from the play of her child patients that the superego was operative much earlier than described in classical theory and that it had both fantastically idealized and very primitively punitive characteristics. She found that the savage oral, anal, and urethral characteristics of her patients' superegos were very important determinants of serious psychopathology.

Klein found that intense oedipal conflict often resulted in her patients regressing to forms of relationship with their parents, and with her in the transference relationship, that reinstated her patients' earlier relationship to their parents as part objects, split into all-good and all-bad characteristics. As part of this process, she also discovered the defense mechanisms that predated the establishment of repression as the primary mechanism of defense. These included, most importantly, introjection, projection, projective identification, denial, and splitting.

Klein discovered that anxiety generated in relationships with external objects led her child patients to introject aspects of their external objects in fantastically distorted forms, and, through this process, the child built up a complex world of internalized objects. These internal objects were experienced by the child as quite concrete and real and as having ongoing relationships with one another, with external objects, and with the child. Klein learned that there was a complex interplay between the child's conscious and unconscious fantasies and actual experiences and that only gradually did a child develop a realistic view of, and relation to, his or her internal and external objects. For children with serious psychopathology, this process goes horribly awry.

Klein felt some internal objects were depersonified and incorporated into ego and superego structure. Thus, she advanced a theory of intrapsychic structure formation predicated on the depersonification, synthesis, and integration of aspects of internalized object relationships. It was because of her theory of an internal object world and of intrapsychic structures derived from internalized object relations that she came to be referred to as an object-relations theorist.

Those aspects of Klein's early formulations found useful by Kernberg (1980) are 1) her observations on the primitive defense mechanisms predating repression, especially the operations of splitting, introjection, projection, and projective identification; 2) her description of the primitive fears and fantasies characterizing the life of troubled children and adults; 3) her focus on the condensation of oedipal with preoedipal conflicts and the overriding influence of aggression on libidinal conflicts for deeply troubled patients; 4) her formulation of primitive object relationships, especially the activation of need-gratifying, split, part-object relationships in the transference, all of which Kernberg sees as factors operative in individuals with narcissistic and borderline personality disorders.

The second phase of Klein's work involved investigation of manic-depressive psychosis and its implications for development (1935, 1937, 1940), a study that led her to de-emphasize and then abandon the psychosexual theory of development and to substitute for it a theory of development in terms of "positions."

Klein postulated that there are two developmental positions, the paranoid/schizoid and the depressive. The paranoid/schizoid position is operative from birth to about 6 months of age. It is characterized by 1) need-gratifying, split, part-object relations; 2) annihilation anxiety; and 3) the use of the defense mechanisms of splitting, projection, introjection, denial, and projective identification.

Beginning around 6 months of age, the paranoid/schizoid position gradually shifts to the depressive position, which is characterized by 1) ambivalent, whole-object relations; 2) all situations of anxiety other than annihilation anxiety; and 3) the use of the defense mechanism of repression and other higher-level defenses, e.g., reaction formation, intellectualization, and isolation. The depressive position, however, never fully supercedes the paranoid/schizoid position. In the course of development, these two developmental positions are internalized and become dialectically related intrapsychic constellations operative throughout life. Thus, whenever an individual comes into conflict, he or she experiences that conflict in terms of the anxiety, defenses, and object-relation patterns that characterize either the paranoid/schizoid position or the depressive position.

Klein felt manic-depressive psychosis revived the conflicts and anxieties that characterized the depressive position. An individual who has achieved the depressive position in development has ambivalent whole-object relations with others whom he or she has come to love, value, and depend on. Actual or threatened separations from and/or loss of relatedness to these individuals are sources of sadness, grief, mourning, pining, anxiety, and conflict. Conflict in this position concerns the acceptability of expressions of anger and hate evoked when someone loved leaves, disappoints, frustrates, or deprives an individual. The primary anxiety is that anger and hate will become overwhelming and lead to total destruction of the loved object or the loving relationship. This motivates the individual to repress anger, hate, and all other aspects of relatedness to the loved object that would threaten the continuity of the relationship. In this context, individuals come to experience guilt and concern when their anger does, in fact, hurt someone they love, and these affects motivate them to undo the effects of aggression through acts of reparation.

If depressive-position conflicts become too intense, however, manic defenses are operationalized. These defenses are of particular importance in the understanding of narcissistic psychopathology. A manic relationship to objects is characterized by a triad of feelings: control, triumph, and contempt, which are directly related to and defensive against depressive feelings associated with valuing the object, depending on it, fearing its loss, and guilt. Thus, when manic defenses are operationalized, dependency is denied or reversed, ambivalence is lost, and splitting is reinstituted with the result that objects are again perceived as all good or all bad. When a good object becomes bad because frustrating, it is totally devalued, rage and contempt are justified, and one is entitled to attack and destroy them without feeling concern, sorrow, or guilt, because the good qualities are split off and denied. There is no grief associated with the loss of the now all-bad object and no concern about providing for oneself what the lost relationship once provided. Individuals experience themselves as omnipotently self-sufficient and/or as capable of effortlessly providing for themselves all that they need from others who are again experienced on a need-gratifying, split, part-object relationship basis. Kernberg has demonstrated how these features are operationalized in individuals with narcissistic personality disorders. He has also specified ways in which aspects of the paranoid/schizoid position are operationalized in individuals with narcissistic disorders. Exploration of these features characterized the final phase of Klein's contributions to psychoanalysis (Klein 1946, 1957).

In addition to clarifying the nature of the anxiety, the defenses, and the object relations operative in this developmental position, Klein also discovered the important role of envy in normal and pathological development. Klein carefully distinguished between envy and jealousy. Jealousy is operative in the Kleinian schema in the depressive position. It is based on love and aims at the possession of the loved object and the removal of the rival; thus it pertains to triangular relationships and therefore to the time of development when whole objects are clearly recognized and differentiated from one another. Envy, on the other hand, was according to Klein an earlier emotion, one of the most primitive and fundamental. She felt it was first experienced in relation to part objects but subsequently persisted in whole-object relationships. Envy's aim is to be as good as a good object. If this is felt to be impossible, then envy's aim is to spoil the goodness of the good object in order to remove the painfully envious feelings. It is this spoiling aspect of envy that is so destructive to development as it results in a good object becoming bad precisely because it is good. This is in contrast to a good object becoming bad because it has become frustrating or depriving.

Klein felt envy was a direct manifestation of the death instinct. She felt that if early envy was intense it interfered with development from the paranoid/schizoid position, and especially with the process of splitting objects into good and bad part objects, as now good objects can become bad, and thus all objects can become bad and persecutory. If good objects cannot be preserved, introjected, and identified with, obviously all subsequent development is interfered with.

Aspects of Klein's work on the paranoid/schizoid position that Kernberg applies to the understanding of the genetic, dynamic, and structural features of individuals with narcissistic character disorders include 1) the enormous conflict involved in valuing and depending on others; 2) dread of experiences of helplessness, needfulness, and of being vulnerable, especially with regard to dependency needs; 3) the experience of intense paranoid and persecutory anxiety, and the operationalization of splitting, projection, projective identification, and primitive idealization to cope with these anxieties; 4) the persistence of a style of relating to others on a need-gratifying, split, part-object relationship basis; and 5) the destructive role envy plays in the lives of these individuals.

A Kleinian whose work Kernberg found particularly helpful in developing his own views with regard to narcissistic psychopathology is Herbert Rosenfeld. In fact, Kernberg feels Rosenfeld developed "the first contemporary theory of pathological narcissism" (Kernberg 1984, p. 179) in a series of articles published between 1964 and 1978 in which Rosenfeld detailed the structural characteristics of narcissistic personalities and their transference developments in the course of psychoanalysis from a Kleinian perspective. Kernberg integrated many of Rosenfeld's clinical observations, though not his metapsychological explanations of them, into his own work.

Contributions of the Hungarian School

In this section, I explore the contributions made by members of the "Hungarian School of Psychoanalysis" to the concept of "deficit disorders" as originating in faulty parenting, relating their findings to self psychology. I believe theories originating in the Hungarian school were as important and influential for self psychologists as the work of Klein was for Kernberg. I will focus primarily on the work of Michael Balint because of the many ways his work appears to have anticipated, adumbrated, and contributed to self psychology, but I will relate his work to the preceding and parallel work of his fellow Hungarian analysts, Sandor Ferenczi, Imre Hermann, and Alice Balint.

It was no doubt Ferenczi who imparted to members of the Hungarian Psychoanalytic Society a special interest in investigating pathological parenting as the etiologically significant factor leading to the character problems found in treatment-resistant patients. Ferenczi was a therapeutic zealot to whom patients who had failed in analysis with others were frequently referred. Thus, he became the "analyst of last resort" for numerous patients.

Ferenczi often experimented with modifications of psychoanalytic technique in his efforts to help his deeply troubled patients (Ferenczi 1920, 1929a, 1931). A part of this work involved pioneering explorations of the countertransference contributions on the part of the analyst to treatment impasses. Ferenczi became convinced his patients reexperienced in their relationship to him early infantile traumas that were at the root of their disorders and that he unwittingly played a part in his patients' retraumatization in the analytic relationship. Although well intentioned, some of Ferenczi's experiments were ill-advised and got him into trouble. He barely managed to avoid a break with Freud over them. Nonetheless, he anticipated many of the modifications in technique later advocated by self psychologists.

Another source of controversy and friction with Freud was Ferenczi's increasing conviction of the importance of trauma in the genesis of severe psychopathology (Ferenczi 1927, 1929b, 1933). He stressed, as Freud had not since abandoning his seduction theory of neurosis, that many individuals are in fact traumatized by bad parenting. Ferenczi came to feel that this was the primary etiological factor operative in treatment-resistant disorders, as opposed to conflict over sexual and aggressive drive expression. Hence he (1933) wrote of his

> stress on the traumatic factors in the pathogenesis of the neuroses which had been unjustly neglected in recent years. Insufficiently deep exploration of the exogenous factor leads to the danger of resorting prematurely to explanations—often too facile explanations—in terms of "disposition" and "constitution." (p. 156)

This is a point of view with which self psychologists would agree.

Another important influence on Balint was the work of Imre Hermann, an analyst with an extraordinarily wide range of interests. Unfortunately, most of his writings are unknown to the English-speaking world because they have not been translated. Hermann's best-known article in English is probably "Clinging—Going-in-Search: A Contrasting Pair of Instincts and Their Relation to Sadism and Masochism," originally published in 1936. In this article, Hermann postulates a state of "dual-union" between mother and child as the first postnatal state from which a child subsequently separates and differentiates. "What we see in the infant's urge to cling to the mother's body is the instinctual feeling he has that only together with her is he whole. Child and mother are said to be fused, after birth, in a dual-unit" (Hermann 1936, p. 7). Hermann's notion of the "dual-union" enduringly influenced Balint's work and is clearly reflected in self psychology theory.

In the 1930s, Balint wrote a series of articles (1932, 1935, 1937) that anticipated, adumbrated, and contributed to many ideas later incorporated into self psychology. I am going to focus on Balint's concepts of "primary love," "the basic fault," and the "new beginning" phase of treatment with its important differentiation between "benign" as opposed to "malignant" regression.

Writing in the 1930s, Balint made the then-startling and revolutionary assertion that there was no such thing as primary narcissism: "The earliest phase of extra-uterine existence is not narcissistic: it is directed toward objects" (1937, p. 98). As he expressed it later: "The individual is born in a state of intense relatedness to his environment . . . self and environment are harmoniously "mixed up" . . . they interpenetrate each other" (1968, p. 67). This archaic primitive object relationship was called by him "primary love." It is a "mother-child unit" coexisting (ideally) in a harmonious interpenetrating mix-up. No one looking at the mother-infant pair can or even tries to say where, from the infant's point of view, one ends and the other begins. Alice Balint, in 1939, made the point that what was true for the infant was also true for the mother, that is, the mother is receiver and giver to the same extent as her child. She experiences her child as part of herself in the same way that the child regards the mother as part of itself.

The infant's developmental task is to gradually develop out of this harmonious interpenetrating mix-up. The detachment from the mother involves a dissolution of the primitive attachment and reconciliation with the fact that the mother is a separate being with her own interests. All later object relations can be traced back to this primary object relationship, and, from Balint's point of view, the ultimate aim of human striving is to reestablish an all-embracing harmony with one's environment.

Balint's concept of primary love with its assertion of an

object relation present from birth has had far-reaching ramifications, especially because, as early as 1935, Balint also explicitly separated the original object relation and the subsequent line of development of object relations from Freud's theory of psychosexual drive development.

Balint felt some of the hypothesized phases in psychosexual development were only artifacts. As corollaries to this line of thought, Balint asserted that all narcissism was secondary, as were autoeroticism and hate. These phenomena were disintegration products, reactions to and/or adaptations to frustrations arising in the primary object relationship. This is a view, especially with regard to hate, with which Kohut would agree but Kernberg would disagree.

The implications of the concept of a progressive differentiation of an infant from a mother-infant unit for Mahler's work are obvious, but these are not the current focus. Instead, echoes of this concept in Kohut's theory of the differentiation of a cohesive self from an originally undifferentiated self-selfobject matrix will be discussed. Kohut seems to conceptualize an original interpenetrating mix-up between the child and the adults who constitute the child's self-selfobject developmental matrix.

Resemblances between Kohut's and Balint's work are even stronger when descriptions of the characteristics of the object relation in the state of primary love and of self-selfobject relationships are compared. The form of object relating and of intrapsychic organization in the state of primary love is subsumed by Balint under the heading of functioning at the level of the "basic fault," one of the three areas of the mind and the level operative at the beginning of mental life (Balint 1968). It is the intrapsychic corellate of the interpersonal relationship called by him "primary object love." The two other areas of the mind develop from the basic fault: the area of the oedipal complex develops out of this level as a more complex differentiation of the basic fault; the area of creation evolves as a simplification of the basic fault.

In addition to being the foundation for the two other areas

of the mind, the basic fault is also the precursor of all later object relations, and as long as it is active, it determines the form of object relationship available and possible. At this level, all events belong exclusively to a two-person relationship. The nature of this relationship has unique, clear, definite, recognizable characteristics. Only one of the two partners can have needs and wishes. The other partner, though powerful, is important only insofar as he or she is gratifying or frustrating and is not to have needs and wishes of his or her own. Control over the other is expected to be absolute. Ongoing gratification is hard to recognize as it is associated only with a quiet, tranquil sense of well-being. Frustration, on the other hand, evokes stormy protest. If it is too intense or continues for too long, frustration can lead to anger, rage, paranoid fear of retaliation, despair and depression, or to flight into a hypochondriacal, autoerotic, narcissistic state.

Balint compared the relationship to a primary object with the relationship to air. One needs air to live and simply expects it to be there as needed. One expects to be able to breathe freely, unself-consciously, and heedlessly. One does not take into account the air's feelings about being breathed; one takes it for granted and expects to have unlimited use of it. An individual operating at the level of the basic fault has this same type of relationship to the people who constitute his interpersonal matrix. The nature of the dynamic force operating at this level is not that of a conflict; it is in the nature of an ongoing needfulness for an environmental provision to the individual of what he cannot yet provide for himself. The individual feels it is his due to receive what he needs automatically, without asking for it, and without any question of earning it, deserving it, or being grateful for it.

These same characteristics of object relatedness are echoed almost verbatim by Kohut and other self psychologists as characteristics of self-selfobject relationships, especially early in development and as a characteristic of the ongoing object relatedness of primitively organized individuals with primary disorders of the self, and as characteristics of the transference in the treatment of individuals with a primary disorder of the self.

Striking parallels between Balint's work and subsequent theory by self psychologists are also to be noted in their respective views about the origin and nature of character pathology. For Balint, progressive healthy separation and differentiation from the state of primary love depends on good-enough active environmental adaptation to the infant's needs. If there is a failure in the earliest mothering, one in which there is not adequate input of love (i.e., interest, affection, and enjoyment at the personal level) and/or one in which there are repeated instances of ill-timed, over- or understimulation of the child, then there is a traumatic disruption of the harmonious interpenetrating mix-up, and a developmental arrest occurs at the level of the basic fault. Sufficient lack of fit between the child and the people who constitute his or her environment results in a developmental arrest that leaves the child with a structural defect or deficit carried into adulthood, where it determines character and the characteristics of object relationships. An important theoretical point to note here is Balint's assertion that it is the conscious and unconscious character of the parents and their actual behavior that determines the issue here, and not, at least initially, vicissitudes and conflicts in the child's libidinal and aggressive drive development that are etiologically significant. The extent of distortion in development is directly proportional to the degree of failure of care. Again, this is a theoretical point of view with which Kohutian self psychologists appear to agree and which they incorporate in their description of "mirror-hungry," "ideal-hungry," "merger-hungry," and "contact-shunning" personalities.

Further parallels between Balint's work and the work of self psychologists are found in the similarity between the recommendations with regard to modifications in therapeutic technique for treatment of individuals with primary disorders of the self proposed by self psychologists and the modifications in therapeutic technique first proposed by Balint in 1932 for treatment of individuals later defined as having basic-fault pathology. Balint spoke of the necessity for the analyst to create conditions within the analytic situation allowing the patient to regress to the level of object relating at which the developmental arrest occurred. He felt the patient had to become free to recover awareness of, and to express directly, long-repressed, archaic, but developmentally normal desires. Only if the patient could get back to the point of arrest was there any hope that "a new beginning" toward healthier maturation could begin. To achieve this, the analyst's role in certain periods of the "new beginning" requires him to take on, in many respects, the characteristics of a primary substance or object and in this sense to be gratifying. That is, the therapist must be there, must be pliable, must not offer too much resistance, and must be indestructible. The therapist must allow the patient to exist with him or her in a sort of harmonious interpenetrating mix-up. All this means consent, participation, and involvement but not necessarily action, only understanding and tolerance.

It is in this context that Balint made his distinction between "benign" and "malignant" regression in analysis (1968). Benign regression is characterized by the patient's need to feel that he or she is being recognized and responded to as an individual, that his or her existence, individuality, and inner life are recognized as unique and valuable. The patient does not wish for instinctual gratification. Malignant regression, on the other hand, is aimed at gratification of instinctual cravings. These wishes are not to be gratified by the analyst.

The wishes associated with regression for the sake of recognition can in some senses be gratified, as they presuppose nothing more than an environment that accepts and consents to sustain and care for the patient. With benign regression the task is to help patients develop in the analytic situation the primitive relationship corresponding to their repetitive pattern and to maintain it in undisturbed peace until they can discover the possibility of new forms of object relatedness. Thus, to heal the fault, a new type of object relationship is offered that can repair, to the extent possible, the core defect originally due to a lack of active adaptation by the environment to meeting the child's normal developmental needs.

Balint noted that if all went well, development was taken up again at the point of diversion from its original course because of the trauma from the environment. The patient then is progressively able to recognize and accept newly refelt wishes and either realize or eventually renounce them. In a successful treatment, rigid ego structures, character traits and defense mechanisms, ossified behavior patterns, and ever-repeated forms of object relations become analyzable, understandable to patient and analyst, and finally adaptable to reality.

Balint's conceptualizations with regard to the etiology and pathogenesis of adult character pathology and many of his recommendations for conducting therapy with these individuals are echoed clearly and directly by self psychologists. For example, the central problem in the primary disorders of the self is conceptualized as faulty development in either the grandiose self or the idealized parent imago pole of the bipolar self. This faulty development is seen as primarily due to parental pathology in the capacity of the parents either to mirror or to offer themselves for idealization. The result is an adult with a primary disorder of the self who lives with a "deficit disorder" in which selfobjects continue to be required to provide functions for the individual that the individual cannot provide for himself or herself because of the absence of intrapsychic structure.

The task of the therapist is conceptualized as the provision of a milieu wherein the patient can regress and remobilize archaic but developmentally normal needs and find in the analyst the empathic selfobject missing in his or her infantile development. In the therapy of a patient at the level of the basic fault, as in the psychoanalytic treatment of an individual with a primary disorder of the self, repetition precedes recollection. Successful treatment depends on the analyst first providing appropriate gratification of the patient's need for empathic self-selfobject relatedness. Over time, with increasing clarification and interpretation of the nature of the self-selfobject relationship, its genetic determinants, and its characteristics and functions in the present, and with repeated instances of transmuting internalization of the selfobject functioning of the analyst by the patient as a result of nontraumatic failures on the part of the analyst, healing of the structural defect (or fault) results as intrapsychic structure and functioning gradually replace self-selfobject relating. Thus, Kohut's formulations seem a rich and original extension of Balint's preliminary outline of the etiology, pathogenesis, and therapeutic modifications required for the treatment of individuals with primary "deficit," as opposed to "conflict," disorders.

Contributions of W.R.D. Fairbairn

W. Ronald D. Fairbairn was a British analyst who spent virtually his entire professional life working in relative isolation in Edinburgh, Scotland, exploring the nature and function of schizoid phenomena. Although he began his investigations as a classical drive theorist, his findings led him ultimately to call for abandonment of drive theory as he came to disagree with Freud's view that the primary motivational force in development was the pursuit of drive gratification. He felt, instead, that an individual's wish to establish and maintain ongoing good relationships with others was the primary motivational force in development. This, in turn, led him to advocate a revision of psychoanalytic theory replacing drive theory with an object-relations theory of development.

Fairbairn sketched out the influence of Freud and Klein on his thinking in his article "Steps in the Development of an Object-Relations Theory of the Personality" (1949). Fairbairn felt Freud's "The Ego and the Id" (1923) outlined a theory of superego formation predicated on the internalization of a parent. The superego is "an endopsychic representative of parental figures internalized during childhood at the instance of an inner necessity for the control of the oedipus situation" (Fairbairn 1949, p. 153). Thus, it is an instance of an originally external object relationship being internalized and contributing to enduring intrapsychic structure formation. In "Group Psychology and the Analysis of the Ego" (Freud 1921), Fairbairn felt Freud explained the cohesion of the social group in terms of common loyalty to a leader conceived as functioning as an outer representative of the individual's superego conceived as a father figure. Here we see external object relationships being determined by the projection of an internal object. Fairbairn felt that in these papers were the beginnings of a theory of the personality conceived in terms of the relationship between the ego and objects, both external and internal.

Fairbairn noted that Melanie Klein's analytical researches led her to ascribe ever-increasing importance to the influence of internal objects in the development of the personality. Klein went beyond conceptualizing the superego as the sole internal object to envisage the presence of a multiplicity of internalized objects, good and bad, benign, idealized, and persecuting, whole and part objects. She also expanded the role of introjection and projection in such a way as to represent mental life in terms of a constant interplay between the internalization of external objects and the projection of internalized objects. Thus, the form assumed by the personality comes to be largely explained in terms of object relationships.

Fairbairn (1949) wrote:

> Klein's views seemed to me to represent an important advance in the development of psychoanalytic theory . . . however . . . she failed to push her views to their logical conclusion . . . if the introjection of objects and the perpetuation of such objects in the inner world are as important as her views imply . . . it seems to point inevitably to the conclusion that libido is not primarily pleasure-seeking but object-seeking. (pp. 154–155)

Fairbairn articulated a theory of the personality conceived in terms of object relations, in contrast to one conceived in terms of instincts and their vicissitudes (1941, 1944). Fairbairn retained the use of the word *libidinal* to describe the object-seeking tendency of the person. He felt the ultimate goal of libidinal striving was the establishment and maintenance of good ongoing object relationships, and not, as Freud and Klein had claimed, drive gratification. Fairbairn felt an "ego" was present from birth and that the object-seeking tendency of the person was a function of the ego, not the id. (Fairbairn's use of the term *ego* seems closest to, and better understood by substituting for it, the term *self*). Fairbairn did not feel there was an initial objectless phase. He felt all autoerotic and all narcissistic behaviors were secondary, reflecting the enactment of an object relationship with an internalized object. Similarly, Fairbairn did not feel there was any evidence for the death instinct. He felt that aggression was a reaction to frustration or deprivation and did not reflect the activity of a drive. It was, like anxiety, an ego reaction to any interference with maintaining good ongoing relationships with others.

Because the aim of libidinal gratification is the establishment and maintenance of ongoing good relationships with others, Fairbairn felt that when pure pleasure seeking on the part of a child emerged, it was secondary and a sign of difficulties in maintaining ongoing good relationships with others, especially the parents, and did not, in other words, reflect primary drive activity. Fairbairn felt the earliest and original form of anxiety as experienced by the child was separation anxiety. Throughout life, this is the primary source of anxiety, both as directly experienced and expressed and as symbolically elaborated.

Fairbairn felt the theory of psychosexual development and of erotogenic zones should be abandoned. In place of the theory of infantile sexuality and psychosexual development, Fairbairn formulated a theory based on the nature of dependence on objects, outlining a developmental schema in terms of which an original state of infantile dependence passes through a transition stage, and ends in a stage of mature dependence.

Fairbairn's stage of infantile dependence corresponded to Freud's and Abraham's early and late oral stages. Fairbairn felt the only natural part object was the breast and that the early oral stage was characterized by part-object relatedness. The late oral stage for Fairbairn was characterized by ambivalent whole-object relatedness. Fairbairn accepted Klein's formulations with regard to the paranoid/schizoid and depressive positions as reflecting the earliest object relations situations and their associated characteristic anxiety situations and defenses. He also continued to relate schizophrenia and manic-depressive psychosis to fixation to these two stages.

Fairbairn acknowledged that in the stage of mature dependence, owing to the constitution of the human organism, the genital organs provided one path to the object, but this path paralleled a number of others. The genital channel was an important path, but by no means the exclusive channel governing mature adult object relations. Thus, he did not feel it was correct to describe the libidinal attitude of the adult as genital; he felt it was more properly described as reflecting mature dependence. In this context, Fairbairn understood the emergence of an oedipal conflict and of castration anxiety in the course of development as, in effect, a breakdown product, reflecting some problem in the relationship between the child and his or her parents. He did not feel that an oedipal conflict and castration anxiety would be present if the child's ongoing object relationships with both parents were satisfactory.

The final area of revision of psychoanalytic theory by Fairbairn was in the nature of endopsychic structure formation. Fairbairn abandoned thinking in terms of the id, the ego, and the superego, replacing these with a theory of dynamic structure based on internalized object relationships. The ego was the original structure, conceptualized as initially unitary and governed in its functioning by its need for establishing and maintaining ongoing good object relationships. Fairbairn felt that when difficulties were encountered in the relationship between the child and the mother, the child's wish to maintain an ongoing good relationship with the mother led him or her to progressively repress aspects of object relating that were disapproved of by the mother and that led her to become rejecting, depriving, frustrating, critical, attacking, disapproving, or abandoning. Thus, to quote Sutherland (1963): "The conflicts within the primary relationship of the infant and its mother lead to a splitting off or segregation within the original unitary ego of the intolerable aspects of the relationship. Such a split involves a division of the pristine ego into structures each of which contains a) a part of the ego, b) the object that characterizes the related relationships, and c) the affects of the latter" (p. 114). As we shall see, this tripartite unit of internalization became a central part of Kernberg's thinking but not Kohut's.

The repressed systems reflect both a repressed needs and desires system and a repressed primitive control system. These systems are constantly seeking an outlet in ordinary relationships and thus serve as scanning apparatuses that seek potential objects in the outer world to participate in the enactment of the repressed object relationships. However, enactments of the repressed needs and desires system, either in fantasy or in actual behavior, are of course very evocative of the primitive control systems; that is, they are accompanied by varying degrees of anxiety and guilt because their aims continue to be felt by the individual as incompatible with the preservation of the ego-syntonic relationship with the needed person. Thus, each enactment is ordinarily followed by prompt re-repression in order to avoid the feared loss of the object relationship. Once re-repressed, these aspects of object relations, of course, again press, now unconsciously, for actualization. Thus, Fairbairn provided a model that attempted to describe "the functioning of the person in his social relationships and . . . provide at least the outline of a model for human interaction, particularly for conflict in social behavior" (Sutherland 1963, p. 118).

The relevance of Fairbairn's work to that of Kernberg and Kohut seems obvious. Kohut's theory, like Fairbairn's, seems primarily an object-relations theory placing the establishment and maintenance of good ongoing relationships with others at the center of theories of human motivation and development. Kohut, like Fairbairn, feels 1) all aggression is secondary to frustration or deprivation; 2) primary pleasure seeking, like rage, reflects a reaction to a traumatic disruption in a vitally sustaining relationship and not the workings of a primary instinct; 3) oedipal conflict and the emergence of castration anxiety are secondary breakdown phenomena, reflecting a traumatic disruption in the relation between a child and its parents in their roles as selfobjects; and 4) the central etiological factor operative in serious psychopathology is defective parenting.

Fairbairn felt serious schizoid pathology originated in a disturbed mother-infant relationship characterized by a situation in which the child is not really loved for himself as a person by his mother. The child also comes to realize that his own love for his mother is not really valued and accepted by her. This traumatic situation results in the child coming to regard his mother as a bad object insofar as she does not seem to love him and the child comes to regard outward expressions of his love as bad.

As we shall see, Kohut, like Fairbairn, postulates that it is the conscious and unconscious aspects of parental character and of their parenting that are the principal etiological agents in the genesis of the primary disorders of the self. Parental conflicts and deficiencies in mirroring and in accepting idealization traumatize the developing child, leading to the dynamic repression of various aspects of the child's self-selfobject relationships to his or her parents.

Kernberg, also, has found much of value in Fairbairn's work. He is critical of Fairbairn for his rejection of libido and aggression as drives. Kernberg feels it is important to consider the role of pure pleasure seeking, along with the central role of establishing and maintaining good ongoing object relationships, in human motivation. Kernberg also feels Fairbairn seriously underrates the roles that aggression, hate, and envy play from the beginning of life in both normal and pathological development. He disagrees with Fairbairn that only bad objects are internalized and criticizes Fairbairn's developmental model for telescoping development into the first few months of life and for neglecting, relatively speaking, all subsequent phases of development. Similarly, Kernberg feels that Fairbairn ignored or neglected the lack of differentiation between the self-representations and object representations characterizing earliest development, out of which differentiated self-representations and object representations emerge. What

Kernberg finds valuable, though, is Fairbairn's model of progressive endopsychic structuralization deriving from the internalization of object relationships and the importance of dynamically interrelated internalized object relationships in normal and pathological functioning.

Kernberg adopts Fairbairn's unit of internalization, consisting of a self-representation in relation to an object representation linked by the affect operative in the object relationship at the time of internalization. As we shall see, Kernberg retains the terms the id, the ego, and the superego but spells out a different timetable and process of development than originally proposed by Freud, relating the development of these structures to object relationships internalized in the tripartite units first proposed by Fairbairn. Finally, Kernberg finds valuable Fairbairn's explorations of the conflicts over loving and being loved. Klein emphasized conflicts over aggression, Fairbairn over loving, in ways that Kernberg found usefully complementary. Kernberg (1980) spoke admiringly of Fairbairn as "the theoretically most profound, consistent, and provocative writer of the British 'middle group' " (p. 79).

Work of Otto Kernberg

Kernberg's theories with regard to normal and pathological narcissism can best be understood in the context of his more general theory of development. Kernberg (1976) has outlined an object-relations theory of development combining the drive theory of ego psychology with aspects of object-relations theories formulated by Klein and Fairbairn. His schema affirms the fundamental importance both of drive gratification and of establishing and maintaining good ongoing relations with others. Kernberg has outlined a five-stage theory of normal development and, following Freud, relates different types of psychopathology to fixation and arrest at and/or regression to each of these different stages of development. In this brief outline, I shall mention only those points of fixation felt to contribute to the development of narcissistic personality disorders.

Kernberg follows Mahler's theory of separation-individuation closely, with regard to the timing and the processes involved in earliest development. In addition, he adopts as his "unit of internalization" the structural unit Fairbairn first described, consisting of a self-representation in relation to an object representation and bound to it by the affect operative in the relationship at the time of its internalization.

During stage one of development, the infant is slowly achieving a capacity to perceive, relate to, and internalize experiences with the world primarily as mediated by its experience of its mother. These experiences are alternately pleasurable and unpleasurable. Kernberg feels that the pleasurable, gratifying experiences of the infant in interactions with its mother are internalized first as a good self-object-affect intrapsychic constellation—though at this stage there is not yet differentiation between self and other.

Stage two of development begins with consolidation of the undifferentiated good self-object-affect representational unit. This, for Kernberg, becomes "the nucleus of the self-system of the ego and the basic organizer of integrative functions of the early ego" (Kernberg 1976, p. 60). Simultaneous with the consolidation of the undifferentiated good self-object-affect representational unit is the building up of a bad self-object-affect representation unit which integrates experiences of a frustrating, painful nature. These good and bad intrapsychic constellations are organized separately under different affective circumstances and determine two separate constellations of "affective memory." They are organized separately, initially, because they occur at different times and the infant's ego cannot yet integrate them. Later, though, they are kept separate actively through splitting mechanisms.

Stage two ends when the infant achieves a stable capacity to differentiate self-representations from object representations in the core good self-object-affect representational unit. The capacity to do so in the bad self-object-affect representational unit lags, however, due to the anxiety associated with this differentiation.

During stages one and two, the affects associated with the internalization process are primitive, crude, global, and intense. Kernberg feels more differentiated affects and the specific drive dispositions of libido and aggression emerge only gradually subsequently in the course of development. The developmental series of good self-object-affect representational units become the intrapsychic structures invested with libido, whereas the developmental series of bad self-object-affect representational units become those invested with aggression. "From a clinical viewpoint, one might say that the evolving affect states and affect dispositions actualize, respectively, libidinal and aggressive drive derivatives" (Kernberg 1976, p. 64). This aspect of Kernberg's theory represents a significant change from Freud's theory of drive and affect development but it follows Edith Jacobson's work quite closely.

Stage three of development begins with the completion of the differentiation of the self-representations from the object representations within the core good self-object-affect representational unit and includes the later differentiation of self-representations from object representations within the core bad self-object-affect representational units. With the achievement of stable differentiation of self from others, ego boundaries are established and the child begins to build up an ever-widening number and type of self-representations and object representations. However, at this stage, good and bad self-representations and object representations coexist without being integrated, and, in fact, the separation of libidinally and aggressively invested self-representations and object representations becomes strengthened by active utilization of the mechanism of splitting, which is geared toward "protecting" the good self-representations and object representations from "contamination" by bad self-representations and object representations. This is the stage in which need-gratifying, split, part-object relationships predominate. Here, Kernberg is following Kleinian theory quite closely. There is not yet an integrated concept of self or others. Normally, splitting mechanisms gradually decrease but, under pathological circumstances, splitting may actually increase, as is the case for individuals with borderline and narcissistic personality disorders. Kernberg feels narcissistic personality disorders are a subtype of borderline personality disorders. He feels these two disorders share the anxieties, defenses, and object relationships characteristic of stage three of development. What distinguishes narcissistic from boderline disorders for Kernberg are the structures created in stage four of development.

Stage four of development is characterized by the integration of libidinally and aggressively invested self-representations into an integrated self system and of libidinally and aggressively invested object representations into an integrated representation of others. Integrative processes decrease recourse to splitting mechanisms, and repression and other higher-level defense mechanisms become the primary defense mechanisms utilized by the ego. Repression results in establishing the dynamic repressed contents of the id, and, for Kernberg, the id as a psychic structure comes into existence only at this point. This is a significant revision of Freudian theory, but here Kernberg follows Fairbairn closely.

Similarly, Kernberg feels stage four marks the beginning of the integration of the superego as an independent intrapsychic structure:

> The earliest superego structure derives from the internalization of the fantastically hostile, highly unrealistic object-images, reflecting "expelled," projected and reintrojected "bad" self-object representations.... [These structures are akin to Klein's primitive, sadistic superego and Fairbairn's anti-libidinal object.]
>
> The second superego structure is derived from the ego's ideal self and ideal object representations.... The condensation of... ideal self and ideal object representations constitutes the kernel of the ego ideal. The sadistically determined superego forerunners and the early ego ideal formation... are then integrated. Thus the superego has to repeat the process that is already started in the ego, namely, the integration of internalized object relations of libidinal and aggressive characteristics. (1976, p. 71)

Within the ego, an ego identity is established in stage four through processes first described by Erikson (1950). Kernberg feels individuals with narcissistic personality disorders form a specific and pathological structure during this stage of development, a pathological "grandiose self" combining aspects of the real self, the ideal self, and the ideal object. This pathological structure interferes with subsequent ego and superego development and promotes a regression to stage three object relationships, anxieties, and defenses. Thus, for Kernberg, narcissistic personality disorders combine characteristics of both stages three and four.

During stage five of development, the ego identity established in stage four is consolidated and reshaped. Both self-representations and object representations undergo continuous reshaping on the basis of a reciprocal interaction between real experiences with others and experiences with the internal world of objects. As a result of this process, one gains an increased capacity for realistic appreciation of self and others and reshapes one's internal representations of self and others on the basis of such realistic appraisals.

Turning now to Kernberg's theories of normal and pathological narcissism (1975), following Hartmann and Jacobson, Kernberg defines normal narcissism as the libidinal investment of the self. This begins for Kernberg with the libidinal investment of the good self-object-affect representational unit that serves as the nucleus of ego development. Subsequently, the contradictory all-good and all-bad self-representations derived from libidinally and aggressively invested self-representations must be integrated and dynamically organized into a comprehensive self-system. A crucial factor for the development of normal narcissism is the predominance of libidinally invested self-representations over aggressively invested self-representations in the composite self-structure—the ego identity—that emerges from the integration of libidinally and aggressively invested self-representations. This allows consolidation of a realistic self-concept incorporating rather than dissociating the component self-representations.

It must be stressed, however, that Kernberg posits that "the libidinal investment of the self," or healthy self-love, self-regard, and self-esteem, does not stem simply from an instinctual source of libidinal energy. Other contributions to "the libidinal investment of the self" include

1. *External factors*, including libidinal gratifications from external objects, gratification of ego goals and aspirations in social effectiveness or success, and environmental sources of gratification of cultural, ethical, intellectual, and aesthetic aspirations.
2. *Instinctual and organic factors.* Good general health increases the libidinal investment of the self as does an ability to gratify one's instinctual needs in a personally and socially acceptable manner.
3. *Superego factors.* Living up to the demands, expectations, and standards of the ego ideal and living in ways that do not evoke the critical or punitive aspects of the superego increase self-esteem and self-regard.
4. *Ego factors.* In addition to superego-originated aspirations against which the actuality of the self is measured, there are also goals originating within the ego itself reflecting various stages of development. Thus, the ego, as well as the superego, exercises self-critical functions toward the self which contribute to self-esteem regulation.
5. *The internal object world.* A predominantly positive loving relationship between the self and the world of internal objects is another source of self-esteem. Good inner objects supply the self with love and confirmation of goodness and value that can be especially important when one meets with disappointments and frustrations in reality.

Thus, for Kernberg, positive regard for oneself, the healthy, mature, loving investment in oneself, has many sources, but is ultimately determined by the nature of the relationships established between the self and external and internal objects, the id, the ego, and the superego. Difficulties in any or all of these relationships can lead to the development of pathological narcissism. Thus, the term *pathological narcissism* for Kernberg covers a wide variety of disorders. Least problematic are the narcissistic disturbances associated with the neuroses and with neurotic character pathology. To the extent that neurotic symptoms and character traits protect self-esteem, they have a narcissistic function that, when explored analytically, activates narcissistic frustrations and conflicts. One can then discover how the content of ego expectations and goals and superego expectations, goals, demands, and prohibitions have remained at infantile levels. Thus, these and only these disorders reflect for Kernberg fixation at or regression to infantile narcissistic goals characteristic of a normal, though excessively infantile, self-structure.

A more severe type of narcissistic disturbance, according to Kernberg, is that which characterizes the object relationships of homosexuals, as first described by Freud. Here, pathological identifications have led an individual to identify himself with a pathogenic, internalized object (for example, his mother), and to relate to others (both internal object representations and external objects) because they stand for an aspect of his (present or past, actual or idealized) self. Within this more pathological relationship between the self identified with an object and an object identified with the self, an object relationship nonetheless still exists both intrapsychically and in external relationships.

It is only for individuals with narcissistic personality disorders that Kernberg feels relatedness to others is abandoned. Here, the relationship is no longer between self and object, but between a primitive, pathological, grandiose self and the temporary projection of that same grandiose self onto objects who are then idealized. The relationship is no longer of self to object, nor of object to self, but of self to self. It is here that a totally narcissistic relationship, defined as a relationship of the self to the self, replaces an object relationship. This, for Kernberg, is the most severe form of pathological narcissism.

The final type of narcissistic pathology described by

Kernberg is characterized by the lack of an integrated self. These are patients who either present with a borderline personality organization or who are psychotic. What differentiates the former from the latter is a capacity to maintain reality testing and differentiation of self from other. What differentiates narcissistic from borderline personality disorders is the presence of a pathological self-structure, the grandiose self, in individuals with narcissistic personality disorders.

Let us examine now in greater detail Kernberg's understanding of narcissistic personality disorders as a specific subtype of narcissistic character pathology (Kernberg 1970, 1974a, 1974b, 1975, 1984).

Descriptively, individuals with narcissistic personality disorders frequently have achieved social and vocational success and often present free of obvious symptoms. It is only as one gets to know these individuals better than one realizes that their emotional life is shallow and driven and that they are often restless and bored, feel empty and depressed, and derive little enjoyment from life. These patients have a characteristic disturbance in self-regard and self-esteem regulation, presenting an apparently contradictory picture of having an inflated concept of themselves while, simultaneously, showing an inordinate need for attention, interest, affection, love, praise, and admiration from others in order to maintain the self-concept. When these needs are not met, these apparently well-functioning individuals can become intensely anxious, angry, depressed, hypochondriacal, and/or paranoid.

Thus, beneath a facade of smooth, effective, and often charming social functioning, these individuals are revealed to be deeply distrustful, suspicious, anxious, and vulnerable people driven by a constant search for gratification of strivings for brilliance, wealth, power, and beauty. They relate to others on a need-gratifying, split, part-object relationship basis and are often only interested in others who gratify their narcissistic needs. Those who do are temporarily perceived as all good and are inordinately idealized. The narcissistic individual appears to value and depend on them. However, if this other fails to meet their narcissistic needs, extreme rage and contempt emerge, with ruthless demandingness and scathingly depreciatory attacks. The ease of the shift from total idealization to total devaluation is an especially important characteristic of individuals with narcissistic personality disorder. Others, including idealized others, are not in fact loved and valued in their own right, but simply as sources of narcissistic supplies. Thus, individuals with narcissistic personality disorders have primarily exploitative relationships with others, feeling entitled to control, possess, and exploit others ruthlessly to obtain narcissistic supplies. These individuals have virtually no interest, affection, love, concern, or empathy for others and can end relationships when they cease to be gratifying without remorse, regret, or guilt. There is often a striking absence of depressive reaction, as individuals with narcissistic personality disorders are especially deficient in genuine feelings of sadness and mournful longing in response to separation and loss. Instead, they respond to loss with either anger, resentment, and wishes for revenge or indifference. In either case, the narcissistic individual ordinarily simply moves on to relate to a new need-gratifying object who is, in turn, subject to cycles of alternating idealization and devaluation.

Individuals with narcissistic personality disorders struggle, often unconsciously, with the conviction that they have basically nothing good and worthwhile to offer others. They deeply envy anyone whom they feel has something to offer to others, including to themselves, making it virtually impossible for them to trust, value, depend on, or profit from relating to others.

Some patients with narcissistic personality disorders present with conscious feelings of insecurity and inferiority, rather than superiority, grandiosity, omnipotence, and entitlement. These feelings, however, usually alternate with grandiose and omnipotent fantasies. The presence of such extreme contradictions in self-concept is often the first clue of the severe psychopathology operative.

Dynamically, Kernberg feels individuals with narcissistic

personality disorders resemble those with borderline personality disorders in struggling with a pathological condensation of genital and pregenital conflicts under the overriding influence of pregenital, and especially oral, aggression. They cope with these conflicts primarily by operationalizing splitting mechanisms as well as primitive forms of projection, projective identification, primitive and pathological idealization, omnipotent control, and narcissistic withdrawal and devaluation, i.e., the defense mechanisms Klein described as operative in the paranoid/schizoid position and the manic defense.

Analytic exploration of the haughty, grandiose, and controlling behavior of these individuals regularly demonstrates that this behavior is a defense against paranoid traits related to the projection of oral rage, which is central to their psychopathology. Kernberg feels these individuals experience themselves as hungry and empty, "full of impotent anger at being frustrated and fearful of a world which seems as hateful and revengeful as the patient himself. This, the deepest level of the self-concept of narcissistic personalities, can be perceived only late in the course of their psychoanalytic therapy" (Kernberg 1970, pp. 57–58).

As previously mentioned, Kernberg (1974a) feels that individuals with narcissistic personality disorders have

> an integrated, although highly pathological, grandiose self, which reflects a pathological condensation of some aspects of the real self (i.e., the "specialness" of the child that was reinforced by early experience), the ideal self (i.e., the fantasies and self-images of power, wealth, and beauty that compensated the small child for the experience of severe oral frustration, rage and envy), and the ideal object (i.e., the fantasy of an ever-giving, ever-loving, and accepting mother, in contrast to their experience in reality—replacement of the devaluated real parental object). (p. 256)

This structure is not present in individuals with borderline personality disorders. Its presence in individuals with narcissistic personality disorders helps to account for their ability to maintain apparently good social and vocational adaptation. Kernberg feels this pathological grandiose self-structure interferes with the consolidation of normal ego and superego structures, especially with the formation of the ego ideal, as well as with external and internal object relationships. For example, normal superego development is interfered with because the ideal self-representations and object representations that ordinarily would contribute to ego-ideal formation are condensed instead into the pathological grandiose-self ego structure. This process interferes with integrating idealized aspects of the ego ideal with the primitive, punitive, punishing aspects of the superego. As a result, primitive, nonintegrated, sadistic superego forerunners persist and are easily projected onto others, thereby contributing to the paranoid persecutory trends seen in these individuals. Similarly, the development of an integrated ego identity is interfered with as the formation of the grandiose self can occur only if many aspects of the real self are dissociated and/or repressed. This is especially true with regard to dependency needs. The projection of these needs and of the oral sadism associated with them contributes further to the development of paranoid trends.

A key question in terms of the etiology of narcissistic personality disorder is, What leads to the genesis of the pathological grandiose self-structure? Put most basically—Does it emerge primarily as a result of conflict over drives, or is it secondary to environmental deprivations due to faulty parenting? According to Kernberg (1970), "It is hard to evaluate to what extent this development represents a constitutionally determined, strong, aggressive drive, a constitutionally determined lack of anxiety tolerance in regard to aggressive impulses, or severe frustration in their first years of life" (p. 58). But despite providing characteristics of parents and their parenting that might account for this pathological development, it seems clear in Kernberg's writings that he favors conflict over drives to environmental explanations with regard to the origin of this type of character pathology. For example, he is particularly wary of narcissistic patients' complaints about their parents as the primary source of their difficulties:

> What regularly emerges is that underlying the patient's consciously remembered or rediscovered "disappointments" of his parents, are devaluation of parental images and real parental figures that the patient carried out in the past in order to avoid underlying conflicts with them. The patient's disappointments in the analyst reveal . . . dramatically the total devaluation of the transference object for the slightest reason and, thus, the intense overwhelming nature of the aggression against the object. . . . The implications of "either you are as I want you or you cease to exist" is also the acting out of unconscious need for omnipotent control of the object and reflects defenses against aggression. (1974a, p. 263)

Thus, it remains for Kernberg

> an open question to what extent inborn intensity of aggressive drive [or] the predominance of chronically cold, narcissistic, and at the same time overprotective maternal figures appears to be the main etiological element in the psychogenesis of this pathology. (1974b, p. 221)

In addition to describing the characteristics of individuals with analyzable narcissistic personality disorders, Kernberg has differentiated several subtypes of narcissistic personality disorders that he feels have a grave prognosis. These include narcissistic patients functioning on an overt borderline level, narcissistic patients with pervasive ego-syntonic antisocial and sadistic trends, and patients characterized by the syndrome of malignant narcissism. Malignant narcissism occurs in

> patients whose grandiosity and pathological self-idealization are reinforced by the sense of triumph over fear and pain through inflicting fear and pain on others, and also cases in which self-esteem is enhanced by the sadistic pleasure of aggression linked with sexual drive derivatives. Narcissistic personalities . . . who obtain a sense of superiority and triumph over life and death, as well as conscious pleasure by severe self-mutilation; and narcis-

> sistic patients with a combination of paranoia and explosive personality traits, whose impulsive behavior, rage attacks, and blaming are major channels for instinctual gratification, all may reflect the condensation of aggression in a pathological grandiose self and may find the treatment situation a welcome and stable outlet for aggression that militates against structured intrapsychic change. (Kernberg 1984, p. 195)

Kernberg feels these patients ordinarily present a contraindication for analysis. He recommends a supportive psychotherapeutic approach to their treatment.

Work of Heinz Kohut

Kohut began his investigations into the nature and function of narcissism as an ego psychologist. His early articles (1966, 1968, 1972) and first book (1971) delineate a theory of normal narcissistic development, of development of specific types of narcissistic psychopathology, and of a psychoanalytic approach to the treatment of these disorders in terms of drive theory and the structural hypothesis. His ideas differed markedly, however, from those of his fellow ego psychologist, Otto Kernberg, even during this period.

Theory of Normal Development

Kohut felt an infant was born into a state of primary narcissism. Unlike Freud, Kohut (1966) defined primary narcissism as a state in which "the baby originally experiences the mother and her ministrations not as a you and its actions, but within a view of the world in which the I-you differentiation has not yet been established" (p. 245). Defining primary narcissism in these terms, beyond reflecting aspects of the work of Hartmann, Jacobson, and Mahler, also clearly reflects Hermann's hypothesis that an individual differentiates out of what is originally a state of "dual-union" between a baby and its mother. It is also similar to Kernberg's stage two of development.

In describing normal development from a state of primary narcissism, Kohut (1966) noted that "the balance of primary narcissism is disturbed by maturational pressures and painful psychic tensions which occur because the mother's ministrations are of necessity imperfect and traumatic delays cannot be prevented" (p. 246). Kohut hypothesized that the baby dealt with these unavoidable disruptions by simultaneously building up two new systems of perfection: the narcissistic self (later termed by him the grandiose self) and the idealized parent imago, two normal narcissistic psychological constellations emerging from the state of primary narcissism with independent lines of development. Within the narcissistic-self (grandiose-self) constellation, "everything pleasant, good, and perfect is considered as part of a rudimentary self, while everything unpleasant, bad, and imperfect is considered as 'outside' " (Kohut 1966, p. 246). Within the idealized parent-imago constellation, by contrast, "the baby attempts to maintain the original perfection and omnipotence by imbuing the rudimentary you, the adult, with absolute power and perfection" (Kohut 1966, p. 246). In the subsequent course of development, if all went well, these two normal narcissistic structures were felt by Kohut to contribute to aspects of ego and superego structure and functioning.

Kohut felt idealization of the parent imago ultimately was transformed into idealization of the superego and ego ideal, while the developmental line of the narcissistic self (grandiose self) was felt to contribute to ego structure and functions. Kohut felt the grandiose fantasies generated by the grandiose self were the ultimate source of the ego's ambitions and were inextricably linked to exhibitionism and therefore to an admiring, mirroring other, originally the mother. However, Kohut felt developmentally normal exhibitionism could become problematic because it was also linked to a vulnerability to the experience of shame. Kohut felt shame was evoked whenever the mirroring other failed to mirror appropriately. Kohut's effort to understand the nature and function of shame in narcissistic disorders is an especially important aspect of his contribution to psychoanalytic theory. Kernberg, by contrast, is virtually silent about this affect and its impact on development.

It is important to note at this point that Kohut and Kernberg disagree fundamentally about the nature of normal narcissistic development. Kernberg does not agree with Kohut's hypothesis of the grandiose self and the idealized parent imago as normal, secondary narcissistic structures emerging from the state of primary narcissism. For Kernberg, the grandiose self is always pathological, having no role or function in normal development.

During this first period of investigation, Kohut (1971) conceptualized the self as

> a structure within the mind since a) it is cathected with instinctual energy, and b) it has continuity in time, i.e., it is enduring . . . the self, then, quite analogous to the representations of objects, is a content of the mental apparatus but it is not one of its constituents, i.e., not one of the agencies of the mind. (p. xv)

Here, Kohut is following Hartmann, Jacobson, and Kernberg closely. However, when he went on to postulate that the self, in its narcissistic dimension, developed in relation to "selfobjects," he introduced a totally new type of "object" to psychoanalysis. Kohut contrasted "selfobjects" with "true objects (in the psychoanalytic sense)." "True objects in the psychoanalytic sense" are objects "loved and hated by a psyche that has separated itself from the archaic objects, has acquired autonomous structures, has accepted the independent motivations and responses of others, and has grasped the notion of mutuality" (Kohut 1971, p. 51). They are, in other words, people from whom the self has fully separated, differentiated, and individuated. Selfobjects, on the other hand, are "objects which are not experienced as separate and independent from the self" (Kohut 1971, p. 3). "The expected control over the narcissistically cathected subject and its function, for example, is closer to the concept which a grownup has of himself and of the control which he expects over his own body and mind than to the grownup's experience of others and of his control over them" (Kohut 1971, p. 33).

This description of the nature of self-selfobject relating strikingly parallels Balint's description of the nature of object relating at the level of the basic fault. Kohut, however, provided a metapsychological concept, i.e., the selfobject, that applies to the object of this type of relatedness and has specifically adapted it to his theory of normal and pathological narcissistic development.

Kohut hypothesized two types of selfobjects: idealized and mirroring, which are functionally related to the idealized parent-imago and to the grandiose-self narcissistic configurations, respectively. Kohut described selfobjects as archaic, prestructural objects whose ongoing presence and functions were necessary for the maintenance of an ongoing sense of self and healthy self-esteem because they perform functions for the self that the self cannot yet perform for itself.

Kernberg does not recognize selfobjects as distinct from "true objects in the psychoanalytic sense," feeling Kohut failed to recognize the aggression associated with relating to an object as if it were part of the self. For Kernberg, this type of relatedness is defensive, pathological, and not an aspect of normal object relationships.

Kohut felt that the formation of intrapsychic structure was linked with minor nontraumatic failures on the part of the selfobjects of childhood through a process of internalization and intrapsychic structure formation termed by him "transmuting internalization." For Kohut, there was an intimate reciprocal relationship between "the formation of psychic structure and the withdrawal of object-instinctual and narcissistic cathexes from object imagos" (1971, p. 49). Kohut (1971) felt that

> preceding the withdrawal of the cathexis from the object there is a breaking up of those aspects of the object imago that are being internalized . . . the withdrawal of narcissistic cathexes takes

> place in a fractionated way if the child can experience disappointments with one idealized aspect or quality of the object after another.... In addition to the just-mentioned breaking up of specific aspects of the object imago, there takes place... a depersonalizing of the introjected aspects of the image of the object, mainly in the form of a shift of emphasis from the total human context of a personality of the object to certain of its specific functions. The internal structure, in other words, now performs the functions which the object used to perform for the child—the well-functioning structure, however, has largely been divested of the personality features of the object. (pp. 49–50)

Thus Kohut differs in a fundamental way from Kernberg with regard to the processes involved in intrapsychic structure formation. Specifically, he eliminates or, at least, downplays the role of internal objects as precursors of eventually depersonified structures and functions and the role of an ongoing world of internalized object relationships as vitally influencing normal and pathological functioning.

Theory of Psychopathology

Kohut attributes narcissistic personality disorders to traumatic events occurring during the course of development of the grandiose-self and/or the idealized parent-imago narcissistic constellation. With regard to the developmental line of the grandiose self, Kohut (1966) noted:

> If the grandiosity of the narcissistic self... has been insufficiently modified because traumatic onslaughts on the child's self-esteem have driven the grandiose fantasies into repression, then the adult ego will tend to vacillate between an irrational overestimation of the self and feelings of inferiority and will react with narcissistic mortification to the thwarting of its ambitions. (p. 252)

Similarly,

> if the child experiences traumatic disappointment in the admired adult, then the idealized parent imago, too, is retained in

> its unaltered form, is not transformed into tension-regulating psychic structure, but remains an archaic, transitional object that is required for the maintenance of narcissistic homeostasis. (Kohut 1968, p. 87)

When this occurs, the child, and subsequently the adult, remains fixated on an external representative of an archaic idealized parent imago. Thus, in narcissistic personality disturbance,

> the ego's anxiety relates primarily to its awareness of the vulnerability of the mature self; the dangers which it faces concern either the temporary fragmentation of the self, or the intrusions of either archaic forms of subject-bound grandiosity or of archaic narcissistically aggrandized self-objects into its realm. The principal source of discomfort is thus the result of the psyche's inability to regulate self-esteem and to maintain it at normal levels. (Kohut 1971, p. 20)

With regard to the etiology of these disorders, Kohut (1968) emphasized that "the essential genetic trauma is grounded in the parents' own narcissistic fixations . . . the parents' narcissistic needs contribute decisively to the child remaining enmeshed with the narcissistic web of the parents' personality" (p. 92).

Thus, Kohut felt narcissistic disorders were derivative of parental failures in their roles and functions as either mirroring selfobjects of their child's grandiose self and/or their roles as an idealized selfobject that could subsequently be internalized as an aspect of the child's idealized parent imago. This line of thinking emphasizing a primarily environmental (i.e., parental) etiology for narcissistic psychopathology places Kohut solidly in the tradition of Ferenczi, Balint, and Fairbairn. This is another point of disagreement between Kernberg and Kohut.

Theory of Therapy

In one of his most unique contributions, Kohut noted that when patients with narcissistic personality disorders came for psychoanalytic therapy, they spontaneously generated two types of pathognomonic narcissistic transferences: the mirroring and the idealizing transferences. These transferences correspond respectively to the therapeutic activation of the grandiose-self or the idealized parent-imago narcissistic constellations and to the mirroring and idealizing self-selfobject relationships associated with them. Kohut felt these pathognomonic narcissistic transferences established themselves spontaneously if the analyst did not interfere with their emergence. Thus, for example, he recommended that the analyst accept the admiration associated with an idealizing transference early on in the analysis to facilitate the establishment of an analyzable idealizing transference. Similarly, and despite the difficulties that it posed for the analyst, Kohut felt the analyst must accept the patient's need for emphathic mirroring and provide it when the grandiose-self narcissistic constellation and mirroring selfobject needs were mobilized in the mirror transference.

The central task of the analyst of a patient with a narcissistic personality disorder, for Kohut, was the facilitation of the mobilization of these two transference paradigms and then the analysis of the dynamic and genetic determinants of these transferences as they became clear to the patient and the analyst after incidents of minor, nontraumatic disruptions of the transference. Thus, the analyst had to be sensitive to disruptions of the transference revealed by the patient becoming anxious, angry, depressed, hypochondriacal, paranoid, or otherwise symptomatic. Then the analyst's task with the patient was to clarify the cause of the disruption and the nature of the effects of the disruption on the patient's sense of self and self-esteem, in the here-and-now context of the relationship to the analyst experienced as a selfobject. This was followed by reconstruction with the patient of how the disruption in the relationship to the analyst and its pathogenic effects in the present paralleled the patient's chronically traumatic experiences of his or her parents in their mirroring and/or idealized selfobject roles in childhood. Kohut (1968) commented:

> As is the case in the idealizing transference . . . temporary disturbances of the (mirroring) transference equilibrium occupy in the analysis of narcissistic personalities a central position of strategic importance which corresponds to the place of the structural conflict in the ordinary transference neurosis; and their analysis tends to elicit the deepest insights and leads to the most solid accretions of psychic structure. (p. 99)

Kohut's postulation of specific pathognomonic narcissistic transferences derivative of a patient's conflicted self-selfobject relatedness with his or her parents, which are separate and distinct from transferences originating in a patient's conflicted sexual and aggressive relationships with his or her parents, is another point of major disagreement between Kernberg and Kohut. Kernberg does not recognize the existence and validity of narcissistic transferences as described by Kohut, feeling that the patient's efforts to elicit mirroring responses to his or her grandiose self and to idealize the analyst are pathological, defensive maneuvers aimed at denying intense conflict over dependency needs and the rage and paranoid and persecutory object relationships and fears associated with the mobilization of these conflicted needs.

Kernberg's and Kohut's disagreement about the nature of the transferences operative in narcissistic personality disorders parallels their disagreement about the relationship of pathological narcissism to normal infantile narcissism. Kohut argues for a continuity between normal infantile narcissism and pathological narcissism. For him, pathological narcissism occurs when normal infantile narcissistic needs for mirroring and idealization are traumatically disrupted by parental failures in their selfobject functions vis-à-vis the child. This leads to dissociation (vertical split) or repression (horizontal split) of normal infantile narcissistic needs which, in turn, determine the type of narcissistic psychopathology that emerges. In analysis, the transferences mobilized reflect normal infantile needs, and, through analysis of their genetic and dynamic determinants, the dissociations and repressions can be eliminated and normal development can proceed from points of fixation and/

or regression. Here, Kohut's theorizing strikingly parallels theories of the formation of psychopathology and its analytic treatment advanced by Ferenczi, Balint, and Fairbairn.

Kernberg, by contrast, feels the form of pathological narcissism operative in individuals with narcissistic personality disorders and the transferences mobilized in analysis are distinct from normal infantile narcissism.

Emergence of Self Psychology

During the years between the publication of Kohut's first book and his second in 1977, Kohut's thinking underwent a revolutionary transformation. The publication of *The Restoration of the Self* (1977) led Kohut to establish a new school of psychoanalysis—self psychology—that advanced an entirely new metapsychological understanding of narcissism, one that paralleled a progressive pulling away from the metapsychology of ego psychology: "In the earlier contributions I presented my findings concerning the psychology of the self mainly in the language of classical drive theory" (Kohut 1977, p. xiii). This volume, however, represents "a move toward a clearly defined psychology of the self, [a psychology] that puts the self at the center, examines its genesis and development and its constituents, in health and in disease" (Kohut 1977, pp. xiv–xv). With this publication, Kohut redefined the self:

> This structure is the basis of our sense of being an independent center of initiative and perception, integrated with our most central ambitions and ideals and with our experience that our body and mind form a unit in space and a continuum in time. This cohesive and enduring psychic configuration, in connection with the correllated set of talents and skills that it attracts to itself or that develops in response to the demands of the ambitions and ideals of the nuclear self, forms the central sector of the personality. (pp. 177–178)

Kohut then outlined a theory of development of the self in terms of a "bipolar self" independent of any relation to the metapsychology of ego psychology. He continued to propose that the grandiose self and the idealized parent imago emerged out of the state of primary narcissism. These two independent but interrelated narcissistic configurations underwent subsequent development from infantile to mature forms. This development required the presence of empathically responsive selfobjects, the mirroring selfobject in relation to the grandiose-self pole of the bipolar self, and an admired and idealized selfobject in relation to the idealized parent-imago pole. Kohut felt these two narcissistic configurations and the self-selfobject relations determined by them were operative in everyone from birth to death. No longer did he hypothesize that the grandiose self contributed to ego contents and functioning or that the idealized parent imago contributed to superego contents and functioning.

In addition to discontinuing theorizing in terms of the structural model, Kohut (1977) also made it clear that he felt "the responses of the mirroring self-object and the idealizability of the omnipotent self-object must not be viewed within the context of the psychology of the drives" (p. 173). Thus, he abandoned drive theory as well as the structural hypothesis as conceptual tools for understanding normal and pathological narcissism. As part of this process, Kohut formulated a radical reevaluation of the role of drives in normal and pathological functioning in general, no longer considering them primary phenomena. They became for him, instead, secondary phenomena, disintegration or breakdown products:

> I believe that man's destructiveness as a psychological phenomena is secondary, that it arises originally as a result of the failure of the self-object environment to meet the child's need for optimal . . . empathic responses. . . . Destructive rage, in particular, is always motivated by an injury to the self. (Kohut 1977, p. 116)

Kohut differentiated between narcissistic rage and "nondestructive aggressiveness." He (1977) felt the latter

> has a developmental line of its own—it does not develop out of primitive destructiveness by educational influences, but develops under normal circumstances from primitive forms of nondestructive assertiveness to mature forms of assertiveness in which aggression is subordinated to the performance of tasks. Normal, primary, nondestructive aggression . . . subsides as soon as the goals that have been striven for are reached. (p. 121)

With regard to sexual behavior, Kohut (1977) wrote:

> . . . the tenets I propose with regard to the experiences of aggression and rage also apply to the libidinal drives. The infantile sexual drive in isolation is not the primary psychological configuration . . . the primary psychological configuration (of which the drive is only a constituent) is the experience of the relation between the self and the empathic self-object. . . . Drive manifestations in isolation establish themselves only after traumatic and/or prolonged failures in empathy from the side of the self-object environment. (pp. 121–122)

In this context, Kohut felt that when intense oedipal conflict emerges, it is a secondary phenomenon, a breakdown product occurring only for children whose parental selfobjects are severely out of touch and unempathically responsive to the child's oedipal self. Kohut's abandonment of drive theory, of course, sharply differentiates him from Kernberg. However, his abandonment of drive theory and emphasis on an object-relations theory of the personality was anticipated by Fairbairn.

In subsequent publications, Kohut (1979, 1984; Kohut and Wolf 1978) extended and deepened his theorizing with regard to normal and pathological narcissistic development and of a psychoanalytic approach to the treatment of narcissistic disorders from a self psychology perspective. The only major change in his theory of normal and pathological narcissism came in his final book (1984). In this volume, he alters his previous theory of the "bipolar self":

> We now conceive of the self as consisting of three major constit-

> uents (the pole of ambitions, the pole of ideals, and the intermediate area of talents and skills)... we subdivide... selfobject transferences into three groups: (1) those in which the damaged pole of ambitions attempts to elicit the confirming-approving responses of the selfobject (mirror transference); (2) those in which the damaged pole of ideals searches for a selfobject that will accept its idealization (idealizing transference); and (3) those in which the damaged intermediate area of talents and skills seeks a selfobject that will make itself available for the reassuring experience of essential alikeness (twinship or alter ego transference).
>
> ... the present decision to posit three rather than two classes of selfobject transferences... must be seen simply as the necessary outgrowth of our broadened clinical experience and our deepened understanding of the clinical phenomena that we observe. (pp. 192–193)

In this volume, Kohut sketched out an outline of the new developmental line of twinship or alter-ego needs. Kohut (1984) felt this involved important self-affirming and self-maintaining experiences in early childhood which result in the child's obtaining the sense of security that comes from feeling himself "to be a human among humans" (p. 200). Self-sustaining alter-ego or twinship experiences allow a feeling that one lives with others who are sufficiently like oneself to understand and be understood by oneself. This represents for Kohut (1984) "one of the major self-object needs of man" (p. 201).

In this final volume, Kohut continued to argue for

> the psychological primacy of phenomena (affection and assertiveness) that are traditionally considered secondary (that is, that are considered sublimated drives) and of the secondary nature of phenomena (lust and destructiveness) that are traditionally considered primary (that is, that are considered unsublimated drives). (p. 12)

Thus, in the end, Kohut considered structural and functional deficiencies of the patient's self as the primary disorder in every type of psychopathology. Baker and Baker (1987) have recently provided a lucid and succinct overview of Kohut's thinking up to the point of his death.

Kohut was a true psychoanalytic revolutionary. Like Fairbairn before him, he advocated an abandonment of drive theory and of the structural hypothesis in favor of an object-relations theory, i.e., a self-selfobject relations theory, of the personality. The question now is whether Kernberg's criticisms of Kohut's theories are as valid as his criticisms of the shortcomings of Fairbairn's theories. It remains for analytic and empirical research to decide.

References

American Psychiatric Association: Diagnostic and Statistical Manual of Mental Disorders, 2nd Edition. Washington, DC, American Psychiatric Association, 1968

American Psychiatric Association: Diagnostic and Statistical Manual of Mental Disorders, 3rd Edition. Washington, DC, American Psychiatric Association, 1980

Baker HS, Baker MN: Heinz Kohut's self psychology: an overview. Am J Psychiatry 144:1–9, 1987

Balint A: Love for the mother and mother love (1939), in Primary Love and Psychoanalytic Technique. Edited by Balint M. London, Hogarth Press, 1952, pp 109–127

Balint M: Character analysis and new beginning (1932), in Primary Love and Psychoanalytic Technique. Edited by Balint M. London, Hogarth Press, 1952, pp 159–173

Balint M: Critical notes on the theory of the pregenital organizations of the libido (1935), in Primary Love and Psychoanalytic Technique. Edited by Balint M. London, Hogarth Press, 1952, pp 49–72

Balint M: Early developmental states of the ego (1937), in Primary Love and Psychoanalytic Technique. Edited by Balint M. London, Hogarth Press, 1952, pp 90–108

Balint M: The Basic Fault: Therapeutic Aspects of Regression (1968) (Classics in Psychoanalysis Ser No 5). New York, Brunner/Mazel, 1979

Erikson EH: Identity and the life cycle (1950), in Identity and the Life Cycle: Selected Papers (Psychological Issues Monograph No 1). Edited by Erikson EH. New York, International Universities Press, 1959, pp 50–100

Fairbairn WRD: A revised psychopathology of the psychoses and psychoneuroses (1941), in Psychoanalytic Studies of the Personality. Edited by Fairbairn WRD. London, Tavistock, 1952, pp 28–58

Fairbairn WRD: Endopsychic structure considered in terms of object-relationships (1944), in Psychoanalytic Studies of the Personality. Edited by Fairbairn WRD. London, Tavistock, 1952, pp 82–136

Fairbairn WRD: Steps in the development of an object-relations theory of the personality (1949), in Psychoanalytic Studies of the Personality. Edited by Fairbairn WRD. London, Tavistock, 1952, pp 152–161

Ferenczi S: The further development of an active therapy in psychoanalysis (1920), in Further Contributions to the Theory and Technique of Psychoanalysis, 2nd Edition. Compiled by Richman J. London, Hogarth Press, 1969, pp 198–217

Ferenczi S: The adaptation of the family to the child (1927), in Final Contributions to the Problems and Methods of Psychoanalysis. Edited by Balint M. New York, Brunner/Mazel, 1980, pp 61–76

Ferenczi S: The principles of relaxation and neocathexis (1929a), in Final Contributions to the Problems and Methods of Psychoanalysis. Edited by Balint M. New York, Brunner/Mazel, 1980, pp 108–127

Ferenczi S: The unwelcome child and his death instinct (1929b), in Final Contributions to the Problems and Methods of Psychoanalysis. Edited by Balint M. New York, Brunner/Mazel, 1980, pp 102–107

Ferenczi S: Child analysis in the analysis of adults (1931), in Final Contributions to the Problems and Methods of Psychoanalysis. Edited by Balint M. New York, Brunner/Mazel, 1980, pp 126–142

Ferenczi S: Confusion of tongues between adults and the child (1933), in Final Contributions to the Problems and Methods of Psychoanalysis. Edited by Balint M. New York, Brunner/Mazel, 1980, pp 156–167

Freud S: Three essays on the theory of sexuality (1905), in The Standard Edition of the Complete Psychological Works of Sigmund Freud, Vol 7. Translated and edited by Strachey J. London, Hogarth Press, 1953, pp 123–245

Freud S: Leonardo DaVinci and a memory of his childhood (1910), in The Standard Edition of the Complete Psychological Works of Sigmund Freud, Vol 11. Translated and edited by Strachey J. London, Hogarth Press, 1957, pp 59–138

Freud S: Psycho-analytic notes on an autobiographical account of a case of paranoia (dementia paranoides) (1911), in The Standard Edition of the Complete Psychological Works of Sigmund Freud, Vol 12. Translated and edited by Strachey J. London, Hogarth Press, 1958, pp 1–84

Freud S: Totem and taboo (1912–1913), in The Standard Edition of the Complete Psychological Works of Sigmund Freud, Vol 13. Translated and edited by Strachey J. London, Hogarth Press, 1955, pp 1–161

Freud S: On narcissism: an introduction (1914), in The Standard Edition of the Complete Psychological Works of Sigmund Freud, Vol 14. Translated and edited by Strachey J. London, Hogarth Press, 1957, pp 67–104

Freud S: Lecture 26 of the introductory lectures: The libido theory and narcissism (1916–1917), in The Standard Edition of the Complete Psychological Works of Sigmund Freud, Vol 16. Translated and edited by Strachey J. London, Hogarth Press, 1963, pp 412–430

Freud S: Group psychology and the analysis of the ego (1921), in The Standard Edition of the Complete Psychological Works of Sigmund Freud, Vol 18. Translated and edited by Strachey J. London, Hogarth Press, 1955, pp 67–143

Freud S: The ego and the id (1923), in the Standard Edition of the Complete Psychological Works of Sigmund Freud,

Vol 19. Translated and edited by Strachey J. London, Hogarth Press, 1961, pp 3–66

Hartmann H: Comments on the psychoanalytic theory of the ego. Psychoanal Study Child 5:74–96, 1950

Hermann I: Clinging—going-in-search: a contrasting pair of instincts and their relation to sadism and masochism (1936). Psychoanal Q 45:1–36, 1976

Jacobson E: The self and the object world. Psychoanal Study Child 9:75–127, 1954

Kernberg OF: Factors in the psychoanalytic treatment of narcissistic personalities. J Am Psychoanal Assoc 18:51–85, 1970

Kernberg OF: Contrasting viewpoints regarding the nature and psychoanalytic treatment of narcissistic personalities: a preliminary communication. J Am Psychoanal Assoc 22:255–267, 1974a

Kernberg OF: Further contributions to the treatment of narcissistic personalities. Int J Psychoanal 55:215–240, 1974b

Kernberg O: Borderline Conditions and Pathological Narcissism. New York, Jason Aronson, 1975

Kernberg O: Object Relations Theory and Clinical Psychoanalysis. New York, Jason Aronson, 1976

Kernberg O: Internal World and External Reality. New York, Jason Aronson, 1980

Kernberg O: Severe Personality Disorders. New Haven, CT, Yale University Press, 1984

Klein M: Early analysis (1923), in Love, Guilt, and Reparation and Other Works 1921–1945, Vol 1 (The Writers of Melanie Klein Ser). Edited by Money-Kyrle R. New York, Free Press, 1984, pp 77–105

Klein M: The psychological principles of early analysis (1926), in Love, Guilt, and Reparation and Other Works 1921–1945, Vol 1 (The Writers of Melanie Klein Ser). Edited by Money-Kyrle R. New York, Free Press, 1984, pp 128–138

Klein M: Early stages of the Oedipus conflict (1928), in Love, Guilt, and Reparation and Other Works 1921–1945, Vol 1

(The Writers of Melanie Klein Ser). Edited by Money-Kyrle R. New York, Free Press, 1984, pp 186–198

Klein M: Personification in the play of children (1929), in Love, Guilt, and Reparation and Other Works 1921–1945, Vol 1 (The Writers of Melanie Klein Ser). Edited by Money-Kyrle R. New York, Free Press, 1984, pp 199–209

Klein M: The importance of symbol-formation in the development of the ego (1930), in Love, Guilt, and Reparation and Other Works 1921–1945, Vol 1 (The Writers of Melanie Klein Ser). Edited by Money-Kyrle R. New York, Free Press, 1984, pp 219–232

Klein M: A contribution to the psychogenesis of manic-depressive states (1935), in Love, Guilt, and Reparation and Other Works 1921–1945, Vol 1 (The Writers of Melanie Klein Ser). Edited by Money-Kyrle R. New York, Free Press, 1984, pp 262–289

Klein M: Love, guilt and reparation (1937), in Love, Guilt, and Reparation and Other Works 1921–1945, Vol 1 (The Writers of Melanie Klein Ser). Edited by Money-Kyrle R. New York, Free Press, 1984, pp 306–343

Klein M: Mourning and its relation to manic-depressive states (1940), in Love, Guilt, and Reparation and Other Works 1921–1945, Vol 1 (The Writers of Melanie Klein Ser). Edited by Money-Kyrle R. New York, Free Press, 1984, pp 344–369

Klein M: Notes on some schizoid mechanisms (1946), in Envy and Gratitude and Other Works 1946–1963. Edited by Money-Kyrle R. New York, Free Press, 1984, pp 1–24

Klein M: Envy and gratitude (1957), in Envy and Gratitude and Other Works 1946–1963. Edited by Money-Kyrle R. New York, Free Press, 1984, pp 176–235

Kohut H: Forms and transformations of narcissism. J Am Psychoanal Assoc 14:243–272, 1966

Kohut H: The psychoanalytic treatment of narcissistic personality disorders. Psychoanal Study Child 23:86–113, 1968

Kohut H: The Analysis of the Self. New York, International Universities Press, 1971

Kohut H: Thoughts on narcissism and narcissistic rage. Psychoanal Study Child 27:377–400, 1972

Kohut H: The Restoration of the Self. New York, International Universities Press, 1977

Kohut H: The two analyses of Mr. Z. Int J Psychoanal 60:3–27, 1979

Kohut H: How Does Analysis Cure? Chicago, IL, University of Chicago Press, 1984

Kohut H, Wolf ES: The disorders of the self and their treatment: an outline. Int J Psychoanal 59:413–425, 1978

Mahler MS, Pine F, Bergman A: The Psychological Birth of the Human Infant. New York, Basic Books, 1975

Reich A: Narcissistic object choice in women. J Am Psychoanal Assoc 1:22–44, 1953

Reich A: Pathologic forms of self-esteem regulation. Psychoanal Study Child 15:215–232, 1960

Schafer R: A New Language for Psychoanalysis. New Haven, CT, Yale University Press, 1976

Segal H: Introduction to the Work of Melanie Klein, 2nd Edition. New York, Basic Books, 1973

Stern DN: The Interpersonal World of the Infant. New York, Basic Books, 1985

Sutherland JD: Object relations theory and the conceptual model of psychoanalysis. Br J Med Psychol 36:109–124, 1963

Chapter 2

Gender Differences in Narcissistic Styles

JUDITH A. RICHMAN, Ph.D.
JOSEPH A. FLAHERTY, M.D.

Editor's Note

Having reviewed psychoanalytic conceptualizations of narcissism, Chapter 2 begins to move us in a different direction. Recent decades have seen a remarkable growth of knowledge about psychiatric phenomena through applications of empirical methodology. In this chapter, Judith A. Richman, Ph.D., and Joseph A. Flaherty, M.D., provide the first data on the presence of narcissistic traits in a normal population of medical students, exploring whether there may be gender bias in the current criterion set for narcissistic personality disorder in DSM-III-R.

Chapter 2

Gender Differences in Narcissistic Styles

Narcissistic personality traits and psychopathology have evoked widespread interest during the last decade among social scientists interested in deciphering apparent changes in American society and national character as well as mental health professionals engaged in clinical practice (Jacoby 1980; Kernberg 1975, 1984; Kohut 1971, 1977; Lasch 1979, 1984). Theoretical perspectives on narcissism since Freud's (1914) classical work have evolved out of clinical work with particular patient populations, frequently those from affluent backgrounds undergoing long-term psychoanalysis (Langman and Richman 1987). More recently, empirically oriented researchers have begun to study personality disorders in varied treatment settings, using standardized diagnostic instruments yielding DSM-III (American Psychiatric Association 1980) and DSM-III-R (American Psychiatric Association 1987) diagnoses (Plakun 1987; Reich 1987). These studies use quantitative methodologies to address the reliability and validity of clinical concepts as well as to begin to study the treated prevalence of these disorders.

Although clinical case studies and the more limited quantitative research to date have helped to clarify the nature and etiology of narcissistic pathology seen by clinicians, minimal knowledge exists regarding the nature and prevalence of narcissism in the general population. This knowledge gap is particularly significant insofar as epidemiologists consistently find that treated disorders represent the "tip of the iceberg" in terms of the overall magnitude of psychopathology in populations. Thus, many psychologically distressed individuals never seek mental health treatment (Mechanic 1982). Of additional importance is the growing interest in comorbidity, particularly between affective disorders, substance abuse, and personality disorders. For example, there has been a long-standing interest in those personality traits or disorders that make individuals particularly vulnerable to depression. These lines of inquiry lead to the question of whether patients with narcissistic personality disorder are particularly prone to depressive episodes or substance abuse, especially when faced with a severe narcissistic injury.

Finally, although clinicians frequently diagnose psychopathological conditions without regard to social status characteristics, epidemiological research points to sizable relationships between social characteristics such as gender, social class, or ethnicity and the relative prevalence and differential mode of expressing various disorders (Dohrenwend and Dohrenwend 1981). In sum, we know little about the occurrence of narcissistic traits and psychopathology and related disorders in the general population or about the relative prevalence of these traits across different social groups in either the general population or in mental health treatment settings.

This chapter focuses on gender differences in narcissistic styles of expression insofar as gender has been a key variable associated with the differential expression of psychopathology. Although virtually no empirical research has yet addressed the question of gender differences in narcissism, provocative theoretical formulations argue that narcissism takes on very different forms in men and women. This chapter first reviews alternative theoretical perspectives regarding the salience of gender in relationship to the manifestation of narcissism. We then present empirical data examining gender differences in the manifestation of narcissistic traits in a particular nonclinical population, a medical school setting.

Theoretical Perspectives

Psychology of Women Perspectives

During the last decade, while narcissism was becoming a major focus of interest within psychiatry, a parallel literature on the psychology of women was rapidly developing within psychology and the other social sciences. Much of this literature suggests that there are profound personality differences between the sexes. These differences are seen to result from differing childhood socialization experiences, the differing adult work and familial roles of men and women, and the political-economic distribution of status, wealth, and power in the society (Herman 1983). Within the context of childhood socialization, differing parent-daughter and parent-son relationships are seen to produce female personalities embodying a stronger sense of and need for interpersonal attachments and empathic relatedness, in contrast to male personalities characterized by stronger needs for autonomy and differentiation from others (Chodorow 1978; Gilligan 1982; Jordan and Surrey 1986; Miller 1976).

With the perspective of object-relations psychoanalytic theory within a sociology of gender roles context, Chodorow (1978) provides one of the most detailed analyses of familial processes that are seen to give rise to gender differences in personality. Her main argument is that male and female adult personalities develop out of very different preoedipal and oedipal object-relational experiences that reflect the centrality of the mother as the major parenting figure in the nuclear family and the corresponding relative absence of the father within the family setting. During the preoedipal period, mothers experience their daughters as more like and continuous with themselves, whereas they view their sons as more opposite. For girls, the later resolution of the oedipal complex involves the retention of the intense preoedipal emotional bond with the mother, with the father playing a much more limited, mainly erotic, role. For boys, the oedipal complex involves the shift to an identification with the father who represents a more distant, less present relationship, and the need to deny or reduce the earlier preoedipal attachment to the mother.

The overall thrust of Chodorow's argument is that women emerge from these processes with a sense of self more continuous with others and the capacity to experience another's needs or feelings as one's own. By contrast, men come to define themselves as more separate and distinct, with a greater sense of rigid ego boundaries and differentiation. In addition, the relative absence of the father in the traditional family leads sons to experience their mother's presence as overwhelming and intrusive, giving rise to men's resentment and dread of women.

Whereas Chodorow linked traditional gender roles in the family to sex-differentiated personality development without regard to pathology per se, Philipson (1985) used a similar mode of analysis to suggest that traditional family structures give rise to sex-differentiated expressions of narcissistic psychopathology. Following Kohut, she sees narcissism as deriving largely from inadequate empathic responses by the mother in relation to the child's developing sense of self. However, she argues that faulty maternal empathy takes different forms in relation to sons versus daughters. Unempathic mothers are more likely to treat daughters rather than sons as extensions of themselves. This is seen to produce female narcissistic issues involving the quest for self-esteem through fusion and merger with omnipotent others. By contrast, sons are more likely to be treated as other objects rather than extensions of the mother. Thus, male narcissism is seen to be manifested by a defensive separateness from the mother, characterized by grandiosity, extreme self-centeredness, and the need for admiration. In summary, low self-esteem and a deficient psychic structure are viewed by Philipson as the root of both male and female narcissism. However, the mode of narcissistic expression will vary by gender: women are more likely to need to attach themselves to outstanding figures, whereas men will desire to be those figures.

Sociohistorical Analyses

Social historians interested in the relationship between social structure and personality have used clinical theory and case studies from Freud through contemporary psychoanalytic writings to attempt to document the changing modes of psychopathology linked to changing social structures. Lasch (1979) provides the major analysis of the changing economic organization of society from early capitalism to the current corporate-bureaucratic organization of work and corresponding family structures which he views as resulting in narcissistic psychopathology.

Lasch's main argument is premised on the notion that pathology represents a heightened version of normality. Thus, "each age develops its own peculiar forms of pathology which express in exaggerated form its underlying character structure" (p. 41). Lasch's psychoanalytically informed descriptions of contemporary narcissistic personality traits and styles encompass a broad survey of contemporary literature and journalism depicting various institutions and social movements in contemporary society. Although his theoretical analysis ignores gender as a major variable influencing the manifestation of narcissism, many of his examples appear congruent with perspectives suggesting that men and women will express narcissism in different ways. For example, he (1979) quotes and then analyzes a woman involved in the radical politics of the 1960s:

> "I felt I was part of a vast network of intense, exciting and brilliant people." When the leaders she idealized disappointed her, as they always did, she looked for new heroes to take their place, hoping to warm herself in their "brilliance" and to overcome her feeling of insignificance. (p. 7)

By contrast, he (1979) describes male managers in the corporate world by quoting from Michael Maccoby's study:

> The new executive, boyish, playful, and "seductive," wants in Maccoby's words "to maintain an illusion of limitless options."

> He has little capacity for "personal intimacy and social commitment." . . . In his upward climb, this man cultivates powerful customers and attempts to use them against his own company. . . . In all his personal relations, the gamesman depends on the admiration or fear he inspires in others to certify his credentials as a "winner." (pp. 44–45)

Consistent with Philipson's argument, the female radical appears to seek her esteem through the idealization of and fusion with powerful figures, whereas the male corporate executive manifests a defensive separateness from others through relationships that are mainly exploitative, gaining his esteem through the admiration he seeks from others on the basis of his own actions.

Sociological Perspectives

Mainstream sociology has, for the most part, remained silent in the debates regarding the "culture of narcissism" (Valadez and Clignet 1987). However, sociological perspectives suggest a different set of issues for understanding the prevalence and etiology of narcissism. With regard to gender differences in narcissism, a major question involves the nature of the macroscopic and microscopic social forces giving rise to a high prevalence of unempathic mothering and the consequent high prevalence of narcissism in male and female offspring at a given historical period (Valadez and Clignet 1987). Lorber et al. (1981), for example, critiqued Chodorow's argument for presenting a view of mothering that appeared to her to be culture and time bound.

The psychology of women literature has most extensively analyzed the twentieth century "traditional" nuclear family as the microsetting for the genesis of (gender-linked) personality styles as well as modes of expressing narcissistic pathology in particular. However, the last few decades have witnessed gender role changes characterized by the widespread exit of women from full-time family roles and into occupational roles along with some, though apparently much more limited, realignment of male familial roles to include increased male household and parenthood involvement (Coverman and Shelley 1986; Ross 1987).

Interestingly, when Kohut (1977) digressed from a focus on clinical theory per se to speculation regarding the sociohistorical etiology of narcissism (in both sexes), he partially implicated the increased employment of women outside the home as a factor in the creation of emotionally depriving families that failed to fulfill their childrens' selfobject needs. In a different vein, Lasch (1984) cited the "emergence of the egalitarian family" and weakening of paternal power as contributors to the emergence of the "culture of narcissism." The extent to which particular cohort-linked familial gender roles are associated with gender differences in narcissistic psychopathology in offspring constitutes an important area for empirical investigations.

In addition, given the traditional societal bias favoring the birth of male infants, it is likely that very early parental and extended family attitudes, hopes, and aspirations have been differentially linked to boys and girls. As a result of the transmission of societal values through familial socialization, boys may emerge from the first year of life with an exalted sense of self, entitlement, and grandiosity, whereas girls may be left with a feeling of being less deserving or important. The fact that these attitudes may be conveyed and incorporated into boys' and girls' developing selves before gender identity emerges strengthens the effect. By such a process, girls may emerge into oedipal and adolescent development with a preverbal and unconscious sense of inferiority, boys with an exalted sense, without the verbal and cognitive memory sets that might later, such as through psychotherapy, allow them to comprehend and work through the genesis of these states. However, the extent to which more recent cohorts of children may have experienced familial socialization processes encompassing more gender-neutral attitudes remains to be addressed on an empirical level.

Psychoanalytic Perspectives

A detailed survey of the vast clinical literature addressing narcissistic pathology or the drawing of in-depth contrasts between different perspectives such as those of Kohut (1971, 1977) and Kernberg (1975, 1984) is beyond the scope of this chapter. However, to broadly characterize the clinical psychoanalytic literature as a whole, gender status has not been viewed as playing a major role in influencing either the relative prevalence of narcissism or the particular ways in which it is manifested. Philipson (1985) argued that psychoanalytic case studies of narcissism have predominantly focused on men. She suggests that, as a consequence, psychiatric conceptualizations of narcissism tend to highlight male styles involving grandiosity, extreme self-centeredness, and the great need to be admired. By contrast, the (more predominantly) female search for esteem through the fusion with omnipotent objects receives relatively less attention.

One clear exception to the disproportionate focus on male cases of narcissism can be found in Kernberg's interesting commentary "Barriers to Falling and Remaining in Love" (1976, pp. 185–213). This material encompasses psychoanalytic theory with explicit references to gender as well as contrasting male and female cases depicting narcissistic and borderline pathologies affecting love relationships. In discussing pathology in men, Kernberg wrote: "Devaluation of female sexuality by these male patients, plus denial of their own dependency needs for women, contributes to their incapacity to sustain any deep personal and sexual involvement with them" (p. 195). By contrast, he described borderline women as clinging "desperately to men idealized so primitively" (p. 197). Describing one female patient, he wrote: "Her ruthless exploitation of most people contrasted sharply with her complete dedication and submission to a young man she had met in another hospital and to whom she daily wrote long, passionate love letters" (p. 198). These descriptions of male and female expressions of narcissistic and/or borderline traits would appear consistent with Philipson's depiction of contrasting male and female styles of expression.

Empirical Assessments of Gender Differences in Narcissistic Traits

Given the theoretical formulations and selected clinical case materials suggesting that narcissistic modes of expression are gender linked, we sought to more systematically address this issue by operationalizing diagnostic criteria characterizing narcissistic psychopathology and by examining sex differences in the prevalence of these traits in one nonclinical setting: a population of medical students. We first summarize the results of an earlier study in which we operationalized DSM-III criteria for narcissistic personality disorders (Richman and Flaherty 1988) and then present our current research in which we operationalized DSM-III-R criteria.

Earlier Research With DSM-III Narcissistic Personality Disorder Criteria

Our first study (Richman and Flaherty, in press) involved a population of medical students (*N* = 195, 89% of the overall class) surveyed at the end of their first year of medical school training in March 1986. They were administered a questionnaire consisting of various self-report instruments including the Narcissistic Traits Scale (NTS) that we developed and assessments of depressive symptomatology as measured by the Center for Epidemiologic Studies Depression Scale (CES-D) (Radloff 1977; Weissman et al. 1977), and self-esteem as measured by the Rosenberg items previously used in epidemiologic research (Pearlin and Schooler 1978). The symptoms composing the CES-D represent the major symptoms in the clinical syndrome of depression, though the CES-D is most representative of dysphoric mood and does not correspond to a clinical diagnosis of depression. The CES-D provides for a possible range of scores from 0 to 60, taking into account both the prevalence and persistence of each symptom. The self-esteem items included 1) I feel that I have a number of good qualities. 2) I feel that I'm a person of worth, at least on an equal plane with others. 3) I am able to do things as well as most other people. 4) I take a positive attitude toward myself. 5) On the whole, I am satisfied with myself. 6) All in all, I am inclined to feel that I'm a failure. The self-esteem items are rated on a 4-point scale from strongly disagree to strongly agree (with item 6 reversed).

The NTS included the following items primarily intended to tap each of the DSM-III criteria for narcissistic personality disorder and, in one case, to reflect a Kohutian perspective: 1) He/she has often felt that others haven't been aware of his/her true capabilities (grandiosity). 2) His/her ideal fantasy in life would be to achieve national prominence (fantasies of unlimited success, power, etc.). 3) He/she tends to feel bad when he/she is around people who are clearly brighter (exhibitionism, requirements for constant admiration). 4) He/she sometimes feels really angry when not acknowledged for his/her accomplishments (reactions to the indifference of others—hypothesized to reflect male narcissism). 5) He/she gets really upset over little slights from others that shouldn't bother him/her (reactions to the indifference of others—hypothesized to reflect female narcissism). 6) He/she frequently feels angry because people (or places) don't deliver on things that he/she feels entitled to (entitlement). 7) He/she sometimes wishes that people were more willing to do what he/she would like them to do rather than pursuing their own ideas (interpersonal exploitativeness). 8) He/she has known a number of people who seemed really terrific at first but turned out to be the opposite (idealization/devaluation). 9) It is annoying for him/her to be around people who frequently talk about their problems (lack of empathy). 10) He/she is likely to feel empty or lost after breaking up with a close friend or leaving a place, e.g., college, for good (deficit in central structure of the personality). These items were rated on a 4-point scale from "very unlike" to "very like," tapping "the extent to which this person is similar to yourself."

From a psychometric perspective, we first examined the reliability of this scale in terms of its internal consistency as measured by coefficient alpha: the alphas were .66 for the overall sample, .59 for men, and .75 for women. To address its validity on a preliminary basis, we drew on the DSM-III characterization of narcissistic personality disorder as encompassing fragile self-esteem and frequent depressed mood. We calculated the Pearson correlations of the narcissism score with the CES-D and the Rosenberg self-esteem measures for the entire sample and for men and women separately. The correlations of the NTS with depressive mood were .39 ($P < .001$), .42 ($P < .001$), and .38 ($P < .01$) for the entire sample, men, and women respectively. The correlations of the NTS with low self-esteem were .27 ($P < .001$), .23 ($P < .01$), and .35 ($P < .01$), respectively. These data suggest that the overall DSM-III conceptualization of narcissistic personality disorder (as operationalized by the NTS) is equally valid for men and women in a medical student population.

Analyses of gender differences in narcissistic traits revealed no significant difference between the sexes on the overall scale. However, men scored significantly higher on 3 of the 10 items: He/she has often felt that others haven't been aware of his/her true capabilities (grandiosity); His/her ideal fantasy in life would be to achieve national prominence (fantasies of unlimited success, power, etc.); and It is annoying for him/her to be around people who frequently talk about their problems (lack of empathy). By contrast, one item was more strongly endorsed by women: He/she gets really upset over little slights from others that shouldn't bother him/her (reactions to the indifference of others).

The correlations between each NTS item and low self-esteem for men and women separately showed that more of the narcissistic traits were associated with low self-esteem in women (7 of the 10 items) than in men (4 of the 10 items). In addition, some items were clearly linked to low self-esteem in one sex but not in the other. For example, the item reflecting the lack of empathy toward others (It is annoying for him/her to be around people who frequently talk about their problems) significantly related to low self-esteem in men ($r = .17$, $P < .05$) but not in women. By contrast, the items reflecting anger at the indifference of others (He/she sometimes feels angry when not acknowledged for his/her accomplishments) and sense of entitlement (He/she frequently feels angry because people [or places] don't deliver on things that he/she feels entitled to) significantly related to low self-esteem in women ($r = .27$, $P < .05$, and $r = .21$, $P < .05$, respectively) but not in men. These data thus suggest that the overall conceptualization of narcissistic character traits is applicable to both sexes, but that some of the traits have greater significance for one sex alone. In particular, lack of empathy for the feelings of others appears to be a primarily male form of pathology, whereas vulnerability to slights and indifference from others may be the more typical female style.

The correlations between each NTS item and depressive symptomatology also provided support for the assumption that narcissistic pathology is frequently accompanied by depressive mood in both sexes: eight items were associated with depressive mood for men, whereas six items were associated with depressive mood for women. For men, depressive mood was most strongly associated ($r = .35$, $P <.001$) with the item: He/she has often felt that others haven't been aware of his/her true capabilities. By contrast,the strongest association ($r = .37$, $P <.001$) for women was with the item: His/her ideal fantasy in life would be to achieve national prominence. This latter characteristic was more likely to be manifested by men, but when manifested in either sex, it was more strongly linked to depressive mood in women than in men. In a similar manner, the item tapping feelings of inner deadness at the loss of an object or other environmental support was highly linked to depressive symptoms in men ($r = .33$, $P <.001$), but not at all linked to depressive symptoms in women, though the trait is equally prevalent in both sexes.

We concluded from this first study that the DSM-III conceptualization of the narcissistic personality as a whole, as operationalized by the NTS, is equally applicable to both sexes, but that individual traits appear to be sex linked in prevalence and in their differential association with deficits in self-esteem and dysphoric mood states. In particular, the greater male prevalence of grandiosity, fantasies of unlimited success, and lack of empathy in contrast to the greater female experience of distress in response to the indifference or criticism of others could be interpreted as consistent with the thesis that early object-relational patterns give rise to exaggerated male needs for differentiation from objects (expressed in terms of grandiosity and lack of empathy toward others) and female needs for merger with objects (expressed in terms of difficulties tolerating indifference or criticism from others).

These sex differences in personality were also seen to correspond to deficits deriving from two early selfobject-relational needs elaborated by Kohut (1971): the need to display and be admired for one's evolving capabilities and the need to experience a sense of merger with an idealized parental imago. However, whereas Kohut used the imagery of "Tragic Man" to depict the ostensibly gender-neutral psychic deficits resulting from parental deviations from optimal selfobject functions, we suggested that deficits related to grandiose needs may be more prevalent in men, whereas deficits related to needs for merger with an idealized parental imago may be more prevalent in women.

In addition, congruent with a more sociological perspective, we suggested that the finding that grandiosity as manifested by fantasies of achieving national prominence was linked to depressive mood in female but not in male medical students may be a consequence of the extent to which educational and occupational environments respond more "supportively" to certain healthy or pathological narcissistic needs in men compared with women. Some researchers have depicted medical schools as providing greater instrumental and emotional support for the occupational aspirations of male medical students compared with that provided for female students (Lorber 1984). From this perspective, certain narcissistic traits in men may be less depressogenic or devastating in relation to self-esteem in contrast to those traits in women insofar as the social environment provides relatively greater means for men to gratify the underlying needs.

Alternatively, there is evidence from our previous work that female medical students are more likely than male medical students to list a male faculty member as a major source of social support (Blumberg et al. 1984). This may suggest their greater need to identify with a valued authority figure. Adding to the usual burden of successful advancement in the medical profession, female medical students are still expected or expect themselves to also achieve success in their family lives as wives, daughters, and mothers, whereas male students and doctors are given a "reprieve" from domestic roles to concentrate on their professional success. These high expectations in women, rather than providing a richness of role-related rewards, may more commonly constitute a broader array of vulnerabilities and possible narcissistic injuries as female students and doctors try to achieve this enviable ideal of the "superwoman."

Gender Differences in Narcissistic Styles Corresponding to DSM-III-R Criteria

The data presented here represent a further exploration of gender differences in narcissistic styles in a medical student population as assessed by the Narcissistic Traits Scale—Revised Version (NTS-RV). This instrument was developed with the goal of expanding the number of items (from 10 to 18) to tap gender differences in greater depth. The items were written to correspond to each of the nine DSM-III-R criteria (with two items per criterion).

Sample. The sample was drawn from the first-year medical students (N = 184) entering a state college of medicine in the fall of 1987. During the initial registration period, the entire class was administered a self-report questionnaire focusing on various psychosocial variables and psychiatric symptom states. Participation was defined as confidential and voluntary. The final response rate (following a second request for participation 2 weeks later) was 91% of the cohort (N = 167). The sample was 66.5% male and 33.5% female, similar to the sex distribution of the total population. The mean age of the men was 23.9 and the mean age of the women was 23.5, with most of the respondents in their 20s. Both the men and women were predominantly single (89.27 and 83.6%, respectively) and from socioeconomic backgrounds characterized by parents with at least high school education and, in many cases, college and postgraduate training.

Measures. Table 1 presents the 18 NTS-RV items along with their correspondence to DSM-III-R criteria for narcissistic personality disorder. The items are rated on a 4-point scale from "very unlike" to "very like," tapping "the extent to which this person is similar to yourself."

As in the earlier study, the questionnaire included assessments of depressive symptomatology measured by the CES-D (Radloff 1977; Weissman 1977) and self-esteem measured by the Rosenberg items previously used in epidemiologic research by Pearlin and Schooler (1978).

To assess the reliability of the NTS-RV in terms of its internal consistency, we calculated alpha coefficients for the sample as a whole and for men and women separately. The alphas were .76, .75, and .77, respectively.

Our assessment of validity to date is similar to that of the previous study: the degree to which the overall NTS-RV significantly correlates with depressive mood and low self-esteem. In contrast to the results from our earlier study, the NTS-RV is significantly linked to depressive mood and low self-esteem in men only: $r = .37$ ($P < .001$) and $r = .28$ ($P < .01$), respectively. The contrasting female correlations with depressive mood and low self-esteem were .14 and .07, respectively.

Table 1. Narcissistic Traits Scale—Revised Version (NTS-RV): items and diagnostic criteria

DSM-III-R diagnostic criteria[a]	NTS individual items
(1) Reacts to criticism with feelings of rage, shame, or humiliation (even if not expressed)	1. He/she can feel incredibly angry when people criticize something he/she does.
	2. He/she gets upset over little slights that shouldn't really bother him/her.
(2) Is interpersonally exploitative: takes advantage of others to achieve his/her own ends	3. If he/she were hiring employees, he/she would look for people who would advance his/her goals and not pursue their own interests.
	4. He/she tends to seek out people he/she likes to be with because of their exceptional attractiveness, talent, or success.
(3) Has a grandiose sense of self-importance, e.g., exaggerates achievements and talents, expects to be noticed as "special" without appropriate achievement	5. He/she has often felt that others haven't been aware of his/her true capabilities.
	6. He/she often gets positive feedback from others on his/her exceptional skills or unique ways of understanding things.
(4) Believes that his/her problems are unique and can be understood only by other special people	7. He/she might have difficulty finding kindred spirits or confidants because many people are not sophisticated enough to appreciate his/her unique qualities.

	8. He/she often finds it difficult to find people able to understand his/her problems because they are so complex.
(5) Is preoccupied with fantasies of unlimited success, power, brilliance, beauty, or ideal love	9. His/her ideal fantasy in life would be to achieve national prominence.
	10. He/she expects to have a perfect love relationship even if many people he/she knows have relationships that don't seem to be all that great.
(6) Has a sense of entitlement: unreasonable expectation of especially favorable treatment, e.g., assumes that he/she does not have to wait in line when others must do so	11. He/she gets very irritated when minor bureaucrats try to enforce petty regulations on him/her (e.g., parking violations, library fines).
	12. He/she often feels that he/she should be able to skip long waits or lines in stores, restaurants, etc., when his/her time is especially precious.
(7) Requires constant attention and admiration, e.g., keeps fishing for compliments	13. He/she has a classy or somethat flamboyant style of dress and likes to be complimented for his/her taste.
	14. He/she tends to feel best when regarded as one of the brightest or most talented people in his/her social setting.

continued

Table 1. Narcissistic Traits Scale—Revised Version (NTS-RV): items and diagnostic criteria *(continued)*

DSM-III-R diagnostic criteria[a]	NTS individual items
(8) Lack of empathy: inability to recognize and experience how others feel, e.g., annoyance and surprise when a friend who is seriously ill cancels a date	15. It is annoying for him/her to be around people who frequently talk about their problems.
	16. He/she feels irritated when people cancel plans because of illness, since he/she manages to fulfill obligations even when sick.
(9) Is preoccupied with feelings of envy	17. He/she would feel very bad if most of his/her friends did better in school than he/she.
	18. He/she tends to feel jealous of people who are more attractive or successful than he/she.

[a] Reprinted with permission from American Psychiatric Association 1987. Copyright 1987 American Psychiatric Association.

Gender Differences Across NTS-RV Components. To determine the extent to which the prevalence of narcissistic traits as measured by the NTS-RV are linked to gender status, we performed several analyses. First, a one-way analysis of variance was computed to determine whether there was a significant difference between men and women on the overall NTS-RV. Second, we performed similar analyses for each item, addressing the extent to which the component parts of the overall NTS-RV discriminate between men and women. Last, to the extent that narcissistic pathology is assumed to reflect low self-esteem and relate significantly to depressed mood, we calculated Pearson correlations of the relationships between each narcissistic trait and both depressive symptomatology and low self-esteem. These correlations were calculated separately for men and women to further assess the extent to which particular traits more clearly reflect gender-linked narcissistic styles.

Results. First, as shown near the bottom of Table 2, the analysis of variance examining sex differences in the overall NTS-RV score showed no significant difference between the two sexes. Thus, the male and female medical students in our sample do not appear to vary in their overall manifestation of narcissistic traits, as measured by the NTS-RV.

The analyses of sex differences on the individual items comprising the NTS-RV, shown in Table 2, provide support for the thesis that men and women express narcissistic issues in different ways. Six of the 18 items discriminated between the men and women at a significant or trend level, with the men scoring higher on all but one of those items. The items in which men scored higher included 1) If he/she were hiring employees, he/she would look for people who would advance his/her goals and not pursue their own interests (exploitativeness), ($P < .05$). 2) He/she tends to seek out people he/she likes to be with because of their exceptional attractiveness, talent, or success (exploitativeness) ($P < .05$). 3) He/she might have difficulty finding kindred spirits or confidants because many peo-

Table 2. Gender differences in narcissistic traits

Narcissistic traits	Men (mean ± SD)	Women (mean ± SD)	*F* (df = 1)
Reactions to criticism			
1. Angry when people criticize something	2.12 ± 0.74	2.05 ± 0.82	.257
2. Upset over slights	2.01 ± 0.83	2.25 ± 1.0	2.767*
Interpersonally exploitative			
3. Hires to advance self	1.97 ± 0.80	1.66 ± 0.82	5.620**
4. Seeks out exceptional people	2.28 ± 0.90	1.96 ± 0.87	4.678**
Grandiose sense of self			
5. People not aware of true capabilities	2.11 ± 0.82	2.05 ± 0.72	.675
6. Gets feedback on exceptional skills	3.08 ± 0.66	3.12 ± 0.69	.159
Uniqueness of problems			
7. Hard to find sophisticated confidants	1.93 ± 0.90	1.54 ± 0.76	7.785***
8. Problems are so complex	1.84 ± 0.82	1.64 ± 0.69	2.108
Fantasies of unlimited success			
9. Achieve national prominence	2.12 ± 0.93	1.91 ± 0.86	1.923
10. Have perfect love relationship	2.58 ± 0.95	2.50 ± 1.0	.232
Sense of entitlement			
11. Irritated by petty regulations	2.68 ± 0.97	2.30 ± 0.99	5.377**
12. Should skip waits or lines	1.77 ± 0.79	1.77 ± 0.89	.002
Requires attention/admiration			
13. Compliments for dress	1.95 ± 0.91	2.04 ± 0.99	.340
14. Regarded as brightest	2.55 ± 0.82	2.43 ± 0.93	.742
Lack of empathy			
15. Annoyed by people's problems	2.19 ± 0.71	1.98 ± 0.77	2.991*
16. People shouldn't cancel plans when ill	1.76 ± 0.82	1.77 ± 0.81	.007
Feelings of envy			
17. Feels bad if friends do better in school	2.37 ± 0.92	2.59 ± 1.02	1.91
18. Feels jealous of attractive/ successful people	2.04 ± 0.77	2.07 ± 0.99	.064
Overall scale	39.36 ± 6.50	37.75 ± 7.15	2.100

$^{*}P < .10$. $^{**}P < .05$. $^{***}P < .01$.

ple are not sophisticated enough to appreciate his/her unique qualities (views problems as unique) ($P < .01$). 4) He/she gets very irritated when minor bureaucrats try to enforce petty regulations on him/her, e.g., parking violations, library fines (entitlement) ($P < .05$). 5) It is annoying for him/her to be around people who frequently talk about their problems (lack of empathy) ($P < .10$). In sum, these reflect the dimensions of interpersonal exploitativeness, sense of uniqueness, entitlement, and lack of empathy. By contrast, the one item on which women manifested a higher score was He/she gets upset over little slights that shouldn't really bother him/her ($P < .10$). This reflects the dimension of oversensitivity to criticism.

Table 3 presents the Pearson correlations of each NTS-RV item with low self-esteem and depressive symptomatology separately for men and women. First, as shown near the bottom of the table and already noted with regard to evidence for the validity of the instrument and DSM-III-R construct for narcissistic personality disorder, the overall NTS-RV score is significantly linked to low self-esteem and depressive symptomatology for men but not for women ($r = .28$, $P < .01$, for self-esteem; $r = .37$, $P < .001$, for depressive symptomatology). To the extent that the NTS-RV adequately captures DSM-III-R criteria, these data are supportive of the perspectives suggesting that the overall conceptualization of narcissistic pathology focuses disproportionately on male issues.

Second, focusing on the relationship between individual narcissistic traits and low self-esteem (assumed to reflect the core deficit underlying narcissistic pathology), Table 3 indicates that 11 of the 18 items relate to low self-esteem in men and that 7 of the 18 items relate to low self-esteem in women at the significant ($P < .05$ or better) or trend ($P < .10$) levels. Interestingly, the one dimension in which both items manifested a strong link to low self-esteem for men and women was in the area of envy. In addition, the one dimension in which both items manifested a strong link to low self-esteem in men but no relation to female self-esteem was in the area involving the sense of uniqueness.

Table 3. Pearson correlations relating narcissistic traits to low self-esteem and depressive symptoms in men and women

	Psychopathology			
	Low self-esteem		Depressive symptoms	
Narcissistic traits	**Men**	**Women**	**Men**	**Women**
Reactions to criticism				
1. Angry when people criticize something	.19**	.13	.07	.00
2. Upset over slights	.16**	.42****	.30***	.32***
Interpersonally exploitative				
3. Hires to advance self	.11	.13	.40****	−.10
4. Seeks out exceptional people	.19**	.05	.18**	.00
Grandiose sense of self				
5. People not aware of true capabilities	.15**	.22**	.16**	.10
6. Gets feedback on exceptional skills	.07	.17*	−.06	.05
Uniqueness of problems				
7. Hard to find sophisticated confidants	.32****	.07	.34****	.07
8. Problems so complex	.43****	.04	.42****	.44****
Fantasies of unlimited success				
9. Achieve national prominence	.06	.09	.02	−.03
10. Have perfect love relationship	.03	.15	.00	.01
Sense of entitlement				
11. Irritated by petty regulations	.06	.19*	.16**	.07
12. Should skip waits or lines	.18**	.14	.13*	.09
Requires attention/admiration				
13. Compliments for dress	.02	.19	.04	.06
14. Regarded as brightest	.10	.13	.02	.04
Lack of empathy				
15. Annoyed by people's problems	.13*	.27**	.09	.19*
16. People shouldn't cancel plans when ill	.17**	.01	.18**	.10
Feelings of envy				
17. Feels bad if friends do better in school	.19**	.32***	.30****	.11
18. Feels jealous of attractive/ successful people	.32****	.43****	.27***	.37***
Overall scale	.28***	.07	.37****	.14

* $P < .10$. ** $P < .05$. *** $P < .01$. **** $P < .001$.

Third, focusing on depressive symptomatology, data in Table 3 indicate that 11 of the 18 items relate to depressive mood in men, but only 4 of the 18 items relate to depressive mood in women at the significant or trend level. Here it is apparent that each of the questions tapping two narcissistic personality disorder dimensions (interpersonal exploitativeness and sense of entitlement) are linked with depressive mood in men but not in women. For women and men, depressive mood is strongly associated with the item tapping jealousy as a component of envy and the item tapping difficulty finding people who can understand his/her problems since they are so complex. Finally, for the dimension pertaining to the lack of empathy, it is interesting to note that the item tapping annoyance at people's problems relates at the trend level to female depressive mood, whereas the item tapping the nonfulfillment of obligations relates significantly to male depression.

Discussion. Relative to the contemporary portrayal of narcissism as both a clinical disorder and a character style widely prevalent throughout society, this study represents one of the first empirical investigations of the extent to which men and women in a nonclinical population manifest similar or divergent narcissistic personality traits. More specifically, we addressed the extent to which the DSM-III-R conceptualization of narcissistic pathology as measured by the NTS-RV constitutes a sex-linked mode of expression in a medical student population. These data as a whole provide some empirical support for the notion that current conceptualizations of narcissism are disproportionately reflective of male modes of expressing psychopathology. In contrast to our earlier study operationalizing DSM-III criteria, this study showed that the DSM-III-R criteria overall, as measured by the NTS-RV, do not relate to low self-esteem or dysphoric mood in women. This suggests that the *overall* construct as measured by the NTS-RV is applicable to men but not to women. At the same time, subcomponents, most notably that of envy, do appear to be valid indicators of narcissism for both sexes.

Additional evidence for the disproportionate DSM-III-R

focus on male manifestations of narcissism can be found in the greater number of items in this study on which men manifested higher scores. At the same time, the lack of a significant gender difference on the overall instrument does suggest that the women in this particular population do manifest many traits that are theoretically considered "male" (although many of these traits correlate with low self-esteem and/or dysphoric mood only for men).

The content areas in which men manifested higher scores—those involving interpersonal exploitativeness, entitlement, and lack of empathy—can be interpreted, as in the earlier study, as reflecting exaggerated male needs for differentiation from objects. Moreover, the item tapping difficulty of finding sophisticated confidants due to the uniqueness of problems is probably most consistent with this perspective insofar as men scored higher than women, while manifesting a significant relationship between this trait and both low self-esteem and dysphoric mood. By contrast, the higher score for women on reactions to slights from others might again reflect greater female needs for merger with objects. At the same time and contrary to the psychology of women perspective, several categories, including grandiosity, fantasies of unlimited success, requirements for admiration, and feelings of envy, are manifested to the same extent by both sexes in this particular sample.

The overall interpretations of the data presented here and general conclusions drawn should be viewed as preliminary, given a number of methodological limitations of this research. First, this particular population of medical students is clearly nonrepresentative of the general population. In particular, women remain underrepresented among both medical student and physician populations proportionate to their representation in the general population. It is conceivable that women with more masculine personality traits are more likely to be selected into medicine. Thus, our research may underestimate the extent to which narcissistic character traits as currently conceptualized clinically are *more* strongly (male) sex-linked in the general population. In this respect, our tests of the hypothesized gender differences were clearly conservative.

Second, this study operationalized the narcissistic character style by developing a scale that primarily corresponds to the DSM-III-R narcissistic personality disorder construct. The NTS-RV manifested reliability in terms of the internal consistency of items and preliminary evidence for validity for men but not for women in terms of its ability to significantly correlate with both low self-esteem and dysphoric mood. We have not assessed the degree to which the scale discriminates between individuals manifesting a clinically diagnosed narcissistic personality disorder, other psychiatric disorders, or no psychiatric disorder. In addition, beyond the need for further validation of the NTS-RV is the question of the extent to which narcissism constitutes a clinical state discrete from "normality" or, alternatively, the end point of a continuum of traits (as argued by theorists such as Lasch). We developed a scale corresponding to DSM-III-R criteria but rating individual items on a continuum rather than as present or absent. This was based on the implicit view that pathology in the area of personality disorders as found in either treatment or general population settings is less reflective of "health" versus "illness" than of relative degrees of personality traits or styles. Relative to this perspective, some of our findings of gender differences in narcissistic styles in a particular community population appear similar to gender differences in narcissism apparent in clinical case descriptions.

Finally, from a sociological and epidemiological perspective, the extent to which the findings in this study are generalizable to other age groups and social classes remains to be addressed in future studies. With regard to age in particular, this sample represents a cohort likely to have grown up in families characterized by traditional gender-differentiated parental roles. To the extent that it is this particular family structure that gives rise to gender-differentiated narcissistic styles as argued by theorists such as Philipson, an interesting question for future empirical studies involves the extent to which younger individuals currently growing up in *relatively* less gender-differentiated families develop different (less gender-linked) manifestations of narcissism.

References

American Psychiatric Association: Diagnostic and Statistical Manual of Mental Disorders, 3rd Edition. Washington, DC, American Psychiatric Association, 1980

American Psychiatric Association: Diagnostic and Statistical Manual of Mental Disorders, 3rd Edition, Revised. Washington, DC, American Psychiatric Association, 1987

Blumberg P, Flaherty JA, Morrison A: Social support networks and psychological adaptation of female and male medical students. J Am Med Wom Assoc 39:165–167, 1984

Chodorow N: The Reproduction of Mothering. Berkeley, University of California Press, 1978

Coverman S, Shelley JF: Change in men's housework and childcare time, 1965–1975. Journal of Marriage and the Family 48:413–422, 1986

Dohrenwend BP, Dohrenwend BS: Socioenvironmental factors, stress, and psychopathology. Am J Community Psychol 9:128–164, 1981

Freud S: On narcissism (1914), in The Standard Edition of the Complete Psychological Works of Sigmund Freud, Vol 14. Translated and edited by Strachey J. London, Hogarth Press, 1957, pp 69–102

Gilligan C: In a Different Voice. Cambridge, MA, Harvard University Press, 1982

Herman M: Depression and women: theories and research. J Am Acad Psychoanal 2:493–512, 1983

Jacoby R: Narcissism and the crisis of capitalism. Telos 11:58–65, 1980

Jordan JV, Surrey JL: The self-in-relation: empathy and the mother-daughter relationship, in The Psychology of Today's Woman. Edited by Bernay T, Canton D. Hillsdale, NJ, Analytic Press, 1986

Kernberg O: Borderline Conditions and Pathological Narcissism. New York, Jason Aronson, 1975

Kernberg O: Object Relations Theory and Clinical Psychoanalysis. New York, Jason Aronson, 1976

Kernberg O: Severe Personality Disorders. New Haven, CT, Yale University Press, 1984

Kohut H: The Analysis of the Self. New York, International Universities Press, 1971

Kohut H: The Restoration of the Self. New York, International Universities Press, 1977

Langman L, Richman JA: Psychiatry as a vocation, in Current Research on Occupations and Professions, Vol 4. Edited by Lopato HZ. JAI Press, 1987

Lasch C: The Culture of Narcissism. New York, WW Norton, 1979

Lasch C: The Minimal Self. New York, WW Norton, 1984

Lorber J: Women Physicians. New York, Tavistock, 1984

Lorber J, Coser R, Rossi AS, et al: On the reproduction of mothering: a methodological debate. Signs 6:482–514, 1981

Mechanic D: Symptoms, Illness Behavior, and Help-Seeking. New York, Neale Watson Academic Publications, 1982

Miller JB: Toward a New Psychology of Women. Boston, MA, Beacon Press, 1976

Pearlin LI, Schooler C: The structure of coping. J Health Soc Behav 19:2–21, 1978

Philipson I: Gender and narcissism. Psychology of Women Quarterly 9:213–228, 1985

Plakun EM: Distinguishing narcissistic and borderline personality disorders using DSM-III criteria. Compr Psychiatry 28:437–443, 1987

Radloff LS: The CES-D scale: a self-report depression scale for research in the general population. Applied Psychology Measurement 1:385–401, 1977

Reich J: Sex distribution of DSM-III personality disorders in psychiatric outpatients. Am J Psychiatry 144:485–488, 1987

Richman JA, Flaherty JA: "Tragic Man" and "Tragic Woman": gender differences in narcissistic styles. Psychiatry (in press)

Ross C: The division of labor at home. Social Forces 65:816–831, 1987

Valadez J, Clignet R: On the ambiguities of a sociological analysis of the culture of narcissism. Sociological Quarterly 28:455–472, 1987

Weissman MM, Sholomskas D, Pottenger M, et al: Assessing depressive symptoms in five psychiatric populations: a validation study. Am J Epidemiol 106:203–219, 1977

Chapter 3

Empirical Overview of Narcissistic Personality Disorder

ERIC M. PLAKUN, M.D.

Editor's Note

This chapter reviews recent developments in the empirical understanding of narcissistic personality disorder as defined in DSM-III and DSM-III-R. Empirical psychiatric methodology is used to test the validity of this new diagnostic entity by comparing it to other well-established psychiatric diagnoses and to another closely related personality disorder, borderline personality disorder. It is through such empirical investigation of reliably diagnosed patients that psychoanalytic conceptualizations can be tested, scrutinized, and refined in light of the empirical reality of patients' lives, an essential step if narcissistic personality disorder is to move from an exclusively psychoanalytic concept into the realm of empirical psychiatry.

Chapter 3

Empirical Overview of Narcissistic Personality Disorder

The publication of the third edition of the *Diagnostic and Statistical Manual of Mental Disorders* (DSM-III) by the American Psychiatric Association in 1980, with its introduction of a separate axis for personality disorder diagnoses, has been an event heralding much empirical research into the personality disorders, especially borderline personality disorder (BPD). DSM-III has by now given way to the 1987 revision of the third edition, DSM-III-R, which has made subtle but significant changes in the Axis II personality disorders. These changes have included a reduction in criterion overlap among personality disorders, a decrease in the degree of diagnostic inference required to rate some criteria, and the use of an entirely polythetic diagnostic system for personality disorders, in which a specified minimum number of diagnostic criteria from a larger set is required to establish a diagnosis (Widiger et al. 1988). The monothetic diagnostic system sometimes used in DSM-III had required all criteria to be present for such diagnoses as schizoid, avoidant, dependent, and compulsive personality disorders.

Although narcissism has long been a subject of interest in psychoanalysis, especially in the decade preceding the publication of DSM-III, little empirical data about the disorder are available and there have been frequent calls for empirical data by authors of psychoanalytic papers on narcissism (Akhtar and Thomson 1982; Bursten 1982; Goldstein 1985; Nurnberg 1984; and others). The adoption of discrete diagnostic criteria for narcissistic personality disorder (NPD) in DSM-III has permitted the first systematic study of this disorder, but such data have lagged behind that available for BPD, the most extensively studied of the Axis II disorders. NPD as defined in DSM-III has become a useful benchmark, but the criterion set has been criticized for its lack of empirical support (Gunderson 1983; Vaillant and Perry 1985) and for not including recognition that NPD may be manifested in more ways than simply overt grandiosity, exhibitionism, and entitlement (Akhtar and Thomson 1982; Bursten 1982; Cooper 1987). In DSM-III-R, NPD has been altered significantly. A criterion concerning envy has been added, a separate criterion concerning the belief that one's problems are unique has been separated from its prior inclusion in the DSM-III "grandiosity" criterion, and "cool and indifferent response to criticism" has been deleted because of its overlap with a BPD criterion. Just as important as these criterion changes has been the shift to a fully polythetic diagnostic format for NPD requiring five of a set of nine criteria to be present to make the diagnosis, a distinct improvement over the DSM-III format requiring four criteria to be monothetically present and then at least two of the remaining four to be present. Despite these diagnostic refinements, though, little empirical data have been available about NPD until quite recently. Indeed, according to Siever and Klar (1986), "There are to our knowledge no empirical studies of the criteria for [NPD]. Its inclusion in DSM-III was based on the consensus of clinicians regarding its existence. . . . While [NPD] is widely discussed in the psychodynamic literature, there are no data supporting the coherence, validity or reliability of this diagnostic grouping" (pp. 299–301).

There are probably several reasons why empirical research has lagged in NPD. The diagnosis has been of primary interest to psychoanalysts and psychoanalytically oriented psychiatrists who historically have shown little interest in empirical research. Further, many narcissistic patients are relatively high functioning and either do not present for treatment at all or present as outpatients. Indeed, hospital treatment of NPD may be relatively rare in short-term hospital settings unless there is significant comorbidity with an Axis I diagnosis such as a major affective disorder, substance abuse and/or dependence, or another Axis II disorder, such as BPD with attendant physically self-damaging acts, self-destructiveness, and impulsivity leading to hospitalization.

At this writing, Gunderson, Perry, and others are in the process of collecting data on samples of narcissistic patients which will be welcome additions to the empirical data available on NPD. Gunderson and Ronningstam (1987) have been developing a semistructured diagnostic interview for narcissism (the DIN) assessing five dimensions of narcissism (grandiosity, interpersonal relations, reactiveness, affects and mood states, and social and moral adaptation), which overlap but are not identical to DSM-III NPD criteria. Ronningstam and Gunderson (1987) have reported that the DIN discriminates narcissistic from nonnarcissistic clinician-rated patients. The fully developed DIN should allow refined, reliable clinical diagnoses of NPD comparable to those now possible through use of the Diagnostic Interview for Borderlines (Gunderson et al. 1981).

Pfohl et al. (1986) at the University of Iowa have studied the internal consistency of individual DSM-III criteria. Of their 131 patients with personality disorder, only 5 met criteria for NPD. They were unable to calculate an overall kappa coefficient for interrater reliability for the presence of the diagnosis. Following the mixed monothetic and polythetic model of NPD found in DSM-III, Pfohl et al. studied the positive predictive value of each NPD criterion for the diagnosis—that is, the probability that a patient will meet criteria for NPD if a given criterion is present. The low positive predictive value of DSM-III criterion D (response to criticism), with its low interrater reliability (kappa = 0.20), was noteworthy. They speculate that the low reliability of this item resulted from the fact that "the full text of the criterion mentions six possible reactions to three possible situations: 'Cool indifference or marked feelings of rage, inferiority, shame, humiliation, or emptiness in response to criticism, indifference of others, or defeat.' [DSM-III, p. 317]" (Pfohl 1986, p. 29). Indeed, in DSM-III-R, this criterion is reworded to "reacts to criticism with feelings of rage, shame, or humiliation (even if not expressed)" (p. 351). DSM-III criterion E4 (lack of empathy) also showed poor reliability with a positive predictive value of only 20% and a kappa of 0. As has also been noted in numerous psychoanalytic articles, Pfohl et al. commented on the close relationship between NPD and BPD.

Recently, Stone (1989) and McGlashan and Heinssen (1989) have published studies of narcissism in patients with BPD. Stone (1989) found that long-term outcome of those P.I.-500 patients with BPD who had narcissistic traits falling short of or fulfilling criteria for NPD was similar to outcome in the overall group of BPD patients. Stone noted that BPD patients with NPD tended to be male and to be at greater risk for completed suicide than BPD patients without NPD. McGlashan and Heinssen (1989) evaluated the impact of narcissistic traits on long-term outcome of BPD patients from the Chestnut Lodge follow-up study. Although the authors found little difference at long-term follow-up between noncomorbid BPD patients and BPD patients with some narcissistic traits, at baseline, BPD patients with narcissistic traits showed a nonsignificant trend to have had more and longer hospitalizations and to be older at onset of illness and at index hospitalization than noncomorbid BPD patients. At follow-up, there was a nonsignificant trend for BPD patients with narcissistic traits to be functioning more poorly socially and vocationally, to have more problems with alcohol, to have been more likely to attempt suicide in the follow-up interval, and to have performed more poorly in terms of global functioning at follow-up than noncomorbid BPD patients. Both these studies are valuable contributions to the empirical understanding of personality disorders, but they do not offer data about NPD patients per se, because few if any patients with NPD who did not also meet criteria for BPD were found in the locked long-term settings under study. Nevertheless, the hints they provide that narcissistic traits are more often seen in male BPD patients and that BPD patients with narcissistic traits seem to show a consistent if nonsignificant trend toward worse outcome than noncomorbid BPD patients foreshadow some of the differences reported below about NPD patients with comorbid BPD.

Richman and Flaherty's interesting work on gender differences in narcissistic styles was presented in Chapter 2. The remaining empirical studies of NPD available in the literature to date are based on a group of former psychiatric inpatients who participated in a follow-up study after a mean of 14 years from admission at the Austen Riggs Center in Stockbridge, Massachusetts, a long-term, fully open psychiatric hospital emphasizing intensive psychoanalytic psychotherapy. Because the hospital's treatment emphasis is intensive psychoanalytic psychotherapy, it is more common than in other inpatient settings to find patients meeting the NPD diagnosis. Often these NPD patients have been unable to sustain outpatient treatment and are unlikely to benefit from short-term hospitalization.

Four pertinent empirical studies have emerged from the Austen Riggs Center follow-up study. In the first of these (Plakun 1987), I examine the frequency of BPD and NPD criteria in each of the two diagnoses, report phi coefficients of correlations for each BPD or NPD criterion with each diagnosis, and use a stepwise multiple-regression technique to assess the relative predictive power of the 16 total BPD and NPD criteria for each diagnosis. In the second of these studies (Plakun 1989), the validity of the NPD diagnosis is examined by comparing and contrasting NPD patients to those meeting DSM-III criteria for schizophrenic disorder or major affective disorder in terms of longitudinal course and mean 14-year outcome. In the third study (also Plakun 1989), I compare and contrast NPD and BPD patients, shedding light on similarities and differences between the two disorders, which have been conceptualized to be closely related and along the same diagnostic continuum. In the fourth study, correlates of outcome in NPD and BPD are reported and compared (Plakun 1988). Before summarizing the findings of these studies, a few words about methodology are appropriate.

Methods

All subjects were originally inpatients at the Austen Riggs Center, a long-term, fully open psychiatric hospital emphasizing intensive psychoanalytic psychotherapy at which the mean stay approaches one and a half years. Patients at the center have generally failed to benefit from prior short-term hospitalization and/or outpatient treatment with or without medication, leading to referral for longer-term inpatient treatment. Despite generally being treatment failures, patients are selected for their ability to work in a completely open setting and therefore are relatively high functioning. The most frequent diagnosis is BPD, with or without superimposed major affective disorder, but substantial numbers of patients also meet criteria for schizophrenic spectrum disorders or other severe personality disorders including NPD. There is no privilege system and no restriction of patients' freedom, and there are no closed units. There is 24-hour nursing coverage and a doctor on call, a voluntary activity program, and a self-governing patient community with staff consultants. During the index hospitalization, patients receive 4 or 5 hours of individual psychotherapy each week from an experienced board-eligible or -certified psychiatrist or doctorate-level clinical psychologist. Patients are referred from throughout the United States and from other countries. In 1979, an effort was made to contact by mail the 878 patients treated for at least 2 months between 1950 and 1976 to compare their current functioning to that preceding admission. A 2-month stay was determined to be the minimum period to have permitted collection of adequate data to make retrospective DSM-III diagnoses. Of the former patients, 252 could not be located, 262 failed to respond to requests for participation, 33 refused participation, and 94 had died, primarily in the oldest group of patients treated between 1950 and 1960.

Thus, from a domain of 878 former patients, 237 or 27% of the total group, but 45% of living former patients who could be located, responded to an invitation and completed mailed follow-up questionnaires. This response rate compares favorably with the 25–30% for mailed questionnaires preferred by Warner et al. (1983) in their study of follow-up methods. Warner et al. note that the lower response rate with mailed questionnaires, compared with in-person or telephone interviews, is more than compensated for by the minimization of responses intended to please the interviewer.

The sample consisted of 89 (38%) men and 148 (62%) women with a mean age of 24.5 years (SD 7.7 years) at admission. The mean length of stay during the index hospitalization was 16.6 months (SD 10.6). The mean interval between admission and follow-up was 13.6 years (SD 6.6). The sample proved representative of the entire population on the basis of respondent versus nonrespondent comparisons of admission variables, suggesting no significant difference between groups.

Each subject's hospital record contained preadmission and admission summaries, a detailed case history, nursing notes, and activities reports. Only variables for which blind raters could achieve adequate interrater agreement were used. Retrospective DSM-III diagnoses based on portions of the case record were made by two raters blind to patient identity and clinical diagnosis for the 237 respondents. Interrater reliability was established on 25 patients leading to kappa coefficients of 0.81 ($Z = 2.79$, $P < .01$, two tailed) and 0.69 ($Z = 2.02$, $P < .05$, two tailed) for Axis I and Axis II disorders, respectively. These compared favorably with the kappas of the DSM-III field trials in which Axis I and Axis II kappas were 0.68 and 0.56, respectively. The kappa for BPD alone among the jointly rated group of charts was 0.78 ($Z = 0.81$, $P < .05$). For NPD, kappa was 1.0 ($Z = 1.47$, $P = .07$), indicating complete rater agreement on the presence or absence of NPD in all cases in the sample of 25 charts. The kappa of 1.0 falling just short of significance reflects the infrequency of the NPD diagnosis in the sample; that is, most of the "agreement" in the kappa is about the absence of NPD. Certainly, kappa would not likely prove to be 1.0 for NPD among all 237 charts, but agreement of this degree in the reliability sample suggests adequate interrater agreement. DSM-III does not report kappas for individual Axis II diagnoses, so no comparison can be made. The two raters were in agreement about the presence or absence of individual NPD criteria between 75% (for "preoccupation with fantasies of success") and 90% (for "response to criticism") of the time. The 90% agreement on response to criticism is particularly noteworthy in light of the report of low interrater agreement for this criterion in the study by Pfohl et al. (1986). There was agreement about BPD criteria between 70% (for "unstable and intense relationships") and 95% (for "intolerance of being alone") of the time. Based on adequate demonstration of interrater agreement, the remaining patients were assigned DSM-III diagnoses, but were also rated for the presence or absence of each Axis II criterion by one of the two raters. In recognition of the problem posed by the mixed monothetic and polythetic diagnostic system of DSM-III, which confounds study of individual criteria, NPD was diagnosed with a polythetic model requiring the presence of at least five of the eight total DSM-III NPD criteria, A–D and E1–E4. Thus, although it was DSM-III criteria that were rated for NPD, the diagnosis was made with the polythetic system later adopted in DSM-III-R. The BPD diagnosis also required at least five of the eight DSM-III BPD criteria.

Forty-four patients met criteria for BPD but were free of major affective disorder (MAD) and NPD. Nineteen patients met criteria for NPD, but were free of MAD and BPD. Eight patients met criteria for both BPD and NPD while free of MAD and were excluded from subsequent comparisons. For the first study, which examined the ability of NPD and BPD criteria to distinguish between the two diagnoses, inclusion of BPD and NPD patients who nearly met criteria for the other diagnosis by meeting four of its criteria was desirable. Thus, all 44 BPD and all 19 NPD patients were included. For the remainder of the studies, though, where part of the focus was on comparing and contrasting BPD and NPD, the use of as "pure" a group of BPD and NPD subjects as possible was desirable. Further, it is probably true that long-term NPD inpatients are more likely to display borderline traits than outpatients, a factor also favoring elimination of patients meeting four criteria from the reciprocal diagnosis from the BPD and NPD groups. Two NPD patients were thus eliminated, leaving a group of 17 NPD patients, among whom 3 met five, 2 met seven, and 12 met six NPD criteria. Of these 17 NPD patients, 5 met three BPD criteria, 11 met two, and 1 met one. The most common BPD criterion found in 11 of the 17 NPD patients was "a pattern of unstable and intense relationships," probably reflecting the similarity of this criterion to the NPD criterion for "overidealized and devalued relationships." Since 14 of the 17 NPD patients met six or more of the eight NPD criteria, they were a strongly narcissistic group despite the presence of some borderline traits.

Eleven patients were eliminated from the original BPD group because they met more than three NPD criteria. Of the resulting group of 33 BPD patients, 2 met three NPD criteria, 8 met two, and the remainder met one or none. Thus, more than two-thirds of the "pure" BPD patients were free or nearly free of NPD traits.

Distinguishing NPD and BPD With DSM-III Criteria

Each BPD and NPD criterion was correlated with each of the two diagnoses and with all other BPD and NPD criteria for the less "pure" group of 44 BPD patients and 19 NPD patients. Phi correlation coefficients with χ^2 were used because the presence or absence of a criterion or diagnosis is categorical data. In addition, maximum R^2 and minimum R^2 improvement stepwise regressions rank ordering the ability of each BPD or NPD criterion to predict the presence of BPD were performed.

Table 1 lists all 16 NPD and BPD criteria, their frequency of occurrence in each of the two diagnoses, and the phi correlation coefficients of each criterion with each diagnosis. Among

Table 1. Narcissistic personality disorder (NPD) and borderline personality disorder (BPD) DSM-III criteria: frequency in NPD and BPD patients and phi correlation coefficients

	NPD patients (n = 19)		**BPD patients (n = 44)**			
	Frequency	**% with each criterion**	**Frequency**	**% with each criterion**	**Phi correlation coefficient**	**P of χ^2**
NPD criteria					vs. NPD	
A. Grandiose sense of self-importance	18	95	7	16	0.74	.0001
B. Preoccupation with fantasies of success	16	84	12	27	0.54	.0001
C. Exhibitionism	17	89	7	16	0.70	.0001
D. Cool indifference or overreaction	18	95	21	48	0.46	.0001
E1. Entitlement	9	47	1	2	0.52	.0001
E2. Interpersonal exploitativeness	16	84	10	23	0.58	.0001
E3. Overidealized and devalued relationships	6	32	8	18	0.16	.2
E4. Lack of empathy	9	47	5	11	0.41	.001
BPD criteria					vs. BPD	
A1. Impulsivity	8	42	40	91	0.44	.0001
A2. Unstable and intense relationships	12	63	39	89	0.21	.08
A3. Inappropriate, intense anger	4	21	26	59	0.31	.01

A4.	Identity disturbance	9	47	36	82	0.28	.02
A5.	Affective instability	5	26	29	66	0.32	.01
A6.	Intolerance of being alone	0	0	13	30	0.31	.01
A7.	Self-damaging acts	5	26	29	66	0.32	.01
A8.	Chronic emptiness or boredom	1	5	15	34	0.28	.02

Source. Adapted from Plakun 1987 with permission from publisher. Copyright Grune & Stratton 1987.

the NPD criteria, "grandiosity," found in 95% of NPD patients and only 16% of BPD patients, was the most highly predictive, with a phi correlation coefficient of 0.74 ($\chi^2 = 36.7$, $P < .0001$). "Overidealized and devalued relationships" had the only nonsignificant correlation with NPD (phi = 0.16, $P = .2$). It is immediately apparent that among the BPD criteria the correlations are considerably lower than is the case for NPD. "Unstable and intense relationships" was frequent in both BPD and NPD, leading to a phi coefficient of correlation of only 0.21, $P = .08$.

Table 2 reports results of a maximum R^2 improvement stepwise regression rank ordering the 16 criteria for BPD and NPD in terms of their ability to predict the presence of BPD. The same sequence emerged from the use of a minimum R^2 improvement stepwise regression. Table 2 shows the sequence of the regression and the rank by phi correlation coefficient alone for comparison. Because the multiple regression takes intercorrelations between individual criteria into consideration, the rank by phi correlation coefficient alone is not duplicated. For example, "grandiosity" and "exhibitionism" have the highest individual correlations with the NPD and BPD diagnoses overall (phi = ± 0.74 and phi = ± 0.70, respectively), but are also highly intercorrelated (phi = 0.71, $\chi^2 = 3.12$, $P < .0001$), thereby diminishing the predictive power of each criterion in the overall stepwise regression.

The predictive power gained by adding variables fell off sharply after the first five, so an additional maximum R^2 improvement stepwise regression was performed to extract the best five-variable model for distinguishing BPD and NPD. This model accounts for 81% of the total variance in discriminating between the two diagnoses (df = 62, $P = .001$). Table 2 also shows the sequence of this regression. Note that the sequence is not the same as the first five criteria of the best 16-variable model. It is worth noting that NPD criteria appear to have the greatest power to discriminate between NPD and BPD, four of the five criteria proving to be NPD criteria.

This study demonstrates that DSM-III BPD and NPD cri-

Table 2. Sequence of maximum R^2 stepwise regressions of 16- and 5-criteria models for prediction of borderline personality disorder (BPD) with rank by phi correlation coefficient

Rank in 16-variable model (beta weight; *P*)	Rank in 5-variable model (beta weight; *P*)	Rank by phi alone	DSM-III criterion	
1 (−.29; .0001)	1 (−.36; .0001)	5	NPD E1	Entitlement
2 (−.27; .0004)	4 (−.23; .004)	2	NPD C	Exhibitionism
3 (.23; .003)		13	BPD A8	Emptiness or boredom
4 (−.21; .004)	2 (−.35; .0001)	1	NPD A	Grandiosity
5 (.18; .0004)	5 (.22; .0001)	11	BPD A3	Inappropriate, intense anger
6 (.16; .002)		10	BPD A7	Self-damaging acts
7 (.15; .02)		7	BPD A1	Impulsivity
8 (−.13; .03)		3	NPD E2	Exploitativeness
9 (−.11; .06)	3 (−.23; .0001)	4	NPD B	Preoccupation with fantasies of success
10 (.07; .2)		9	BPD A5	Affective instability
11 (.07; .2)		15	BPD A2	Unstable and intense relationships
12 (.06; .3)		16	NPD E3	Overidealized and devalued relationships
13 (.05; .4)		12	BPD A6	Intolerance of being alone
14 (.04; .5)		6	NPD D	Cool indifference or overreaction
15 (.01; .8)		8	NPD E4	Lack of empathy
16 (−.01; .8)		14	BPD A4	Identity disturbance

Note. $n = 63$ patients with BPD or narcissistic personality disorder (NPD). df = 62.
Source. Adapted from Plakun 1987 with permission from publisher. Copyright Grune & Stratton 1987.

teria can reliably discriminate between the two diagnoses. NPD criteria had more predictive power than BPD criteria in discriminating between the two diagnoses whether one looked at phi coefficients of correlation or stepwise regressions. NPD criteria may simply be more specific than BPD criteria, which in a number of respects describe a generic personality disturbance rather than the kind of specific mental content or focused interpersonal impairment delineated in NPD. It is also possible that the greater predictive power of NPD criteria in this sample reflects the likelihood that NPD patients disturbed enough to present for treatment at a long-term hospital may have significant borderline liability despite meeting few BPD criteria. This would suggest that these NPD patients may differ from NPD outpatients. Kernberg (1975, 1980) and Adler (1981, 1986) have written of a range of severity of pathology in narcissistic patients. The relatively high frequency of such BPD criteria as "impulsivity," "unstable and intense relationships," and "identity disturbance" in NPD patients is consistent with this explanation. In any case, the data available from these patients do suggest that DSM-III criteria for NPD and BPD can reliably distinguish between the two diagnoses, even in a patient sample in which the difference between the diagnoses may be minimal. As a cautionary note, it is important to remember that these data shed no light on discrimination of any other diagnosis from either NPD or BPD.

It is worth noting that the correlations in Table 1 and the regressions in Table 2 do not lead to the same sequences in rank ordering the predictive value of individual criteria for these two diagnoses. The stepwise regressions take intercorrelations between criteria into account in a way that simple rank ordering of correlations cannot. An example of this has been cited above for NPD "grandiosity" and "exhibitionism." The findings of this study support the decision implemented in DSM-III-R to minimize the degree of intercorrelation in the BPD criteria for "impulsiveness" and "self-mutilating behavior" by specifying that the same behavior cannot be used to meet both criteria. The phi correlation coefficient for the

DSM-III version of these two criteria was significant (phi = 0.36, $\chi^2 = 8.50$, $P = .004$). Similarly, these data support the decision implemented in DSM-III-R to eliminate the NPD criterion for "overidealized and devalued relationships," which is quite similar to the BPD criterion for "unstable and intense relationships." This feature of relationships is so much more prototypic of the BPD diagnosis that the NPD version of the criterion failed even to approach significance in discriminating between the two diagnoses, as shown in Table 1.

Validity of NPD

A decade before the introduction of DSM-III, Robins and Guze (1970) made an important contribution to psychiatric diagnosis by proposing steps required in establishing the validity of new diagnostic entities. One of their essentials in exploring the validity of new diagnostic entities is long-term follow-up in comparison with other disorders. Since the publication of DSM-III, studies by Pope et al. (1983), McGlashan (1983, 1986), Stone et al. (1987), Paris et al. (1987), and Plakun et al. (1985, 1987) have presented longitudinal course and outcome data on BPD compared with other diagnostic groups, which have gone a long way toward establishing the validity of BPD as defined in DSM-III. Indeed, despite the inherent methodologic weaknesses of retrospective psychiatric research, it has proven an extremely valuable technique in assessing diagnostic validity because the look back can provide data about longitudinal performance of patients in newly introduced diagnostic categories. NPD and the other personality disorders have not received as much interest as BPD heretofore. Recently, I (1989) have provided the first longitudinal course and outcome data on NPD, comparing it with schizophrenia and MAD, thereby following the procedure recommended by Robins and Guze for establishing the validity of new diagnostic entities, and following the course already charted for BPD.

As described above, two NPD patients meeting four BPD criteria were excluded from the study, as were patients meeting criteria for MAD, to provide as pure a group of NPD patients as possible. These 17 "pure" NPD patients were compared with 19 schizophrenic patients and 26 patients with MAD in terms of preadmission, index hospitalization, and follow-up measures. Categorical variables were compared using an overall χ^2 distribution with post hoc analysis of individual-cell χ^2 where relevant. The continuous variables were studied with a one-way analysis of variance with post hoc comparison of the means with Duncan's multiple-range test.

Although statistically significant differences were relatively few, the preponderance of the data suggest that NPD, as has been previously demonstrated for BPD by McGlashan, Plakun et al., and Stone, tends to be more easily distinguished from schizophrenia than from MAD. NPD tended to differ from schizophrenia and/or MAD on 19 of the 25 preadmission measures used (Table 3), 3 of the 7 index hospitalization measures (Table 4), and 15 of the 19 follow-up measures (Table 5). Significant differences were noted in terms of preadmission social functioning (11% of schizophrenic patients were married versus 54% of MAD and 41% of NPD patients, $\chi^2 = 9.01$, $df = 2$, $P = .01$), preadmission hospitalization history (mean Strauss-Carpenter hospital scale score at admission higher in NPD patients at 3.7 than in schizophrenic patients at 2.9, Duncan's multiple-range test, $F = 3.19$, $df = 2$, $P < .05$), and greater preadmission chronicity in schizophrenia, where the mean age at first mental health contact was 16.2 versus 23.0 in MAD and 22.6 in NPD (Duncan's multiple-range test, $F = 4.07$, $df = 2$, $P = .02$). Two measures of global functioning at admission were significant. The mean admission Global Assessment Scale (GAS) score in schizophrenic patients was significantly lower at 30.2 than in MAD patients at 34.9 or NPD patients at 35.4 (Duncan's multiple-range test, $F = 8.76$, $df = 2$, $P < .001$). Significantly more schizophrenic patients presented at admission with major impairment as defined by a GAS score below 30 (58% of schizophrenic patients versus 19% of MAD and 18% of NPD patients, $\chi^2 = 9.6$, $df = 2$, $P < .01$).

Significant differences were found at follow-up in terms of

Table 3. Validation summary of preadmission measures for narcissistic personality disorder (NPD) versus schizophrenia and major affective disorder (MAD)

Variable	NPD trend distinct from schizophrenia	NPD trend distinct from MAD	NPD unique	NPD indistinguishable from either	Row total
Social functioning	2*	0	0	1	3
Vocational functioning	0	0	1	2	3
Outpatient treatment	0	1	2	0	3
Hospital treatment	2*	0	4	1	7
Symptoms	1*	3	0	2	6
Global functioning	2**	0	1	0	3
Column total	7*****	4	8	6	25

*Statistically significant difference at $P < .05$ or better.

Table 4. Validation summary of demographic, family history, and index hospitalization measures for narcissistic personality disorder (NPD) versus schizophrenia and major affective disorder (MAD)

Variable	NPD trend distinct from schizophrenia	NPD trend distinct from MAD	NPD unique	NPD indistinguishable from either	Row total
Demographic	0	1	0	1	2
Family history	0	0	1	0	1
Index hospitalization	3	0	0	4	7

Table 5. Validation summary of follow-up measures for narcissistic personality disorder (NPD) versus schizophrenia and major affective disorder (MAD)

Variable	NPD trend distinct from schizophrenia	NPD trend distinct from MAD	NPD unique	NPD indistinguishable from either	Row total
Social functioning	1	2*	1	1	5
Vocational functioning	0	1	1	0	2
Outpatient treatment	0	1	1	1	3
Hospital treatment	3**	0	0	0	3
Symptoms	0	0	1	2	3
Global functioning	2	0	1	0	3
Column total	6**	4*	5	4	19

*Statistically significant difference at $P < .05$ or better.

rehospitalization history. Schizophrenic patients were rehospitalized a mean of 2.6 times in the mean 14-year follow-up interval compared to 0.8 time in MAD and 0.4 time in NPD patients (Duncan's multiple-range test, $F = 4.87$, df = 2, $P = .01$). The mean Strauss-Carpenter hospital scale score at follow-up, a 0–4 scale measuring the amount of hospitalization in the year before follow-up, showed schizophrenic patients to be significantly lower at 3.7 (i.e., more likely to have been hospitalized in the past year) than MAD patients at 4.0 or NPD patients at 4.0 (Duncan's multiple-range test, $F = 4.51$, df = 2, $P = .01$).

The tendency of NPD to differ more from schizophrenia than from MAD does not demonstrate a fundamental similarity between NPD and MAD, but only the lack of measurable difference on these variables. Trend-level differences between NPD and MAD existed in sex distribution, where NPD was as common in men as in women, whereas three times as many MAD patients were women, but also in terms of preadmission outpatient treatment, where NPD patients tended to have had 2 years of outpatient treatment at the time of admission compared to 3 years for MAD patients, and where three times as many NPD as MAD patients had had more than 6 months of psychoanalysis before the index admission. Similarly, NPD patients tended to differ from MAD patients in terms of the absence of preadmission history of either electroconvulsive therapy (ECT) or involuntary hospitalization: 15% of MAD patients had previously received ECT and 4% had previously been committed involuntarily. Although NPD patients were the same age as MAD patients at onset of illness (22.6 years versus 23.0 years), NPD patients tended to be younger (25.9 years) than MAD patients (30.4 years) at the time of index admission. NPD patients showed a strong trend-level difference from MAD patients insofar as only 65% reported satisfactory intimate relations (≥ 2 on a 0–4 scale) compared to 92% of MAD patients at mean 14-year follow-up ($\chi^2 = 5.75$, df = 2, $P = .06$). Certainly, one retrospective study cannot completely delineate the validity of a new diagnosis, but the overall trends in the data lend support to the hypothesis that NPD is a valid diagnostic entity.

Longitudinal Comparison of NPD and BPD

Psychodynamic conceptualizations of narcissistic personality disorder have long included the notion that NPD is closely related to BPD and may share a single diagnostic continuum (Adler 1981, 1986; Bursten 1982; Kernberg 1975, 1980; Rinsley 1985). It was in part the recognition of this relationship that led to the inclusion of BPD and NPD within the same personality disorder cluster in DSM-III and DSM-III-R. No empirical study of NPD would be complete, then, without a comparison with BPD. The two are so closely related that it should be manifestly clear from the outset that statistically significant differences are likely to be few. The only reported comparison of longitudinal course and outcome data on NPD and BPD patients is that of Plakun (1989), based on the sample of 17 "pure" NPD patients and 33 "pure" BPD patients described above. As elsewhere, categorical variables were compared with an overall χ^2 distribution with post hoc analysis of individual-cell χ^2 where relevant. Continuous variables were studied with a one-way analysis of variance with post hoc comparison of the means by Duncan's multiple-range test where appropriate. Tables 6–15 report the NPD versus BPD comparisons.

Table 6 demonstrates a nonsignificant trend for family history of psychiatric illness to be twice as common in borderline as in narcissistic patients. Although the samples were too small for the difference to achieve significance, the trend is for a female preponderance among patients meeting criteria for BPD but a roughly equal sex distribution in NPD.

Tables 7–10 report preadmission comparisons of NPD and BPD along several dimensions. There were strong trend-level differences suggesting NPD patients were at a social disadvantage at the time of index admission on the basis of a lower mean Strauss-Carpenter social scale score (Duncan's multiple-range test, $F = 3.69$, df = 1, $P = .06$) and more glob-

Table 6. Preadmission demographic features and family history of narcissistic personality disorder (NPD) and borderline personality disorder (BPD) patients

	Diagnosis	
Variable	**NPD (n = 17)**	**BPD (n = 33)**
Percentage who are women	52	70
Mean Hollingshead-Redlich social class (1 highest, 5 lowest)	2.2	1.9
Percentage with family history of psychiatric illness in parents or grandparents	18	36

ally impaired than BPD patients because of a greater percentage of patients with an admission GAS score below 30 ($\chi^2 = 3.3$, df $= 1$, $P = .07$). In general, though, at index admission, NPD patients were more likely to have been married, but were more socially isolated and were more likely to have achieved successful independent living than BPD patients. Vocationally, as can be seen in Table 7, NPD patients seemed to

Table 7. Preadmission social and vocational functioning of narcissistic personality disorder (NPD) and borderline personality disorder (BPD) patients

	Diagnosis	
Variable	**NPD (n = 17)**	**BPD (n = 33)**
Social		
Percentage ever married at admission	41	27
Mean Strauss-Carpenter social scale score at admission (0, no meetings with others, to 4, weekly meetings)	2.5	3.2[a]
Percentage living in dorm or apartment apart from parents	47	61
Vocational		
Percentage unemployed at admission	24	30
Mean Strauss-Carpenter employment scale score at admission (0, unemployed, to 4, full-time employed)	2.5	2.8
Mean number of years of education	14.3	14.4

[a] In BPD versus NPD comparison, BPD > NPD, analysis of variance with post hoc comparison of means by Duncan's multiple-range test, $F = 3.69$, df $= 1$, $P = .06$.

have more difficulty than BPD patients despite comparable levels of education and similar socioeconomic status (see Table 6). NPD patients tended to have a few months less preadmission outpatient treatment than BPD patients, but were more likely to have had their outpatient treatment as psychoanalysis (Table 8). The index admission was the first hospitalization for nearly 60% of BPD patients and 40% of NPD patients, but the mean number of previous hospitalizations was virtually identical for the two diagnoses. NPD patients had, on average, spent nearly a month more in total duration of hospitalization before the index admission and were a year younger than BPD patients when first hospitalized. Hospitalization for more than 3 months in the year before index hospitalization was rare in both diagnoses, as were previous history of

Table 8. Preadmission treatment variables in narcissistic personality disorder (NPD) and borderline personality disorder (BPD) patients

	Diagnosis	
Variable	**NPD (n = 17)**	**BPD (n = 33)**
Outpatient treatment		
Mean duration of preadmission outpatient treatment in months	22.8	27.0
Percentage with more than 6 months of preadmission psychoanalysis	24	6
Hospitalization history		
Percentage never hospitalized before admission	41	58
Mean age at first hospitalization	24.0	25.0
Mean number of previous hospitalizations	0.9	0.8
Mean duration in months of all previous hospitalizations	3.9	3.1
Percentage with more than 3 months in hospital in year before index hospitalization	0	3
Mean Strauss-Carpenter hospital scale score at admission (0, more than 75% of past year in hospital, to 4, no hospitalization in past year)	3.7	3.7
Percentage with preadmission history of electroconvulsive therapy	0	3
Percentage ever committed at time of index hospitalization	0	0

ECT or involuntary hospitalization. NPD patients were nearly 2 years older than BPD patients at the time of first mental health contact, but their ages were the same at index admission, perhaps suggesting a shorter and more fulminant course to admission in NPD than BPD patients (Table 9). NPD patients were less likely to have demonstrated preadmission drug or alcohol problems or to have attempted suicide or other self-destructive acts than their BPD counterparts, as would be expected clinically, but self-destructive behavior was relatively frequent in NPD (Table 9).

At the time of index admission, NPD patients seemed at a disadvantage in terms of global functioning (Table 10). Although the mean admission GAS score was practically identical for the two diagnoses, NPD patients as a group had a Strauss-Carpenter sum nearly a full point lower than BPD patients. Nearly one in five NPD patients had an admission GAS score below 30, whereas only 1 in 33 BPD patients scored this low, a difference noted above to approach significance.

Table 11 shows comparisons of NPD and BPD in terms of measures of the index hospitalization. The length of the index hospitalization was marginally longer for NPD than BPD patients. On average, NPD patients were less likely to have changed therapists or to have engaged in self-destructive be-

Table 9. Preadmission chronicity and symptoms in narcissistic personality disorder (NPD) and borderline personality disorder (BPD) patients

	Diagnosis	
Variable	**NPD (n = 17)**	**BPD (n = 33)**
Mean age at first mental health contact	22.6	20.8
Mean age at index admission	25.9	25.4
Percentage with preadmission alcohol abuse or dependence	18	27
Percentage with preadmission drug abuse or dependence	24	30
Percentage with preadmission suicide attempts	18	22
Percentage with preadmission self-destructive acts	29	48

Table 10. Preadmission global functioning in narcissistic personality disorder (NPD) and borderline personality disorder (BPD) patients

	Diagnosis	
Variable	**NPD (n = 17)**	**BPD (n = 33)**
Total Strauss-Carpenter scale score at admission (0–12)[a]	8.8	9.6
Mean admission GAS score	35.4	35.6
Percentage with admission GAS score less than 30	18	3[b]

Note. GAS = Global Assessment Scale.
[a] Symptom scale excluded because of lack of interrater agreement.
[b] In BPD versus NPD comparison, $\chi^2 = 3.3$, df = 1, $P = .07$.

Table 11. Index hospitalization treatment experience of narcissistic personality disorder (NPD) and borderline personality disorder (BPD) patients

	Diagnosis	
Variable	**NPD (n = 17)**	**BPD (n = 33)**
Mean length of index admission in months	16.7	16.2
Mean maximum full-scale IQ achieved	124	120 (n = 31)
Percentage with more than one therapist	18	24
Percentage with clinical review for treatment crisis	6	3
Percentage with self-destructive acts during index admission	12	18
Percentage transferred to another hospital to end index admission	6	3
Percentage with therapeutic goal rated "achieved" by therapist at discharge	71	61

havior during the index admission and were more likely to have had their therapeutic goal rated as "achieved" by the therapist at discharge.

Tables 12–15 report data on NPD and BPD at mean 14-year follow-up. The average NPD patient was less likely to have married or achieved independent living and substantially less likely to have achieved satisfaction in intimate relations than the average BPD patient (Table 12). The vocational differences between the two at follow-up were trivial. In Table 13, rehospitalization is shown to be rare, and total time spent in the hospital in the follow-up interval was low for both diagnoses. On average, NPD patients were rehospitalized more often and for longer periods, although neither NPD nor BPD patients had been hospitalized at all in the year before follow-up. The average NPD patient had sustained outpatient treatment for almost a year longer than the average BPD patient, but

Table 12. Mean 14-year follow-up social and vocational functioning of narcissistic personality disorder (NPD) and borderline personality disorder (BPD) patients

	Diagnosis	
Variable	**NPD (n = 17)**	**BPD (n = 33)**
Social		
Percentage ever married at follow-up	59	73
Percentage living in private residence, apart from parents	76	88
Percentage reporting at least one close friend	88	88
Percentage reporting satisfactory (2 or more of 4) intimate relationships	65	91
Strauss-Carpenter social scale score at follow-up (0, no meetings, to 4, meetings at least once weekly)	3.3	3.1
Vocational		
Percentage satisfied with work more than 75% of the time	31 (n = 16)	35 (n = 16)
Strauss-Carpenter employment scale score at follow-up (0, unemployed, to 4, full-time employment)	3.4	3.3

Table 13. Mean 14-year follow-up treatment experience of narcissistic personality disorder (NPD) and borderline personality disorder (BPD) patients

	Diagnosis	
Variable	**NPD (n = 17)**	**BPD (n = 33)**
Hospital		
Mean number of hospitalizations in follow-up interval	0.4 (n = 16)	0.2 (n = 31)
Mean number of months hospitalized in follow-up interval	1.8	0.6
Mean Strauss-Carpenter hospital scale score at follow-up (0, 75% or more of past year, to 4, none)	4.0 (n = 16)	4.0 (n = 32)
Nonhospital		
Mean number of years in outpatient treatment in follow-up interval	4.6 (n = 11)	3.7 (n = 26)
Percentage with no psychotherapy in follow-up interval	24	12
Percentage receiving medication at any time in follow-up interval	25 (n = 16)	21

NPD patients were also more likely to have had no psychotherapy in the follow-up interval than BPD patients. Medication use in the follow-up interval was found in approximately one in four NPD patients and one in five BPD patients. Suicide attempts during the follow-up interval were rare in both diagnoses, but, surprisingly, were found in a slightly greater proportion of NPD patients (Table 14). Table 15 reports follow-up global functioning. NPD patients had a marginally lower GAS score at follow-up, whereas just under two-thirds of NPD patients and just over three-quarters of BPD patients achieved one benchmark of good follow-up functioning, a GAS score of 60 or higher.

Table 14. Mean 14-year follow-up symptom history of narcissistic personality disorder (NPD) and borderline personality disorder (BPD) patients

	Diagnosis	
Variable	**NPD (*n* = 17)**	**BPD (*n* = 33)**
Percentage with suicide attempts in follow-up interval	12 (*n* = 16)	6 (*n* = 32)
Mean number of suicide attempts in follow-up interval	0.2	0.3
Mean Strauss-Carpenter symptom scale score at follow-up (0, severe, to 4, no symptoms)	2.5	2.5

Table 15. Mean 14-year follow-up global functioning of narcissistic personality disorder (NPD) and borderline personality disorder (BPD) patients

	Diagnosis	
Variable	**NPD (*n* = 17)**	**BPD (*n* = 33)**
Mean GAS score at follow-up	64.7	66.6
Percentage with follow-up GAS score of 60 or higher	65	76
Total Strauss-Carpenter scale score at follow-up (0–16)	12.9	12.8

Note. GAS = Global Assessment Scale.

In summary, NPD and BPD showed more similarities than differences, as expected. Perhaps the most noteworthy difference is the apparent absence of a female preponderance in NPD. At admission, BPD patients showed evidence of better social and global functioning. Such differences as were noted during the index hospitalization probably reflect the greater impulsivity and self-destructiveness expected in BPD. At follow-up, NPD patients, perhaps surprisingly, appeared to be at a disadvantage to BPD patients in terms of social and global functioning, rehospitalization history, and also in terms of a low level of subjective satisfaction with intimate relations approaching statistical significance.

McGlashan (1986) reported that when he studied global outcome as a function of length of follow-up in BPD an "inverted U" pattern results, with poor outcomes tending to occur in the first and third decades of follow-up, but rarely in the second decade. This same "inverted U" pattern is found in the Austen Riggs Center BPD sample when GAS score range is graphed as a function of length of follow-up. No such "inverted U" is found in the Austen Riggs Center sample of NPD patients when GAS score range is graphed as a function of follow-up interval, good and poor outcomes being found throughout all periods of follow-up.

The presence of an "inverted U" pattern of infrequent poor outcomes in the second decade of follow-up in two studies of BPD patients and the absence of an "inverted U" in NPD patients in the Austen Riggs Center sample is an interesting and provocative finding. It may suggest that the psychodynamics or natural history of BPD patients better suits them to deal with the life issues of their late 30s and early 40s than NPD patients. Another possibility worthy of serious consideration is that BPD patients who might have presented with poor functioning in this middle range of follow-up fail to do so because of successful suicide. Neither McGlashan's nor Plakun's studies were able to definitively trace successful suicide in their geographically diverse patient samples, but Paris et al. (1987) and Stone et al. (1987) have suggested that suicide risk in BPD approaches 10%.

Correlates of Outcome in NPD

Empirical studies of outcome in NPD and BPD have made inroads in establishing the validity of these diagnostic entities and have provided substantial descriptive information. One feature common to both diagnoses is marked heterogeneity of outcome, with more difference in longitudinal course and outcome found within each diagnostic group than between them. As noted above, part of this heterogeneity in BPD appears to be a function of length of follow-up, but this does not account for much of the outcome variance. Some work has already been done by McGlashan (1985, 1986) and Plakun (1988) in exploring what accounts for the heterogeneity of outcome in BPD. This work is exciting and provocative to the clinician as well as the empirical psychiatrist because of its implications for psychodynamic understanding and treatment.

Schizophrenia is the diagnosis for which most is known about prediction of outcome. In his effort to understand outcome prediction in BPD, McGlashan (1985) tested the rules of outcome prediction established in schizophrenia, where 1) like tends to predict like (for example, poor premorbid social functioning predicts poor follow-up social functioning); 2) symptoms of the manifest illness are diagnostically useful but are of little value in outcome prediction, unless the illness is already chronic; 3) demographic and background variables have little predictive power; and 4) social, sexual, and vocational functioning are strongly related to outcome throughout the illness course. In his sample of BPD patients, McGlashan found that like predicted like only for hospital outcome. Surprisingly, symptoms of the manifest illness were strong predictors of outcome, and social, sexual, and vocational functioning were of little predictive value. In what follows, outcome prediction in the 17 NPD patients who are part of the Austen Riggs Center sample will be described and comparisons made to outcome prediction in BPD.

Seven different dimensions of outcome were selected for study, as shown in Table 16. They include 1) follow-up interval rehospitalization as measured by the number of months hospitalized in the follow-up interval, 2) vocational functioning as measured by the Strauss-Carpenter employment scale for the year before follow-up, 3) social functioning as measured by the Strauss-Carpenter social scale for the year before follow-up, 4) intimate functioning as measured by the degree of satisfaction with intimate relationships, 5) achievement of marriage or a stable relationship at follow-up (the only categorical rather than continuous outcome dimension), 6) symptoms as measured by the Strauss-Carpenter symptom scale for the year be-

Table 16. Dimensions of outcome

Hospitalization—Number of months hospitalized in follow-up interval
Vocational functioning—Strauss-Carpenter employment scale score for year before follow-up
Social functioning—Strauss-Carpenter social scale score for year before follow-up
Intimate functioning—Degree of satisfaction with intimate relationships at follow-up
Achievement of marriage or stable relationship—achievement of marriage or stable relationship at follow-up
Symptoms—Strauss-Carpenter symptom scale score for year before follow-up
Global functioning—Global Assessment Scale score at follow-up

fore follow-up, and 7) global functioning as measured by the GAS score at follow-up. Table 17 details the four classes of outcome predictors selected for study: 1) demographic background variables; 2) measures of preadmission functioning; 3) psychiatric illness variables, including onset of the manifest illness, the presence of personality disorder criteria, symptoms, and measures of chronicity; and 4) index hospitalization variables. Three sets of correlations were performed for the 17 "pure" NPD patients and the 33 "pure" BPD patients. First, outcome dimensions were correlated with each other to test whether these were indeed relatively independent. Second, predictor versus predictor correlations were performed to test for significant intercorrelations. Finally, the predictors were correlated with outcome dimensions to assess which predictors correlated most highly with the seven outcome dimensions. Most of the correlations were performed using the Pearson *r* coefficient of correlation, appropriate for continuous variables. When the categorical outcome dimension of "achievement of marriage or a stable relationship" was studied against another categorical predictor variable (e.g., sex), a phi coefficient of correlation was used.

Details of the BPD correlations will be published else-

Table 17. Outcome predictor variables

Demographic variables
- Sex
- Hollingshead-Redlich Social Class
- Family history of psychiatric illness in parents, grandparents, or siblings
- Adoption status
- Moves before age 13
- Birth order
- Presence of divorce in parents

Preadmission functioning
- Years of education at admission
- Marital status at admission
- Strauss-Carpenter employment scale score at admission
- Strauss-Carpenter social scale score at admission

Psychiatric illness variables
- Onset variables
  - Age at first mental health contact
  - Age at first hospitalization
  - Time from first contact to first hospitalization
- Personality trait variables
  - Criteria for borderline personality disorder
  - Criteria for narcissistic personality disorder
  - Criteria for schizotypal personality disorder
- Symptom variables
  - Alcohol or drug abuse and/or dependence
  - Preadmission self-destructiveness
- Chronicity
  - Total duration of preadmission outpatient treatment
  - Total duration of prior hospitalizations
  - Hospitalization history in year before index admission (Strauss-Carpenter hospital scale score at admission)
  - Preadmission electroconvulsive therapy
  - Preadmission commitment

Index admission variables
- Age at index admission
- Global Assessment Scale score at admission
- Length of index admission
- Highest IQ achieved during index hospitalization
- Age at follow-up
- Length of follow-up interval
- Psychotherapy helpfulness rating by patient at follow-up
- Discharge from index hospitalization by transfer to another hospital
- Therapeutic goal rated as "achieved" by therapist at discharge
- Self-destructiveness during index admission
- Number of clinical reviews for treatment crises
- Number of therapists during index hospitalization

where but are commented on as relevant. The outcome dimension versus outcome dimension intercorrelations indeed demonstrated their relative independence of one another, with a few notable exceptions. In NPD patients, global outcome was significantly intercorrelated with achievement of marriage or a stable relationship at follow-up ($r = .58$, $P < .05$) and with symptoms at follow-up ($r = .70$, $P < .01$), intercorrelations that are not surprising because global outcome is inevitably a summation of individual outcome dimensions. Hospitalization and vocational outcome were also significantly intercorrelated in NPD, with $r = -.79$ ($P < .001$). In this sample of NPD patients, then, less rehospitalization during the follow-up interval was strongly correlated with better vocational functioning. Predictor versus predictor intercorrelations were rarely significant and will be commented on where pertinent.

Tables 18–24 report the highest correlates of good outcome in NPD for the seven outcome dimensions. Good hospitalization outcome, that is, fewer months rehospitalized during the entire follow-up interval, was associated with the absence of two personality disorder criteria, schizotypal "suspiciousness or paranoid ideation" ($r = .63$, $P = .009$) and BPD "inappropriate, intense anger" ($r = .56$, $P = .02$; Table 18). Having had a planned discharge as opposed to a discharge for external or financial reasons or because of a therapeutic impasse or crisis, a 3-point scale, also correlated with good hospitalization outcome ($r = .45$, $P = .08$). In contrast with outcome prediction in schizophrenia, like did not predict like. Greater duration of hospitalization before the index hospitalization had a negative correlation with the duration of hospitalization in the follow-up interval ($r = -.40$, P NS).

For vocational functioning, better outcome was associated with being eldest in the sibship or an only child ($r = -.53$, $P = .03$; Table 19). Again, the absence of two personality disorder criteria was associated with better vocational outcome. The absence of schizotypal "suspiciousness or paranoid ideation" ($r = -.48$, $P = .05$) and of NPD "lack of empathy" ($r = -.44$, $P = .08$) were both associated with better vocational function-

Table 18. Correlates of good outcome in narcissistic personality disorder: hospitalization

Hospitalization: Number of months hospitalized in total follow-up interval (mean ± SD 1.8 ± 5.1 months, range 0–20)	
Less rehospitalization associated with	
• Absence of schizotypal DSM-III criterion A7 (suspiciousness or paranoid ideation)	$r = .63$, $P = .009$
• Absence of borderline personality disorder DSM-III criterion A3 (inappropriate, intense anger)	$r = .56$, $P = .02$
• Planned discharge versus discharge for external or financial reasons or because of therapeutic impasse or crisis (3-point scale)	$r = .45$, $P = .08$
• Greater duration of prior hospitalization	$r = -.40$, P NS

Note. $n = 16$.

Table 19. Correlates of good outcome in narcissistic personality disorder (NPD): vocational functioning

Vocational functioning: Strauss-Carpenter employment scale score based on year before follow-up (mean ± SD 3.4 ± 1.1, range 0–4)	
Better outcome associated with	
• Being eldest in sibship or only child	$r = -.53$, $P = .03$
• Absence of schizotypal DSM-III criterion A7 (suspiciousness or paranoid ideation)	$r = -.48$, $P = .05$
• Absence of NPD DSM-III criterion E4 (lack of empathy) (Note: Presence of NPD E4 correlated with better social outcome)	$r = -.44$, $P = .08$
• Retrospective patient rating of index psychotherapy as unhelpful	$r = .44$, $P = .09$
Lower admission Strauss-Carpenter vocational scale score	$r = -.16$, P NS

Note. $n = 17$.

ing at follow-up. The correlation of schizotypal "suspiciousness or paranoid ideation" with vocational and hospitalization outcome no doubt reflects in part the significant intercorrelation between hospitalization and vocational outcome noted in the outcome dimension intercorrelations. A retrospective rating by the patient of the index hospitalization psychotherapy as unhelpful was associated with better vocational outcome ($r = .44$, $P = .09$). Again, like failed to predict like. Lower admission Strauss-Carpenter vocational scale score was weakly negatively correlated with Strauss-Carpenter employment scale score at follow-up ($r = -.16$, P NS).

Table 20 shows correlates of good social functioning in NPD patients at long-term follow-up. Fewer moves before age 13 had the strongest correlation with good outcome. Patients in this sample ranged from the highest socioeconomic classes to middle class. Interestingly, lower socioeconomic status at index hospitalization, that is, being middle class rather than upper class, correlated with better outcome. Similarly, the absence of BPD "emptiness or boredom" and the presence of BPD "impulsivity" correlated with better social functioning at outcome, suggesting that in NPD patients greater affective availability and less bored emptiness may be positive signs. It is worth noting here, though, that lower socioeconomic status intercorrelated with fewer moves before age 13 ($r = .55$, $P = .02$), shorter length of index hospitalization ($r = -.52$, $P = .03$), and the presence of BPD "impulsivity" ($r = .52$, $P = .03$). The absence of self-destructive acts during the index hospitalization had a moderate correlation with good social outcome, a finding at variance with the case in BPD patients, in whom self-destructive acts during the index hospitalization were associated with better outcome. A greater duration of hospitalization before the index admission correlated with better social functioning at outcome, as did the presence of NPD "lack of empathy." Again, like failed to predict like, the Strauss-Carpenter social scale at admission having a weak negative correlation with the Strauss-Carpenter social scale at follow-up.

Table 20. Correlates of good outcome in narcissistic personality disorder (NPD): social functioning

Social functioning: Strauss-Carpenter social scale score based on year before follow-up (mean ± SD 3.3 ± 1.0, range 1–4)	
Better outcome associated with	
• Fewer moves before age 13	$r = -.58$, $P = .01$
• Absence of borderline personality disorder (BPD) DSM-III criterion A8 (emptiness or boredom)	$r = -.56$, $P = .02$
• Lower socioeconomic status at index hospitalization (Hollingshead-Redlich middle class > upper class)	$r = .54$, $P = .02$
• Presence of BPD DSM-III criterion A1 (impulsivity)	$r = .54$, $P = .03$
• Being male	$r = -.54$, $P = .03$
• Absence of self-destructive acts during index hospitalization	$r = -.47$, $P = .06$
• Greater duration of prior hospitalizations	$r = .47$, $P = .06$
• Presence of NPD DSM-III criterion E4 (lack of empathy) (Note: Absence of NPD E4 correlated with better vocational outcome)	$r = .42$, $P = .09$
Lower admission Strauss-Carpenter social scale score	$r = -.18$, P NS

Note. $n = 17$.

Table 21 reports the strongest correlates of good intimate functioning at follow-up as measured by satisfaction with intimate relationships at follow-up. Better intimate functioning was associated with being eldest in the sibship or an only child and with the presence of self-destructive acts during the index hospitalization. This latter finding replicates the case in BPD where it predicted good intimate functioning and achievement of marriage or a stable relationship at follow-up.

Table 22 reports correlates of achievement of marriage or a stable relationship at follow-up. A greater duration of outpatient psychotherapy before the index hospitalization predicted achievement of marriage at follow-up, as did a longer follow-up interval. The latter finding may be an artifact of the reality that the likelihood of marriage increases with time. Achievement of marriage or a stable relationship at the index hospitalization had only a low correlation with achievement of marriage or a stable relationship at follow-up, again suggesting like does not predict like. On the other hand, the fact that longer outpatient psychotherapy before index admission correlates with achievement of marriage or a stable relationship at follow-up may suggest that the ability to sustain a close therapeutic relationship earlier in life does predict the same kind of capacity later in life in patients with NPD.

Table 23 shows correlates of good symptom outcome. Shorter index admission had the strongest correlation with good symptom outcome, followed by lower socioeconomic status at index hospitalization (that is, middle-class rather than upper-class status) and the presence of the BPD criterion of "impulsivity." Because satisfactory interrater agreement could not be achieved on the Strauss-Carpenter symptom scale at admission, it was not included in the study. It is thus not possible to examine the question of whether like predicts like along this symptom dimension or whether shorter index admission was associated with fewer symptoms at admission.

Table 24 reports correlates of good global functioning at follow-up. The strongest correlate was again middle-class rather than upper-class socioeconomic status at index admis-

Table 21. Correlates of good outcome in narcissistic personality disorder: intimacy

Intimacy: Degree of satisfaction with intimate relationships at follow-up (mean ± SD 2.1 ± 1.4, range 0–4)	
Better outcome associated with	
• Being eldest in sibship or an only child	$r = -.56$, $P = .02$
• Presence of self-destructive acts during index hospitalization	$r = .44$, $P = .08$
Higher admission Strauss-Carpenter social scale score	$r = .02$, P NS

Note. $n = 17$.

Table 22. Correlates of good outcome in narcissistic personality disorder: achievement of marriage or stable relationship at follow-up

Achievement of marriage or stable relationship at follow-up: (6 patients, or 35%, achieved marriage or stable relationship)	
Better outcome associated with	
• Greater duration of outpatient psychotherapy before index hospitalization	$r = .56$, $P = .02$
• Longer follow-up interval	$r = .47$, $P = .06$
Marriage or stable relationship at index hospitalization	phi = .23, P NS

Note. $n = 17$.

Table 23. Correlates of good outcome in narcissistic personality disorder: symptoms

Symptoms: Strauss-Carpenter symptom scale score based on year before follow-up (mean ± SD 2.5 ± .09, range 1–4)	
Better outcome associated with	
• Shorter index admission (mean ± SD 16.7 ± 9.4 months, range 4–32)	$r = -.65$, $P = .005$
• Lower socioeconomic status at index hospitalization (Hollingshead-Redlich middle class > upper class)	$r = .55$, $P = .02$
• Presence of borderline personality disorder DSM-III criterion A1 (impulsivity)	$r = .55$, $P = .02$

Note. $n = 17$.

Table 24. Correlates of good outcome in narcissistic personality disorder: global functioning

Global functioning: Global Assessment Scale (GAS) score based on year before follow-up (mean ± SD 64.6 ± 11.9, range 44–82)	
Better outcome associated with	
• Lower socioeconomic status at index hospitalization (Hollingshead-Redlich middle class > upper class)	$r = .65$, $P = .005$
• Shorter index hospitalization (mean ± SD 16.7 ± 9.4 months, range 4–32) (Note: Intercorrelation between lower socioeconomic status and shorter index admission, $r = .52$, $P = .03$)	$r = -.60$, $P = .01$
• Absence of schizotypal DSM-III criterion A2 (ideas of reference)	$r = -.42$, $P = .10$
Higher GAS at admission	$r = .13$, P NS
Shorter duration of prior hospitalizations	$r = .02$, P NS
Higher maximum IQ achieved during index admission	$r = .17$, P NS
Being male	$r = -.38$, P NS
Presence of family history of parental divorce	$r = .12$, P NS

Note. $n = 17$.

sion ($r = .65$, $P = .005$). Shorter index hospitalization also had a relatively strong correlation with good global outcome, but here it is worth recalling that lower socioeconomic status intercorrelates with shorter index hospitalization ($r = .52$, $P = .03$), probably accounting for a significant portion of the correlation of shorter index hospitalization with good outcome. The absence of schizotypal "ideas of reference" also correlated with good global outcome. The correlation of higher GAS score at admission with GAS score at follow-up was quite low ($r = .13$, P NS). Several predictors of good functioning reported in BPD patients were not particularly powerful predictors of good functioning in NPD patients, including shorter duration of prior hospitalization, the presence of a family history of parental divorce, and higher maximum IQ achieved during the index admission. This latter predictor of good outcome in BPD patients, high IQ, is reported by McGlashan (1985). The current sample of NPD patients has such a high mean IQ (124, see Table 11) that its potential value as a predictor is proportionately diminished. There was some suggestion that being male was mildly but not significantly correlated with better global functioning in NPD patients.

It is sensible to consider not only how strong and how significant the correlation of a predictor with an outcome variable is, but also with how many different outcome dimensions a predictor correlates. If one looks across all seven outcome dimensions, the strongest predictor of outcome overall for NPD patients would appear to be middle-class rather than upper-class socioeconomic status at the time of the index admission, which correlated with good global ($r = .65$, $P = .005$), symptom ($r = .55$, $P = .02$) and social ($r = .54$, $P = .02$) outcome. Another apparently powerful predictor was shorter index hospitalization, which predicted good symptom ($r = -.65$, $P = .005$) and global ($r = -.60$, $P = .01$) outcome, but the substantial intercorrelation of this with socioeconomic status has already been noted. The absence of the schizotypal criterion for "suspiciousness or paranoid ideation" correlated with good hospitalization ($r = .63$, $P = .009$) and vocational ($r = -.48$,

$P = .05$) outcome. The absence of schizotypal "ideas of reference" correlated with good global functioning. The latter three correlations suggest that paranoid traits may be especially prognostically ominous in NPD. The presence of BPD "impulsivity" correlated with good symptom ($r = .55$, $P = .02$) and social ($r = .54$, $P = .03$) outcome, suggesting that liveliness and affective availability augur well in NPD, but again the intercorrelation of "impulsivity" with lower socioeconomic status must be kept in mind.

Being eldest in the sibship or an only child was associated with achievement of good intimate functioning ($r = -.56$, $P = .02$) and good vocational functioning ($r = -.53$, $P = .03$) at follow-up. This may suggest that greater focus of parental interest or attention or some other related factors associated with being eldest in a sibship or an only child mitigate some of the impairments that unfold later in patients predisposed to NPD temperamentally or dynamically.

In an as-yet unpublished study (Plakun 1988), a similar analysis of predictors of outcome in BPD has been performed. In BPD, the strongest correlate overall was a demographic background variable, the absence of a family history of parental divorce at the time of index admission, which correlated most highly with good vocational outcome ($r = -.67$, $P = .001$), but also significantly with global, social, and symptom outcome. In the only instance in which like predicted like, shorter duration of hospitalization before the index admission correlated significantly with shorter hospitalization during the follow-up interval ($r = .51$, $P = .003$). McGlashan (1985) also found that like predicted like in terms of hospitalization outcome in his sample of BPD patients. The absence of four personality disorder criteria was also moderately associated with good outcome in Plakun's (1988) study of correlates of outcome in BPD. The absence of NPD "entitlement" correlated with good vocational, social, and global outcome. The absence of schizotypal "odd speech" correlated with good intimate functioning, and the absence of "recurrent illusions" was associated with less rehospitalization at follow-up. Perhaps most interesting of all, the presence of self-destructive acts during the index hospitalization was moderately correlated with good intimate functioning at follow-up ($r = .45$, $P = .008$) and with achievement of marriage or a stable relationship at follow-up ($r = .36$, $P = .04$).

In both NPD and BPD patients, demographic background variables are found to be strong predictors of outcome across multiple dimensions. In BPD, the absence of a history of parental divorce in 5 of 33 patients was associated with better outcome across four of seven dimensions. This suggests patients predisposed to BPD may be especially vulnerable to the stress associated with family conflict or divorce, to the interruption of a relationship with one parent, or to the loss of the opportunity provided by having two parents to unlearn splitting behaviors. In NPD patients, the rich may get richer, but the poor (or at least the middle class) get better. Perhaps this is entirely due to the intercorrelation effect of more moves, the absence of "impulsivity," and the longer index hospitalization with higher socioeconomic status in this sample of patients. The possibility that upper-socioeconomic-class children predisposed to NPD may have difficulty learning self-motivation because of the ready availability of material narcissistic supplies is also worth considering. Review of charts of these high-socioeconomic-status poor-outcome patients shows a trend toward great reliance on nonparent caretakers in childhood, which may be relevant. Finally, greater stability and consistency in formative years as measured by fewer moves and being male and an oldest or only child seem assets to the patient at risk for NPD.

Unlike the case in schizophrenia, in BPD and NPD, demographic background variables are highly predictive of outcome. As was true in McGlashan's study, only in prediction of rehospitalization in BPD patients does like predict like. Premorbid social, sexual, vocational, or global functioning show little evidence of ability to predict these capacities at follow-up in BPD or NPD. Again at variance with outcome prediction in schizophrenia, such symptoms of the manifest illness as the presence or absence of specific personality traits appear to have significant predictive value for NPD patients, in whom paranoid trends are found to be particularly ominous, and for BPD patients, in whom narcissistic "entitlement," two schizotypal criteria, and BPD "emptiness or boredom" heralded poor outcome.

Finally, in BPD patients, the presence of self-destructive acts during intensive psychotherapy in a hospital setting was associated with good outcome. This was not true of self-destructive acts before the index admission. In NPD patients, the situation is equivocal, with self-destructive acts during the index hospitalization being associated with poor social functioning, as indicated by fewer meetings with others, but more satisfaction with intimate relationships at follow-up. At least in BPD patients and perhaps in NPD patients, these findings provide empirical support for Winnicott's notion (1965) that, in the course of intensive psychotherapy, acting out that remains containable within the holding environment of the psychotherapy (which in this case includes the open hospital milieu) may be a hopeful sign of useful therapeutic engagement. The key may well be maintaining a psychotherapeutic focus on the behavior, while working with the transference and countertransference factors that are involved, rather than responding coercively or in an unwitting enactment of countertransference anger and hopelessness. It is this former approach that is the unique strength of long-term hospital settings offering intensive psychotherapy.

In conclusion, a cautionary note is appropriate. Although these findings suggest much about NPD and BPD, the samples are small and specialized. It would be premature to assume the findings can be generalized to outpatient or other inpatient samples, but they do indicate interesting and relevant directions for future research. At the very least, these data constitute a first step in exploring NPD empirically, providing evidence for the discriminative validity of BPD and NPD criteria, the validity of the NPD diagnosis, its similarities and differences with regard to BPD, and some empirical notion of predictors of outcome that can be scrutinized by clinicians, researchers, and psychodynamic theoreticians.

References

Adler G: The borderline-narcissistic personality disorder continuum. Am J Psychiatry 138:46–50, 1981

Adler G: Psychotherapy of the narcissistic personality disorder patient: two contrasting approaches. Am J Psychiatry 143:430–436, 1986

Akhtar S, Thomson JA Jr: Overview: narcissistic personality disorder. Am J Psychiatry 139:12–20, 1982

American Psychiatric Association: Diagnostic and Statistical Manual of Mental Disorders, 3rd Edition. Washington, DC, American Psychiatric Association, 1980

American Psychiatric Association: Diagnostic and Statistical Manual of Mental Disorders, 3rd Edition, Revised. Washington, DC, American Psychiatric Association, 1987

Bursten B: Narcissistic personalities in DSM-III. Compr Psychiatry 23:409–420, 1982

Cooper A: Histrionic, narcissistic and compulsive personality disorders, in Diagnosis and Classification in Psychiatry. Edited by Tischler G. Cambridge, Cambridge University Press, 1987

Goldstein WN: DSM-III and the narcissistic personality. Am J Psychotherapy 39:4–16, 1985

Gunderson JG: DSM-III diagnosis of personality disorder, in Current Perspectives on Personality Disorders. Edited by Frosch J. Washington, DC, American Psychiatric Press, 1983

Gunderson JG, Ronningstam E: The diagnostic interview for narcissistic patients. Paper presented at the 140th annual meeting of the American Psychiatric Association, Chicago, IL, May 1987

Gunderson JG, Kolb JE, Austin V: The diagnostic interview for borderlines (DIB). Am J Psychiatry 138:896–903, 1981

Kernberg O: Borderline Conditions and Pathological Narcissism. New York, Jason Aronson, 1975

Kernberg O: Internal World and External Reality. New York, Jason Aronson, 1980

McGlashan TH: The borderline syndrome, I: testing three diagnostic systems, II: is it a variant of schizophrenia or affective disorder? Arch Gen Psychiatry 40:1311–1323, 1983

McGlashan TH: The prediction of outcome in borderline personality disorder: part V of the Chestnut Lodge follow-up study, in The Borderline: Current Empirical Research. Edited by McGlashan TH. Washington, DC, American Psychiatric Press, 1985, pp 63–98

McGlashan TH: The Chestnut Lodge follow-up study, III: long-term outcome of borderline personalities. Arch Gen Psychiatry; 43:20–30, 1986

McGlashan TH, Heinssen RK: Narcissistic, antisocial and non-comorbid subgroups of borderline disorder. Psychiatr Clin North Am 12:653–670, 1989

Nurnberg HG: Survey of psychotherapeutic approaches to narcissistic personality disorder. Hillside J Clin Psychiatry 6:204–220, 1984

Paris J, Brown R, Nowlis D: Long-term follow-up of borderline patients in a general hospital. Compr Psychiatry 28:530–535, 1987

Pfohl B, Coryell W, Zimmerman M, et al: DSM-III personality disorders: diagnostic overlap and internal consistency of individual DSM-III criteria. Compr Psychiatry 27:21–34, 1986

Plakun EM: Distinguishing narcissistic and borderline personality disorders using DSM-III criteria. Compr Psychiatry 28:437–443, 1987

Plakun EM: Outcome correlates of borderline patients. Paper presented at the 141st annual meeting of the American Psychiatric Association, Montreal, Canada, May 1988

Plakun EM: Narcissistic personality disorder: a validity study and comparison to borderline personality disorder. Psychiatr Clin North Am 12:603–620, 1989

Plakun EM, Burkhardt PE, Muller JP: 14 year follow-up of borderline and schizotypal personality disorders. Compr Psychiatry 26:448–455, 1985

Plakun EM, Muller JP, Burkhardt PE: The significance of borderline and schizotypal overlap. Hillside J Clin Psychiatry 9:47–55, 1987

Pope HG Jr, Jonas JM, Hudson JI, et al: The validity of DSM-III borderline personality disorder: a phenomenologic, family history, treatment response, and long-term follow-up study. Arch Gen Psychiatry 40:23–30, 1983

Rinsley DB: Notes on the pathogenesis and nosology of borderline and narcissistic personality disorders. J Am Acad Psychoanal 13:317–328, 1985

Robins E, Guze SB: Establishment of diagnostic validity in psychiatry illness: its application to schizophrenia. Am J Psychiatry 126:983–987, 1970

Ronningstam E, Gunderson JG: Narcissistic traits in psychiatric patients. Paper presented at the 140th annual meeting of the American Psychiatric Association, Chicago, IL, May 1987

Siever LJ, Klar H: A review of DSM-III criteria for the personality disorders, in Psychiatry Update: American Psychiatric Association Annual Review, Vol 5. Edited by Frances AJ, Hales RE. Washington, DC, American Psychiatric Press, 1986, pp 299–301

Stone MH: Long-term follow-up of narcissistic/borderline patients. Psychiatr Clin North Am 12:621–641, 1989

Stone MH, Hurt SW, Stone DK: The PI 500: long-term follow-up of borderline inpatients meeting DSM-III criteria, I: global outcome. Journal of Personality Disorders 1:291–298, 1987

Vaillant G, Perry J: Personality disorders, in Comprehensive Textbook of Psychiatry, 4th Edition, Vol 1. Edited by Kaplan HI, Sadock BJ. Baltimore, MD, Williams & Wilkins, 1985

Warner JL, Berman JJ, Weyant JM, et al: Assessing mental health program effectiveness: a comparison of three client follow-up methods. Evaluation Review 7:635–658, 1983

Widiger TA, Frances A, Spitzer RL, et al: The DSM-IIIR personality disorders: an overview. Am J Psychiatry 145:786–795, 1988

Winnicott DW: The Maturational Process and the Facilitating Environment. New York, International Universities Press, 1965, pp 203–216

Chapter 4

Case Studies

ERIC M. PLAKUN, M.D.

Editor's Note

The following case examples provide detailed life histories of four troubled individuals, permitting the reader a glimpse into the lives of the human beings whose difficulties have been described in previous chapters using empirical methodology or psychoanalytic conceptualizations. The case examples' greatest strength is the detailed longitudinal look at the lives of these troubled individuals from childhood through their treatment at the Austen Riggs Center, to follow-up a decade or more later. Inevitably, this strength is associated with weakness of another kind. Because these treatments were carried out two and sometimes three decades ago and because the data were gleaned from hospital records and anamneses, there is much detail about life history, but relatively little information about the day-to-day vicissitudes of the intensive psychotherapy and the transference relationship because of a dearth of surviving process material from which these can be reconstructed. Similarly, these treatments were carried out in an era when theoretical emphases within psychoanalytic psychotherapy were quite different from current formulations, so the therapists do not necessarily emphasize in their recounting of the therapy those issues that might be of most interest to us today. Nonetheless, these life histories provide a unique opportunity to view narcissistic and borderline patients in the kind of detail usually only available to psychoanalytic therapists who spend many hours with their patients. They also provide a "good-enough," if not perfect, platform for the clinical discussions that follow.

Chapter 4

Case Studies

The preceding review of psychodynamic conceptualizations of narcissism, the presentation of empirical data pertinent to understanding narcissistic personality disorder, especially with respect to its interface with borderline personality disorder, and the description of gender differences in the prevalence of narcissistic traits in a normal population have provided a systematic overview of narcissism. The following four case examples are offered to provide a longitudinal view of the lives of representative patients with narcissistic or borderline personality disorders. The four patients are drawn from the Austen Riggs Center (Stockbridge, Massachusetts) follow-up study. Names have been changed and other identifying data disguised to preserve confidentiality, but the life histories and descriptions of the index hospitalizations are drawn from case records and follow-up information from the questionnaires. Two patients met criteria for narcissistic personality disorder without major affective disorder or more than three borderline personality disorder criteria and two patients met criteria for borderline personality disorder without major affective disorder or more than three narcissistic personality disorder criteria. For each diagnosis, one patient was selected with a good outcome, as indicated by a follow-up Global Assessment Scale (GAS) score greater than 60, and one with a poor outcome, as indicated by a follow-up GAS score below 50.

The four patients, selected after review of more than two dozen, were felt to be representative of the two diagnoses and the differences between them. An effort was made to select patients with a range of pathology but with a resemblance to outpatients despite a significant course of treatment in a long-term hospital. It is worth reiterating that the current focus is not long-term hospital treatment, but rather the lives of four troubled individuals.

Drs. Otto Kernberg and Paul Ornstein are well known and articulate spokespersons for two contrasting views of narcissism. Dr. Kernberg has published his own ego psychology–object-relations views widely, as has Dr. Ornstein, who often is associated with the Kohutian self psychology point of view. In the two chapters that follow, Drs. Kernberg and Ornstein each offer a discussion of the four cases, highlighting their own unique approaches to understanding and treating narcissistic and borderline patients.

Peter: A Man With Narcissistic Personality Disorder and a Good Outcome

At the time of the index admission in the 1970s, Peter was 29 years old, a white, divorced, Jewish man. This 14-month admission was a continuation of Peter's first 7-week hospitalization, occasioned by suicidal ideation associated with the conviction he had a serious physical illness, and by physical collapse, in which he spent days lying on the floor convinced he was physically ill. Despite a negative medical evaluation, Peter remained barely able to move and was brought to the Austen Riggs Center in a wheelchair by his parents.

Life History

Peter was an only child whose mother learned during the pregnancy that she had rheumatic heart disease, and she was advised to have no more children. This one child was to be the best. Peter's father had been deserted by his own mother at age 3 and was raised in an orphanage, developing hatred for and fear of the world, but he eventually earned success in his profession. Peter's mother was a victim of father-daughter incest after her own mother's death. When Peter entered school, she returned to work, meeting with considerable financial success; her earnings supported Peter's hospitalization.

Peter's father's philosophy of child rearing prevailed during the early years, including frequent beatings with a strap. He felt that children, like animals, needed to be taught respect. As examples, before age 2, Peter had been beaten for not properly using a spoon, for spitting out food, and for crying. At age 2, Peter's mother left home with him, threatening never to return if child-rearing practices did not change. The family was reconstituted, and the father-child relationship changed dramatically, father and son becoming "buddies" who did everything together in a way that made other playmates unnecessary. At the time of admission the father recalled he had changed from his son's "master to his servant."

Significant separation difficulties in kindergarten led to a delay in starting school. Peter eventually began to earn good grades and make friends, but avoided bringing friends home. When Peter was 7, the family moved because of demands of the father's career. Peter experienced the move as traumatic and, over the next 2 years, gained much weight. During this period, Peter's father was frequently absent on business trips, leaving Peter and his mother worriedly waiting for his return. The father was phobic about flying, often raising the possibility his plane would crash and generally presenting a view of the world as a dangerous place. When Peter was 12, there was another significant move to the opposite coast in response to which Peter seemed to become withdrawn and reclusive. He had few friends, refused to speak to his parents, and spent most of his time in his room. Suggestions that he socialize occasionally led to rageful outbursts. The separation from home to begin college at age 17 was difficult, with frequent trips home, but in his sophomore year, Peter stopped visiting and had little to do with his parents over the next 10 years. While at college, Peter tended to have one friend at a time in intense, exclusive relationships. One friendship after another would end because Peter was unable to tolerate being disagreed with, often waiting months for an opportunity to get even with someone by whom he felt betrayed. There were numerous infatuations with women which generally ended in periods of intense dysphoria when Peter's interest was not returned.

After college and the near completion of an MBA, Peter entered a successful period as an investment analyst. Peter earned a lot of money, got a series of promotions, lived in an exclusive neighborhood, and purchased an expensive imported sports car. He had friends but was not dating. Ultimately, Peter left his job to return to graduate school despite his success because he felt undervalued and underpaid in light of what he saw as the exceptional quality of his work. It was at this point that Peter first developed anxiety with hyperventilation. When Peter was 26, his mother underwent surgical excision of a tumor which Peter was convinced was malignant despite a benign pathology report. After his mother's illness, Peter engaged in a series of impulsive, short-lived affairs with several young women, eventually settling into a triangular relationship with two women simultaneously. He chose to marry one because of an infantile, little-girl quality he found irresistible. Peter became sexually impotent after the marriage, and the couple divorced within 6 months, only to become friends and lovers again after the divorce. In particular, the couple enjoyed spending hours together baby talking and cuddling.

At age 27, Peter began a doctorate program, but was dissatisfied with his performance during the first year. He consulted a hypnotherapist and a psychiatrist because of increasing somatic symptoms, fearing something was wrong with his breathing or that he had a brain tumor or cardiovascular problem. Negative medical evaluation did not diminish Peter's concerns. After 2 days crawling around on the floor of his apartment terrified he would pass out if he were to stand up and contemplating suicide, Peter was admitted to a psychiatric hospital. It was the recommendation of the treatment team and his outpatient psychiatrist that he pursue long-term inpatient treatment, leading to transfer to the Austen Riggs Center.

Index Hospitalization

At the time of the index admission, Peter's presentation was noteworthy for his hypochondriacal complaints, phobic fear of exertion, and retreat to a wheelchair. He wanted the best in treatment and felt he had come to the place where the best treatment was offered. He spoke of numerous fantasies of being brilliant, creative, and talented, was involved in exploitative relationships with other members of the patient community, and often was vindictive in his efforts to gain revenge when slighted. On several occasions, brief infatuations with female patients ended after mild rejections, with Peter vowing to seek out and kill their children years hence. For a considerable period, Peter engaged in a struggle with the dietary department of the hospital, insisting his special dietary needs required he be served lobster daily, a request with which the hospital was unwilling to comply. He would walk into community meetings late, then sit in a partially hidden spot to read his mail or newspaper. When others found this behavior offensive, Peter responded with haughty arrogance that he was uninterested in the business of the patient community. He was in the hospital to work with his therapist and there was no point expecting anything else from him. Indeed, throughout his hospital stay, Peter seemed more a boarder than a member of the patient community. Low doses of chlordiazepoxide (Librium) were used sporadically for relief of anxiety early in the treatment. Psychological testing supported the clinical diagnosis of a narcissistic character disorder with strong obsessional trends. His retrospective follow-up study DSM-III diagnoses were Axis I, hypochondriasis; Axis II, narcissistic personality disorder (principal diagnosis), for which he met criteria for grandiosity, preoccupation with fantasies, exhibitionism, cool indifference, entitlement, interpersonal exploitativeness, and overidealized and devalued relationships. From among the borderline criteria, Peter was felt to manifest an identity disturbance, particularly concerning gender issues, and a pattern of unstable and intense interpersonal relationships. His admission GAS score was 30.

In the therapy, Peter was initially angry, demanding, controlling, and complaining while also helpless, dependent, and passive. At first, he regularly crawled up the three flights of stairs to his therapist's office dressed in a bathrobe, carrying a blanket, a cup of water, a medicine cup, and a pocketful of Alka Seltzer. He would not sit in a chair, but lay on the floor. Peter stated concerns about his health, was preoccupied with the qualifications of his psychiatrist, and was disappointed to be working with a man close to him in age rather than with a woman. Peter was demanding and insistent, asking for more than the four scheduled psychotherapy sessions weekly and feeling entitled to contact the therapist at any time.

He spoke of the pattern in his relationships of intense exclusivity with a constant expectation of rejection. Inevitably, something would lead to a disappointment, perhaps something as trivial as another not laughing at one of Peter's jokes, and the relationship would fall apart in a storm of bitterness, cruelty, and vindictiveness. Peter felt he needed something special from the therapist, who was able to hold firm to his position but often found the treatment difficult to endure. When the therapist would weather storms of complaint, Peter praised the therapist for handling the situation in the only way that might have preserved the therapy, but, after a brief period of flattery, would begin a new storm of demands over a new issue.

Over the first 3 months of therapy, the battles continued, whereas Peter's preoccupation with death and somatic complaints decreased markedly. He began to go outdoors and to exercise. In the sessions, he began to sit in a chair and to dress appropriately, then stopped bringing the blanket and then the glass of water to the hours. Gradually, he was able to increase his ability to examine the process unfolding between him and the therapist. He did not carry out a threat to request a change of therapist at the time of the latter's vacation.

By 6 months after admission, Peter had formed an idealized view of the therapist and was able to talk about a number of peculiar fantasies, particularly about food, with idiosyncratic ideas about particular ways certain foods needed to be chewed, swallowed, and mixed with saliva in order to be safely eaten. Peter spoke of awareness of his dependency on the therapist and his anxiety over his inability to control the therapist outside of sessions. There was discussion of the original family triangle and of sexual issues as the patient entered a more stable sexual relationship with a female patient. By a year after admission, Peter had made some trips away from the center and was able to discuss hostile and murderous impulses as well as to talk about how getting better posed a problem if it meant the therapist would win his colleagues' admiration.

Fourteen months after admission, Peter was discharged to outpatient status. His hypochondriacal symptoms had lessened gradually over the first few months of therapy as he had developed an idealizing transference. He had become able to leave the center without fearing attack and had made his way through a series of relationships with other patients that had been characterized by a high degree of possessiveness, dependence, and anger for their failure to meet all his needs. Peter had done some work as a substitute teacher, moving to a full-time teaching position after discharge. By 18 months after admission, he had left the immediate area of the hospital but continued with his psychotherapist for another year. Although he had some difficulty adjusting to life outside the hospital and often found himself sad, alone, and on the verge of tears, tending to blame his environment's lack of stimulating activities for these symptoms, this was felt to represent a continuation of his expectation that things be served up to him. Peter was accepted to a doctorate program and engaged in a number of relationships, including sexual ones.

Follow-up Information

Peter participated in the center's follow-up study 8 years after admission. At follow-up, Peter's GAS score was 68, 38 points higher than at admission. Peter reported that in the month before follow-up, his moods varied, he had been bothered by nervousness, and he felt he was experiencing mild feelings of sadness and discouragement. Peter was somewhat dissatisfied with his personal life, but found his life interesting and felt sure of himself much of the time. He had continued to have moderate concerns about his health from time to time. At follow-up, Peter was directing a college dormitory, had completed his doctorate degree, and was employed full-time as a college professor. He rated himself as satisfied with his work performance about three-quarters of the time. He had remained single, belonged to several social organizations, and reported numerous close friends. Since discharge and termination with his therapist, he had neither been readmitted to a psychiatric hospital nor had any individual psychotherapy. He had spent 2 months in group therapy, though. Peter had used no medications since discharge. Peter described himself as a social drinker and acknowledged some marijuana use.

His Strauss-Carpenter scale scores based on the year before follow-up included moderate symptoms (2 of 4), no hospitalization (4 of 4), full-time employment (4 of 4), and frequent meetings with others (4 of 4), giving him a Strauss-Carpenter scale sum of 14 of 16. Peter had made no suicide attempts since discharge.

In a rating of his treatment at the center, Peter reported psychotherapy and relationships with nursing staff had been the most helpful facets of the program for him, with medications, the community program, and other therapy staff relatively unhelpful. Peter felt he had met with unusual success in his career that had led others to have extremely high expectations of him. He felt that psychotherapy had been instrumental in helping him get through his doctorate program and that this had helped turn his life around. Peter felt his job had none of the features that previously made him avoid work and that other satisfying life experiences had resulted from his stable and successful employment situation. Peter's major complaint about his treatment was the lack of help with the transition from the hospital to the demands and pressure of his current life.

Peter typifies the good-outcome narcissistic patient in several respects. Predictors of good outcome he manifests include being male and an only child, probably lacking schizotypal paranoid traits, manifesting impulsivity at least with respect to sexual relationships, having a less than average length of stay, and being from an upper-middle-class rather than an upper-class socioeconomic background. He was not rated as manifesting the borderline personality disorder criterion for inappropriate, intense anger, but he certainly was capable of articulating vengeful fantasies. Among the predictors associated with poor outcome, he manifested frequent moves as a child.

Mary: A Woman With Narcissistic Personality Disorder and a Poor Outcome

At the time of the index admission, Mary was 22 years old, a white, Protestant, college dropout admitted in the 1960s for a total of 20 months. She was followed up 15 years after admission. At the time of the index admission, Mary had dropped out of a competitive women's college in her junior year because of social and academic difficulties, despite a Wechsler Adult Intelligence Scale—Revised (WAIS-R) full-scale IQ of 129. Mary had had difficulty completing assignments, was self-conscious, and avoided classes because she felt professors knew about her procrastination in completing her work and would be critically disapproving of her. She felt disliked, alone, and "left out" by friends and roommates, with whom she had difficulties sharing living space. Eventually she was unable to complete work or to attend classes, and her fear of rejection and haughty and entitled interpersonal style led to considerable isolation. She consulted with the school psychiatrist, who suggested a return home to enter treatment.

For the next year and a half before the index admission, Mary lived with her parents and was in psychoanalysis with a woman. For a while, Mary worked as a secretary at a university, but 6 months before admission had been transferred to a larger office where she felt disliked and left out. Her social life was already marginal, and she often felt she had "nothing to offer a man." She became more interpersonally isolated, spending much time alone, engaging in elaborate fantasies of being in a romantic relationship with a great man whose life would soon end, such as Beethoven. Mary had tried some college courses, but quit when she sensed her professors became even slightly critical of her. Toward her peers at work and school she was either contemptuous or intimidated. She did not date.

Mary began group psychotherapy and for a while was the adored youngest member in a group of primarily middle-aged, depressed people. Mary was described as haughty, arrogant, cold, and highly critical of others, both in person and in her own sadistic revenge fantasies when slighted. She became fearful of impulses to hurt or kill someone without feeling remorse and of her growing rage at her analyst. Although the analyst felt treatment had been going relatively well, she became concerned about the collapse of Mary's life, especially when Mary quit her job just a few weeks before the index admission. Hospitalization at the Austen Riggs Center was recommended because of the collapse of the patient's life and her fears she would lose control of impulses to hurt herself or others.

Life History

Mary was the only biologic child of an obsessional, perfectionistic, highly successful father, who was aloof and unemotional and felt his daughter lacked discipline, and a warm, self-effacing woman who was socially able, a college graduate, and accepting of her role as her husband's intellectual inferior. Mary saw her mother as a subservient "whipping boy" who held the family together. The household included a female foster child 6 years older than Mary who was taken into the family when Mary was 5 because of a crisis in her own family. This volatile, provocative girl caused her foster mother much distress, resented Mary, and was envious of Mary's status as the "real" child in the family.

In addition, Mary had an adopted brother 8 years her junior, adopted because Mary's father wanted a male heir. The initially rivalrous relationship between Mary and her brother became warmer over the years. The brother is described as withdrawn, athletic, and not the intellectual equal of other family members. Other significant members of the extended family included both grandmothers. The paternal grandmother was a polite, shy, wealthy woman who worshipped Mary, her only biological granddaughter, who forcefully lavished gifts on Mary which Mary rejected, as Mary did her paternal grandmother, despite the grandmother's sometimes childish groveling for approval. The maternal grandmother was a poor, hardworking woman who had raised a family on her own after her husband's death. She is described as a firm, supportive woman who made Mary "toe the mark" and was adored by Mary for her self-sufficiency and firmness.

Immediately after Mary's birth by cesarean section, her mother underwent a total abdomenal hysterectomy because of fibroids. The pregnancy had been long hoped for because of difficulty conceiving, but it was clear it would be the mother's last. Mary's mother was described as "scared to death every time the baby cried." Mary was described as a happy and healthy child. When Mary was 2, the family temporarily moved to a new area because of the demands of the father's career. During this year, in a strange environment, Mary wore an eye patch because of amblyopia. Mary enjoyed nursery school, and recalled her first 6 years as happy and herself as a special, spoiled, and fussed-over child and an aggressive tomboy. When she was 5 the household was thrown into turmoil by the arrival of the 11-year-old foster child, who actively competed with Mary for the attention of her mother and grandmother. After a year or two of turmoil the foster sister was sent to a boarding school. Mary was happy about the end of fighting but sorry about the loss of a playmate with whom she had actually spent many happy hours. When Mary was 8 the foster sister returned to full-time residence with the family, and Mary's younger brother was adopted as an infant. Initially,

Mary was intolerant of his constant crying and spitting up. Once her foster sister returned, her relationship with Mary was cooler and more distant than previously. Soon the family moved to a new town, but Mary was rebuffed by peers because of her haughty, condescending comparisons of the new town to the old one. She was critical of teachers she felt were stupid and spent more time at home than with peers, becoming demanding, selfish, and prone to tantrums.

Mary began to immerse herself in a fantasy world of dolls beginning at about age 8, forming elaborate fantasy relationships and games with them and beginning her preoccupation with fantasies of a comforting and loving relationship with a great man, especially with Beethoven during the last year of his life. Mary was shamed into giving up the dolls and the games at age 13, but the fantasies continued secretly. Previously a tomboy, Mary developed ambivalent interest in femininity following menarche at age 13. In her sophomore year of high school, though, she became increasingly self-conscious about sexuality and her body, began to worship boys from afar while feeling discomfort in their presence, and gained 20 pounds after a mild rejection at a school dance. Also, when Mary was 13, her foster sister married, leaving Mary with a sense of loss. Mary's one friendship was with a disturbed, sophisticated girl who had a reputation for fabricating elaborate stories. When Mary realized other students felt her friend was crazy, Mary angrily broke off the relationship. Six months later when her friend left the school, Mary felt it had been her fault. At age 15, Mary's wealthy paternal grandmother died, leaving a substantial inheritance to Mary, who felt self-conscious about the money. The next year, as a high school junior, Mary began to withdraw more, spent more time in her fantasies about Beethoven, and seemed to withdraw from family life as well, taking no part in day-to-day chores. Despite good grades, Mary's acceptance to her first-choice college came as a surprise to her, and offered a chance, she felt, to show people she really was smart.

At age 18, Mary began college as a music major, but felt

lonely and self-conscious and had trouble with relationships. Surrounded by intelligent women, she no longer felt special. Mary had difficulty with several roommates of whom she was constantly critical and by whom she felt constantly criticized. In her sophomore year, Mary's grades began to slip as she spent increasing periods alone in her room listening to recordings of Beethoven, fantasizing about a love affair with him in the last year of his life. Between her sophomore and junior years of college, Mary worked as a camp counselor but was unable to fit in with peers. In her junior year, Mary threw herself into her schoolwork in an effort to turn her life around, earning good grades and dating three boys, but feeling she really had nothing to offer. In the second half of her junior year the relationship with her roommate became extremely antagonistic. Mary became self-conscious in classes, socially awkward, unable to complete her work, and isolated from her peers. It was at this point that she consulted with the school psychiatrist who suggested she leave college to obtain treatment.

Index Hospitalization

At the time of the index admission, her first psychiatric hospitalization, Mary was diagnosed as having a mixed neurotic character disorder with depressive features in a postadolescent with an identity crisis. Once hospitalized, Mary seemed to flee into health, actively involving herself in the community and activities programs. She was subdued, defensive, shy, frightened, and self-conscious on the surface, concealing secret hatred and contempt for her peers. Psychological testing noted her superficially demure and unassuming manner superimposed over underlying contempt, mockery, and counterphobic denial, with envy of masculine strength, horror at her own sense of vulnerability as a woman, and strong competitive and hostile feelings toward other women. Because of her superficially intact presentation, there was considerable discussion about discontinuing the hospitalization at the time of her first evaluation conference, and she was seen as "baffling" by some staff members, who felt she was a neurotic patient who should have been readily treatable as an outpatient. At her evaluation conference, Mary responded to a question by saying she sometimes felt small and sometimes exalted, apparently describing transient moods rather than bipolar mood swings. At a number of points during her hospitalization, there was concern about episodes of drinking, but Mary seemed to make efforts to grapple with this problem, and staff did not focus on drinking as a major problem for her.

In her four-times-weekly psychotherapy with a relatively young male therapist, Mary initially manifested an idealizing transference. She was sweet, warm, and functioning at an apparently high level. Her colorful relationships with other patients were often the topic of discussion in therapy sessions. A second phase of her psychotherapy at the center involved the emergence of an erotic transference toward the therapist, which was interpreted as a resistance to the psychotherapeutic work. In a third phase of the psychotherapy, Mary began to work in a part of the activities program of the hospital in which she volunteered at a Montessori nursery school on the hospital grounds. As she became overinvolved with her doctor's son at the nursery school, Mary entered a period of neediness and proneness to rages and tantrums in her therapy and outside it. Although she was seen as involved in a gratifying fantasy that the doctor's son was her own, it was difficult to deal with this issue in the sessions. Although forbidding her to attend the nursery school was discussed by hospital staff, such a decision was not made. At about this same time, Mary's father had begun to pressure her to leave the hospital, and a discharge date was set. Mary left after 20 months of treatment, then continued as an outpatient in twice-weekly psychotherapy for another year.

In the follow-up study, Mary's DSM-III diagnosis was Axis I, no diagnosis; Axis II, narcissistic personality disorder (principal diagnosis) and avoidant personality disorder. Mary was felt to manifest five narcissistic personality disorder criteria: grandiosity, preoccupation with fantasies of ideal love, exhibitionism, cool indifference or marked feelings of rage in response to criticism, and relationships that characteristically alternated between the extremes of overidealization and devaluation. She was rated as having the identity disturbance criterion of borderline personality disorder. Although she also met all six criteria for avoidant personality disorder, it was felt this diagnosis alone did not adequately capture the importance of her capacity for contempt and condescension, her preoccupation with fantasies of ideal love, her marked indifference or rage in response to criticism, or her grandiosity. At the time of admission, Mary's GAS score was 40.

Follow-up Information

Mary participated in the center's follow-up study 15 years after admission. At follow-up, Mary's GAS score was 44, only 4 points higher than at admission. It was overridingly clear that alcoholism had emerged as a significant problem for Mary. Three years after discharge, she had begun drinking heavily while back at college. Ten years after discharge, she was involved in an accident while driving intoxicated and entered an alcohol detoxification center and then a residential treatment program emphasizing shared communal work but no psychiatric treatment. At the time of follow-up, 13 years after discharge, Mary was living in an alcohol halfway house. She reported that in the month before follow-up she experienced some nervousness and that she often was not in control of her feelings, but denied sadness, discouragement, or hopelessness. She was relatively dissatisfied with her personal life. Mary felt rested, interested in things in her life, often sure of herself, and relatively cheerful.

Mary's Strauss-Carpenter scale scores based on the year before follow-up included moderate symptoms (2 of 4), no hospitalization (4 of 4), employment more than half the previous year (3 of 4), and rare meetings with others (1 of 4), giving her a Strauss-Carpenter scale sum of 10 of 16. Mary had never married and was childless, belonged to no social organizations, and said she had five personal friends, but relatively little contact with them. Intimate relationships were described as moderately unsatisfactory. Mary had been employed in a factory for more than half of the year before follow-up, but had not been continuously employed. She described herself as satisfied with her performance in work about 75% of the time. Her only rehospitalization in the follow-up interval had been for alcohol detoxification for less than a week. Mary was in psychotherapy and had been for 10 of the 12 years since terminating with her Austen Riggs Center therapist, on average having one or two sessions weekly. In addition, she had been involved in Alcoholics Anonymous and group therapy. She had been residing in a halfway house for just over two and a half years at follow-up.

Although not taking medication at follow-up or during the index hospitalization, Mary had had trials of phenelzine (Nardil), amitriptylene (Elavil), and disulfiram (Antabuse) during the follow-up interval. She acknowledged a severe alcohol problem and social use of marijuana. Mary had not carried out suicide attempts or self-destructive acts during the index admission or the follow-up interval.

In her own retrospective rating of her experience at the center, Mary felt nursing staff and her psychotherapy had been less helpful than other components of the program, such as the activities program, community program, and involvement with other patients. She felt the open setting of the center had permitted her to conceal the extent of her drinking during treatment. Interestingly, she identified her foster sister as someone who had been helpful during her hospitalization at the center. Mary recalled that when she left the center she moved to her own apartment, managing to find a job and make friends within the first few months after discharge. She did not feel the center had adequately prepared her for life outside the hospital setting, though.

In retrospect, Mary wished disulfiram (Antabuse) had been prescribed at the center and that she had made some effort to try her hand at college courses before leaving and had moved to a communal living situation rather than life on her own at the time of discharge. Other comments at follow-up included, "I really enjoyed my stay at Riggs. That may seem a strange thing to say, but it was the first place I had felt I belonged since childhood. The only great drawback was that I felt I was playing at living. I did nothing for 18 months but drink, party, attend therapy and meetings, and participate in activities." She went on, "Psychotherapy puzzles me. As you can see, I've had eons of it, but I'm not sure it has been helpful. Of course, it's pleasurable to have someone's full attention one to five hours a week, but perhaps that was the trouble. It was almost all pleasure, even the weeping felt very good. It wasn't tough on me." She felt the mandatory work component of the residential treatment center she had gone to after emergence of her alcohol problems had been helpful to her, but felt the absence of patient input in running the community in which they lived was a problem.

From among the predictors of poor outcome in narcissistic personality disorder, Mary manifested several. She was from an upper-class family, had moved in childhood (only once, but it was a difficult move), and apparently manifested mild paranoid trends (such as feeling that teachers suspected she was behind in work or that others disliked her). Mary's length of stay was also longer than the mean, and, when she did leave, external pressure from her father led to the discharge. Being an eldest child generally predicted good outcome in this sample, but the appearance of an older foster child at age 5 complicated the family constellation considerably. In retrospect, the failure to identify alcohol abuse as a problem probably contributed to her poor outcome, although her drinking apparently increased only some years after discharge.

Susan: A Woman With Borderline Personality Disorder and a Good Outcome

At the time of her 15-month-long index admission to the Austen Riggs Center in the 1970s, Susan was 19 years old, a white, single, Jewish, college dropout. Susan had been seen in consultation at the center 3 months before the actual admission after several years of increasingly rebellious and impulsive behavior associated with drug use and considerable family and interpersonal turmoil.

Life History

Susan was the first of two children and the only daughter born to her parents. Susan's birth came at a time when her mother was depressed because of the death from cancer of the maternal grandmother 2 months earlier. The mother was pleased to have given birth to a daughter after the loss of the primary woman in her own life, but recalled bitterly that the paternal grandmother, with whom she did not get along, had expressed her own and Susan's father's disappointment that the child was a girl. The maternal grandfather was a likable man who had a good relationship with Susan until his death when she was 8 years old. The paternal family had a history marred by numerous deaths. The paternal grandfather had been an immigrant who found a place for his family in the United States but died in an automobile accident 30 years before Susan's birth. The father had become very close to his mother, the paternal grandmother, partly because he had been her first son and because his birth had followed a miscarriage and the perinatal death of another deformed infant. Especially after the paternal grandfather's death, the father's relationship with the paternal grandmother had become quite dependent. The father's eldest sister was also close to him. She became depressed after the death of the paternal grandfather, having a child within a year in a conscious effort to replace her lost object, but developed a postpartum depression which led to psychiatric hospitalization, during which she suicided within 2 years of the death of the paternal grandfather. Although the father and one of his brothers went on to become physicians, another younger brother had recurrent depressions treated with electroconvulsive therapy and another brother hung himself. The paternal family was involved in much blaming of one another for each of these deaths. Susan's father, a physician, was described as a devout Jew, stern, moralistic, and even "mean." He was his mother's favorite and was closely tied to her, but was said not to be liked very much by his patients. Susan's mother was a bright woman who had been educated in an Ivy League college. The marital relationship was described as stormy and probably was held together by a good sexual relationship. Susan had one brother 3 years younger than her who seemed to be the good child in the family, and never a cause for concern.

Susan's early development was precocious but she was seen as an irritable infant and was particularly prone to awaken when left alone in a room. At the time of Susan's birth, her parents were living with the maternal grandfather in a chronically tense situation after the death of the maternal grandmother. When Susan was 8 months old, her father was drafted into the Army, serving in Korea for the next year. At age 20 months, Susan and her mother were reunited with the father in Japan, then continued to live overseas for another year. While overseas, Susan was said by her physician father to have sustained two generalized seizures triggered by breath holding after a traumatic injury to her hand. An abnormal EEG led to prescription of phenytoin and phenobarbital for 5 years. An adult EEG was reported as normal.

When the family returned from overseas, Susan's mother was pregnant with the younger brother. The family lived with the paternal grandmother who had just had major surgery. Susan was described as withdrawn and clinging to her father for a month after their return. The father in particular was quite pleased with the birth of a son. Although Susan is said to have had no particular reaction to her brother's birth, she was soon sent off to nursery school at age 3 with the conscious intent of allowing time for the mother to be with her newborn son.

The period from ages 3 to 8 was volatile, filled with strife, and difficult for the family, who shared a duplex home with the paternal grandmother. During this period the mother was in analysis paid for by the maternal grandfather. From ages 3 to 5, Susan habitually banged her head in the crib. Her concerned parents eventually sent her to a child guidance clinic and the symptom subsided. Susan began school at a Jewish parochial school where English was spoken in the morning and Hebrew in the afternoon. She was called by her first name in the morning and her middle name in the afternoon. As the only Jew in her neighborhood, attendance at a Jewish parochial school contributed to isolation from peers, but Susan had one Gentile neighbor friend. It was her father who pressured for the preservation of a strong Jewish identity. When Susan was 8, her family moved to their own home. That year the maternal grandfather died of a myocardial infarction. Susan had a memory of having been blamed because she got hurt playing that day and needed attention that diverted her mother from the dying maternal grandfather.

Somewhere between the ages of 8 and 12, Susan developed a "phobia" of seeing her brother's hands at the dinner table. At first, the brother was asked to conceal his hands by pulling down his sleeves or by keeping his hands under the table, until it became clear to the family that such an expectation was having a negative effect on him. The father coerced Susan to confront her fear of seeing her brother's hands, forcing her to stay at the dinner table with the brother's hands exposed. She experienced a frightening panic attack, which led the father to insist Susan do something about the symptom, but it is not clear exactly what steps were taken. There was considerable conflict between the parents about how best to deal with this symptom as Susan entered puberty.

Susan began attending a public high school where she was one of only three Jewish students. Her father expected Susan to select her friends from among the children at a Jewish youth center, but Susan preferred her Gentile peers. Although Susan's mother felt this was sensible, the moralistic and rigid father experienced this as a personal attack. In high school, Susan had a series of intense relationships with non-Jewish boys that would involve sex without birth control and much alcohol abuse. A number of the young men she chose were sadistic, and one in particular was rather anti-Semitic. Suicidal ideation emerged in the course of this series of intense relationships, and at one point after the breakup with a boyfriend, she took an impulsive overdose. Although she told no one of the overdose, Susan asked to be hospitalized, but once admitted felt unable to tolerate the locked doors of the hospital and left after less than a week. In the hospital the overdose was never discovered, and Susan was discharged as an adolescent adjustment reaction.

Subsequently, Susan continued her pattern of dating only non-Jewish boys and drinking to excess. She felt her father's shouted epithet that she was simply a "drunken slut" was probably accurate. At home, there were vicious arguments, and she was prone to intense rages that included throwing things at her father. On at least one occasion the police were called. She made impulsive but abortive efforts to run away from home. Susan provocatively flouted efforts to set limits with her. Primarily, but not exclusively, the problem seemed to be with her father. As a high school senior, Susan began to date a Jewish young man for the first time. He introduced her to marijuana and hallucinogens. She continued this relationship after high school graduation, for the first time using birth control pills. Asked by her mother to keep this a secret from her father, Susan would swallow each pill at the dinner table while her father's back was turned, with the mother watching and gasping in horror.

At age 18, Susan entered a large midwestern college, having taken with her a supply of amphetamines and barbiturates from her father's supply of medications with the intent of having drugs to abuse but also to use in a suicide attempt. Although her mother knew about the drugs, she made only an abortive effort to stop Susan from taking them with her. Susan lasted only a few months at school, failing to attend classes and engaging in extensive hallucinogen and marijuana abuse. She returned home before Christmas and tried working as a clerk but quit, feeling bored and empty. She returned to school for the spring semester and did better, earning Bs, but continued drug use and began a romance with a radical student heavily involved in the antiwar movement. Susan was seen as on the fringe of the antiwar movement, apathetic rather than intensely involved. During the summer after her freshman year, Susan accepted her father's offer to visit an Israeli kibbutz. Susan was unhappy at the kibbutz and tried another, having difficulty with peers because of a pattern of unstable and intense relationships and frequent displays of temper as well as affective instability. Unhappy with her experience in Israel, she returned to her boyfriend and the antiwar movement, but quickly lost interest, and the relationship failed. She was depressed without neurovegetative signs, except an increase in suicidal ideation. At the recommendation of her physician uncle, Susan visited the Austen Riggs Center as a possible treatment resource, attracted by what she had heard about the completely open setting. At the consultation, she was lukewarm about the possibility of admission, deciding she probably would not come since there was a several-months-long waiting list. Susan tried living with her uncle in New York while taking some art courses, but frequently felt suicidal, empty, and bored. When offered admission to the center 3 months after the consultation, she accepted.

Index Hospitalization

At the time of the index hospitalization, Susan presented as a potentially attractive, giggly, immature, and unkempt hippy who was noteworthy for her irritability, changeable moods, hyperalertness, and proneness to outbursts of anger. She was shy, frequently self-depreciatory, and prone to see others as condemnatory of her. Within the first week or two of admission, she was overheard telling another patient of her secret supply of amphetamines and barbiturates. Nursing staff approached her to insist she turn these in, a demand with which she complied. During her stay, Susan demonstrated a penchant for entering a string of unstable interpersonal relationships with male patients, displayed outbursts of anger out of proportion to the stimulus, was moody, irritable, and intermittently depressed, but also was capable of a shy, giggly, girlish presentation. She was felt to be likable despite some of the negative aspects of her presentation. She seemed intolerant of situations in which she was not accompanied by other patients or staff.

Low doses of chlordiazepoxide (Librium) or diazepam (Valium) were given perhaps 10 or 12 times during the course of her entire hospitalization, but she was otherwise not treated with medications. Psychological testing supported the diagnosis of "depression in an immature character with borderline features." It was noted that there was a quality of her personality suggesting it to be in a state of flux. The testing was suggestive of marked impulsivity, depression, paranoid trends, and a focus on minute detail. Her thinking was described as highly personalized, and she seemed to expect betrayal. She experienced others as condemning her. Her WAIS-R score suggested superior intelligence with a full-scale IQ of 122. Susan's retrospective follow-up study DSM-III diagnoses were Axis I, mixed substance abuse, dysthymic disorder; Axis II, borderline personality disorder (principal diagnosis), for which she met criteria for unstable and intense relationships; inappropriate, intense anger; identity disturbance; affective instability; intolerance of being alone; and chronic feelings of emptiness or boredom. She was rated as probably meeting the criterion for impulsivity or unpredictability on the basis of substance abuse and sex without birth control, but was felt not to meet the criterion for physically self-damaging acts because there was only one instance of an overdose documented. Among the narcissistic personality disorder criteria, she was rated as manifesting cool indifference or feelings of rage in response to criticism and relationships that characteristically alternated between overidealization and devaluation. Her admission GAS score was 33.

In her therapy, Susan was alternately shy and pleasing and irritable and angry. She worked with a young, Jewish, male therapist who seemed to struggle with feeling off balance with her for much of their work. Early in the treatment, before she was discovered to be concealing drugs, she reported a dream of having extinguished a "joint" when she realized smoking it was wrong. Subsequent to the discovery and confiscation of the drugs she had brought with her to the center, Susan felt singled out and condemned. She often felt her therapist was disgusted with her. Susan was frequently angry at the therapist and voiced envy of her peers when they got more nursing attention than she. Susan experienced whatever the therapist said as an attack and was angry about weekend and other separations or changed appointments, but would react with great pleasure and delight when an extra session was offered. She threatened to leave the center when her therapist announced a 1-month vacation after 3 months of work together. The therapist realized he felt intimidated by her constant angry outbursts and provocativeness toward him. He felt much pressure to offer reassurance when she would ask if he too felt that others were condemning and attacking her, feeling trapped by the position in which she put him. The therapist experienced her as elusive and enigmatic as well as attacking in the hours.

By 6 months into the therapy, Susan felt herself to be the most evil patient at the center, constantly threatening to leave. The therapist felt intellectualized and distant in the work with her. About 7 months into the therapy, the therapist made the interpretation that she was using him as someone to complain to and seek reassurance from that she was not wrong. She missed the next two sessions, then reported her sense that the doctor was tired of her complaints. Susan seemed to change in the hours and began to speak more about a relatively stable relationship with a male patient who resisted entering an intense relationship with her because he insisted she was able to stand on her own. She also began to speak more about a "crush" on her doctor. Nine months into the treatment, Susan's father began to exert pressure for discharge for financial reasons. Susan constantly asked for assistance in setting up discharge plans but would feel abandoned when the therapist made moves in that direction. About a year after admission, she began to speak more openly of her sexual feelings for the therapist and to acknowledge the connection between these feelings and her pattern of upsets. She also spoke of her terrible fear of aloneness and sense of emptiness, acknowledging her wish to have the therapist with her always.

Susan feared if she left the center she would be forgotten. Fifteen months after admission, Susan was discharged to outpatient status. Just before discharge, she reported a dream in which she was expected to walk into a large body of water and drown. Not wanting that to happen, she held her breath in the dream. Susan was discharged but continued to work with her therapist for 5 more months before terminating. When Susan's therapy was discussed in her final conference before discharge, a number of staff members commented that her doctor had seemed afraid to engage with her. The growing intimacy between therapist and patient was seen as possibly threatening to both. It was pointed out, though, that the therapeutic relationship was growing more mature. In addition to having been constantly derided as ineffectual by the patient, the therapist had faced a fair amount of pressure from her father, but had managed to intervene with him in a way that had allowed the therapy to continue.

Follow-up Information

Susan participated in the center's follow-up study 9 years after admission. At follow-up, Susan's GAS score was 88, 55 points higher than at admission. Susan reported that in the month before follow-up she had been in very good spirits despite being under some pressure, but denied feelings of sadness, discouragement, or hopelessness and saw herself as happy and satisfied with her life. She reported a small amount of worry and anxiety but was interested in her life and felt emotionally stable and sure of herself. She saw herself as energetic, relaxed, and relatively cheerful. At follow-up, Susan was married and had a daughter whose birth by cesarean section had been experienced as a difficult stress. Since leaving the center, she had not been admitted to a psychiatric hospital and had had neither further therapy of any kind since terminating with her Austen Riggs Center therapist nor any psychoactive medications. She rated herself as satisfied with work almost all the time and moderately satisfied with intimate relationships. Since leaving the center, she had completed training as a registered nurse and was on leave from nursing to raise her daughter. She described herself as a social drinker, but used no drugs at all. Susan's Strauss-Carpenter scale score based on the year before follow-up included no symptoms (4 of 4), no hospitalization (4 of 4), full-time employment (4 of 4), and at least weekly meetings with others (4 of 4), giving her a Strauss-Carpenter scale sum of 16 of 16. Susan had made no suicide attempts since discharge.

In retrospect, Susan felt the most helpful parts of her stay at the center had been her psychotherapy and the opportunity to be away from home. When asked what she thought had turned her life around, Susan wrote, "Having an excellent therapist and a real desire to work with him and get better. Also having a wonderful husband and daughter. (However, the latter would not have been possible without Riggs.)" Susan's major complaint about her treatment was that nursing staff were not consistently available enough in times of crisis.

From among the predictors of good outcome in borderline personality disorder, Susan manifests several. Although her parents' marriage was stormy, they did not divorce. She was rated as not meeting three of the personality disorder criteria associated with poor outcome when present, specifically the narcissistic personality disorder criterion of "entitlement" and schizotypal "odd speech" and "recurrent illusions." She had spent 1 week hospitalized before the index admission and had no rehospitalizations during the follow-up interval. Susan had two of the predictors of poor outcome derived from this sample: no self-destructive acts during the index hospitalization and manifesting the borderline personality disorder criterion of "chronic feelings of emptiness or boredom." Interestingly, Susan did have the kind of interaction with nursing staff and her therapist associated with self-destructive acts during the index admission when she was discovered early in her stay to be concealing pills for a suicide attempt.

Larry: A Man With Borderline Personality Disorder and a Poor Outcome

At the time of the 18-month-long index admission in the 1960s, Larry was 44 years old, a white, Protestant, twice-divorced father of a 10-year-old daughter. He had never previously been hospitalized but had had numerous failed outpatient psychotherapies. Since adolescence, he had been preoccupied with a fantasy of having an above-the-knee amputation of his left leg, a fantasy that had been essential for sexual gratification and that he had made efforts to implement.

Life History

Larry was the second of three children and the second of two sons born to his parents. His father was a traveling salesman after failure in an earlier business venture and training as a pilot in World War I. The father was described as a womanizer who was an absent figure in the family. Larry's mother was described as an infantile, neurotic woman tending toward invalidism. At the time of the index admission, Larry had an older brother, aged 46, who continued to suffer from enuresis as an adult. A 39-year-old sister was described as hostile, paranoid, and especially angry at men.

The pregnancy with Larry was unplanned but not unwanted. The family hired a teenage girl who served as a maid and caretaker for the children. At age 20 months, while his mother was shopping, Larry had been left in the care of the maid when he accidentally pulled some hot oatmeal off the stove onto his left foot. Frightened and in terrible pain, Larry was inconsolable for an extended period until his mother could be located and brought home. While waiting, he had been unresponsive to the maid and to the doctor who arrived on the scene. Larry had a vague memory from that incident of someone shouting "Cut it off," apparently referring to the bootie he was wearing. There was an extended convalescence over several months as the burn healed, leaving a scar.

Another early experience included genital play with his brother. When Larry was 2, the maternal grandfather died. At age 5, Larry was sent to an aunt's farm for a week, learning of his sister's birth when he returned but not previously having been informed that a baby was expected. He refused to believe the birth had really occurred and was upset with the arrival of this sibling. At about this time, Larry lacerated his scalp in a fall, requiring sutures. About a month after his sister's birth, Larry's mother was seriously burned while using gasoline as a cleaning fluid in the basement. Again Larry was sent to live with his aunt for at least a month. He recalled having been anxious and unhappy about the separation. By the time he began kindergarten, Larry was closely tied to his mother, whereas his father was an absent figure. Larry was seen in a number of respects as a "sissy" in each of the several neighborhoods to which the family moved because of the demands of the father's career. Larry was sad and disconsolate when one of his friends moved away. Once school began, Larry was a teacher's pet but picked on by other children. He became a loner, enjoying long walks exploring the countryside. He recalled having met an older boy whose leg had been traumatically amputated in a railroad accident. In another memory related to amputation, Larry recalled that his father had once shown rare compassion in his facial expression when Larry and his father passed an amputee on the street.

Larry's adolescence was turbulent. At age 14, he developed unilateral gynecomastia which caused him great concern about his sexual identity and was associated with much shyness. It was at about this time that Larry became fascinated with amputation. He became distantly acquainted with a schoolmate peer with a right above-the-knee amputation and a peg leg prothesis. Such details were important to Larry, who recalled having been terrified but mesmerized by the boy, whose exuberance in life contrasted with his own morbid, emotionless, empty depression. All subsequent sexual experience and activity, whether masturbatory, homosexual, or heterosexual, involved a fantasy of amputation at least transiently. Also during adolescence, Larry was involved in homosexual experimentation, including an instance of anal penetration by his brother. Later, he was befriended by a homosexual pastor who identified Larry as a homosexual and counseled him, but avoided homosexual activity with him. Larry graduated from high school, entering the military in mid–World War II. During this period, he was anxious, inhibited, and continuously attracted to men. After 2 years in the service, he was discharged dishonorably after confessing his homosexuality. He sought psychotherapy but stopped after a few sessions. Larry entered and graduated from a competitive midwestern college, engaging in a number of homosexual affairs. On his 21st birthday, he had his first heterosexual experience.

When Larry was 22, his father died of his second myocardial infarction. Larry and his family believed Larry's turbulent, unsettled, promiscuous homosexual life and his inability to find closeness with his father had hastened the father's death. After the father's death, Larry trained as an architect and began once-weekly psychotherapy, which he continued for the next 20 years, although changing therapists every year or two. Larry's marriage to his first wife was unhappy from the beginning for reasons that are not specified, leading to an annulment after 2 years. Larry's homosexual activities increased, and he began his first efforts to injure his leg to require amputation. Although managing to secure employment as an architect, Larry seemed to founder professionally, repeatedly failing the architectural licensing exam. He engaged in promiscuous homosexuality and drug abuse. At age 32, he married his second wife, who gave birth to a daughter 2 years later.

From his early 30s until the time of admission, Larry was often preoccupied with his obsession about amputation. For example, when reading the newspaper, he would scan for stories related to amputation. While in his early 40s, he began to work with a prominent nonanalytic psychotherapist in both individual and group psychotherapy. While in this therapeutic relationship, Larry finally managed to pass his architectural exams. He left group therapy, though, because other group members were put off by his continuing preoccupation with a wish for amputation. Three years before admission, at age 41, Larry entered school for training as a prosthetist, but he was unhappy with his life, chronically depressed with suicidal ideation, and dissatisfied with his poor marriage, frequently manifesting affective instability and evidence of identity disturbance. Two years before admission, he separated from his wife and experienced more depression. Two months later, he accidentally injured his left leg, subsequently making efforts to enact his amputation fantasy by inserting surgical needles into his leg, then hammering them into the bone in an experience of "unbelievable anguish." His specific intent was to induce osteomyelitis, which he succeeded in doing only after repeated attempts, Larry commenting on how "unbelievably resistant" the body was. Larry was hospitalized and surgically treated for osteomyelitis. In the hospital, he made further attempts to injure the leg, opening the wound and attempting to spread the infection, but the injury healed. His efforts to injure the leg continued up to 3 weeks before admission to the Austen Riggs Center. Larry readily accepted that either death or amputation might be outcomes of his activity.

Several months before admission, Larry was disillusioned with psychotherapy. He engaged in a period of increased drug usage, especially hallucinogens. Larry began a period of seeking out psychiatric consultation with well-known experts around the country, eventually following the recommendation that he seek admission to the Austen Riggs Center.

Index Hospitalization

At the time of the index hospitalization, Larry presented as an energetic, sometimes grandiose, imposing man with charismatic, godlike qualities, who also appeared immature and dependent. He was an erudite and esoteric observer who had a dramatic presentation. He immediately challenged hospital rules and female authorities. Psychoactive medications were not prescribed during the entire hospitalization. Psychological testing offered a diagnosis of a "severe narcissistic-obsessive character disorder with hints of depression." There was no evidence of a thought disorder. An "as if" quality was noted. His WAIS-R full-scale IQ was 140.

In the hospital, Larry's presentation included angry outbursts during which he would smash furniture. Early in his stay, he severely bit his tongue. He was demanding and hostile and seemed to have a chip on his shoulder. Larry's retrospective DSM-III diagnoses were Axis I, chronic factitious disorder, atypical paraphilia, hallucinogen abuse; Axis II, borderline personality disorder (principal diagnosis), for which he met criteria for impulsivity; inappropriate, intense anger; identity disturbance; affective instability; and physically self-damaging acts. From among the narcissistic personality disorder criteria, Larry was felt to manifest grandiosity and exhibitionism. His admission GAS score was 34.

Larry worked with a younger male therapist in four-times-weekly psychotherapy for a total of 21 months in a therapy that gradually shifted its focus from the crippled leg to Larry as a crippled person. Larry responded angrily to the therapist's early interpretations of resistance, telling his therapist not to "fuck with my antisuicide kit." Three months after admission, Larry revealed to his therapist that he was engaged in assaults on his leg. Although the therapist made no intervention to thwart this, nursing staff independently confiscated Larry's implements. In a rage, Larry blamed his therapist for having intruded on and manipulated him, avoiding sessions for a while. When he returned, Larry spoke more of his identity as a sick, crippled, and deformed child. He felt like he was "porous" with his mother, by which he seemed to mean something about fearing merger. Toward his father, he experienced only an unbridgeable distance. There was an angry confrontation between therapist and patient when the former discovered

Larry had been lying about marijuana use. The therapist threatened to discontinue the work if lied to, later feeling he had been excessively punitive in this response. Larry responded, though, by making apparently earnest efforts to turn over a new leaf. It was at this point that Larry shaved his beard and began to look rather boyish, but complained of feeling controlled and possessed by the therapist. Shortly after this, when the therapist announced plans for a vacation, Larry became sad and threatened suicide.

By 9 months after admission, Larry was speaking about his rage at his father for having allowed him to be engulfed by his mother. He had never felt claimed by his father. Larry reported a dream in which his father's erection turns Larry into a girl. Later, Larry revealed a masturbation fantasy of amputees exploring each other's deformities. He also revealed some of his own masturbation practices, including drinking his own urine and defecating in a towel wrapped around himself like a diaper. Larry hated the way he had come to see the therapist as forcing him toward health when what he really wanted was to be sick and helpless. Larry consciously refused to relinquish his specialness by becoming like others. As he progressively revealed more in the therapy, Larry's role in the center community shifted from rebel and challenger of authority to high-functioning community member and social conscience of his peers.

About 14 months into the treatment, financial limitations emerged with the news that Larry's insurance coverage would soon be exhausted. Larry felt his therapist had a plot to be rid of him. Although the therapist had not told Larry that he was in the last 6 months of his own fellowship at the center at this point, it seems likely Larry knew such information anyway. A period of rage at the therapist began. Soon the therapist revealed his upcoming departure. Larry reported a dream of jumping into the grave after his father's funeral. Larry's financial situation prevented him from continuing inpatient treatment after 18 months, leading to discharge to outpatient status for continued three-times-weekly psychotherapy with his therapist. He spoke of a plan to become a prosthetist, which he saw as a sublimated partial solution to his preoccupation with amputation. After 2 or 3 months of outpatient treatment, Larry's doctor left the area. Larry's therapist's recommendation had been for Larry to stop therapy when the therapist left, without resumption with anyone else. Larry reportedly disagreed with this plan but acquiesced. After discharge, Larry pursued his goal of becoming a prosthetist.

Follow-up Information

Larry participated in the center's follow-up study 11 years after admission. At follow-up, Larry's GAS score was 50, 16 points higher than at admission. Larry reported he had been in low spirits, sad, discouraged, and dissatisfied with his life in the month before follow-up. He was anxious and tense quite a bit of the time, rarely woke up fresh or rested, and felt depressed much of the time. He reported he had been worried about his health. Larry was living alone in a private residence and had been married and divorced another time since discharge. His one child had been involved in psychiatric treatment. Larry reported that the breakup of his third marriage and the failure of a business venture had been significant stresses for him in the follow-up interval. Larry reported 2 years of further education since leaving the center, but had failed to complete a degree. Larry was unemployed at follow-up. He had had no hospitalizations since discharge but had been in twice-weekly psychotherapy for virtually the entire follow-up interval. Larry reported a medication trial of amitriptylene (Elavil) in the past and currently was using both diazepam (Valium) and flurazepam (Dalmane). Larry felt he had a moderate problem with alcohol but was not using other illicit drugs. He reported having made no suicide attempts and no further efforts to harm himself. He saw his intimate relationships as very satisfactory. Larry's Strauss-Carpenter scale scores based on the year before follow-up included continuous moderate symptoms (1 of 4), no hospitalization (4 of 4), employment more than half the year (3 of 4), and approximately once-a-month meetings with friends (2 of 4), giving him a Strauss-Carpenter scale sum of 10 of 16.

In his rating of treatment at the center, Larry reported that all aspects of the program had been helpful, but contacts with other patients were somewhat less helpful. He saw himself as somewhere between doing well and not doing well. As he put it, "Each day is spent in the crucible, yet one does well to remain alive."

Larry manifests most of the predictors of good outcome in borderline personality disorder: an absence of parental divorce, self-destructive acts during the index hospitalization, and the absence of the narcissistic personality disorder criterion of "entitlement," schizotypal criterion of "odd speech" or "recurrent illusions," and borderline personality disorder criterion of "emptiness or boredom." Nevertheless, his GAS and Strauss-Carpenter scale scores define him as a poor outcome, although his renunciation of efforts to become an amputee or die trying suggests at least some measure of good outcome.

Chapter 5

Case Discussion: The Ego Psychology–Object-Relations Perspective

OTTO F. KERNBERG, M.D.

Editor's Note

Dr. Kernberg is the leading spokesperson for the ego psychology–object-relations point of view in the treatment of narcissistic personality disorder. His important conceptual contributions were summarized by Dr. Sacksteder in Chapter 1, with special emphasis on Dr. Kernberg's psychoanalytic precursors and on the differences between Dr. Kernberg's point of view and the self psychology point of view offered by the late Heinz Kohut. In the following chapter, Dr. Kernberg offers his reflections on the four case histories presented in Chapter 4 from his unique perspective. The absence of process material and of detailed information about the transference and countertransference makes a discussion of the psychotherapy difficult for Dr. Kernberg, but the reader gains a rare opportunity to see how Dr. Kernberg perceives such patients.

Chapter 5

Case Discussion: The Ego Psychology–Object-Relations Perspective

It is difficult to provide a clinical discussion of four cases that, by necessity, were condensed to a bare minimum regarding the patients' past history, diagnostic evaluation, progress throughout treatment, treatment outcome, and long-term follow-up. My comments will therefore necessarily be tentative, focusing on potential avenues of further exploration rather than expressing categorical statements about what happened.

First some general remarks about the patients. The diagnostic assessment of all four patients satisfactorily stressed the key symptoms from which the diagnoses were derived. While agreeing with the diagnostic formulations, I would have stressed further the differential diagnosis of psychosis with hypochondriacal delusions in the case of Peter, and again in the case of Larry, whose atypical perversion might also have masked delusions related to his wishes for self-amputation.

I also missed an emphasis on the diagnostic evaluation of what, in clinical experience, have impressed me as the two most reliable clinical prognostic indicators for intensive psychotherapy with nonpsychotic patients: the quality of object relations and the intensity of antisocial features. Although some information has been provided regarding the past object relations of these four patients and their interpersonal relationships in the hospital, we learn very little about the developments of these relationships in the transference and about the intrapsychic—as opposed to the interpersonal—features of their relations with the most important others in their lives. Because of the prognostic importance of the history of antisocial features, I would explore these systematically in all patients with severe personality disorders. In this regard, it is of interest that dishonesty or deceptiveness was prominent in the treatment of three of the four patients.

The presentation of the patients' past life history raises certain interesting questions. Of course, the history must be condensed to its essentials. But it frequently happens that even these condensations may reflect important aspects of the patient's current psychopathology, his or her conscious "myths" about the past, and the evaluating psychiatrist's theories and biases regarding what is important in the patient's past. I also wonder whether the presentation of the past history may reflect the therapists' developing knowledge about the patients' past derived from the exploration of the transference. In any case, the discrepancy between the relatively extensive information about the patients' past histories and the sparsity of information about their transference developments limits the usefulness of these summaries.

It is important to keep in mind that the past history looks very different at the end of the treatment from the way it did at the beginning, and that, outside the context of well-documented developments in the patient's transference, speculations about the psychodynamic implications of such past history are risky and highly unreliable. It is particularly with patients suffering from severe personality disorder that the current disorganization of ego and superego functions affects their capacity to evaluate their own past. It is only in the course of the treatment that the unconscious history of that past gradually emerges, first in a distorted fashion and later, in advanced stages of the treatment, more realistically.

The major problem with the presentation of the four cases is that so little has been reported about transference developments. Perhaps because the focus of the presentations is on follow-up, interest is centered on the prognostic implications of the patients' past history, initial evaluation, and overall treatment course in the hospital, whereas what happened during the psychotherapeutic treatment itself has received very little attention. This lack of information seriously limits the possibilities of discussing the treatment process itself.

The availability of long-term follow-up many years after the conclusion of the index treatment of these four patients is of great interest. At the same time, in light of my experience of conducting follow-up interviews (between 2 and 3 years after completion of treatment) in the context of the Menninger Foundation Psychotherapy Research Project, I would be somewhat skeptical about accepting at face value the patients' statements. There may be important motivational factors operating in patients who have refused further treatment and who indicate that "everything is well" in order to keep threats of further psychotherapeutic evaluation at bay. Or, to the contrary, they might exaggerate current difficulties to express their disappointment in their past treatment. It is true, however, that the follow-up studies were done at a time so distant from the original treatment that such motivational factors might be less important. By the same token, one would assume that the patients would not show the regressive features during follow-up evaluations that can be seen after relatively brief follow-up periods.

Nevertheless, there are always complex relations between what patients report at follow-up about their treatment and what interviewers know from that past treatment; I would have liked further exploration of this point. Susan, for example, wrote that "Having an excellent therapist and a real desire to work with him and get better" helped her to turn her life around. In the information provided about the treatment, however, the therapist described her as elusive and himself as intellectualized and distant in the work with her, and in Susan's final case conference before discharge a number of staff members commented that her doctor had seemed afraid to engage with her. It may well be that the relationship with her therapist changed dramatically in the 5-month outpatient therapy that followed Susan's discharge from the hospital, but, even under these circumstances, it would have been of great interest to raise the question regarding her changing perception of her therapist with her.

It was striking to me that the two patients who had good outcome had almost no treatment after leaving the Austen Riggs Center, when, on the basis of all evidence, they probably should have continued in outpatient psychotherapy after that time. In contrast, the two patients with poor long-term outcome continued in (rather ineffective) treatments over many years. The implication may be simply that the patients who did well required no further treatment, whereas those who did poorly required further treatment and were not able to improve in spite of such treatment. The situation may be more complicated, however—more about this follows.

Peter

Regarding Peter's diagnostic evaluation, it was not clear to me whether his conviction that he had a serious physical illness was truly delusional or not. I also did not fully understand what was meant by his "physical collapse" at the time of his arrival at the hospital: Was this a form of dramatization, a conversion symptom, a delusion, or the expression of severe and paralyzing anxiety? Why, in short, did he need a wheelchair? The diagnosis of Peter as suffering from a narcissistic personality disorder is convincing; the presence of severe hypochondriacal features is an indication of severe narcissistic pathology, but, as already mentioned, requires the differential diagnosis between narcissistic personality and psychosis. I have seen somewhat similar cases, whose initial diagnosis of narcissistic personality had to be changed to that of an atypical paranoid psychosis.

The past life history of this patient is puzzling. The description of his father, shifting from somebody who frequently beat the patient with a strap to the patient's "buddy," raises the question of whether the father indeed had such dramatically contradictory features. Could it be that the description of the father as well as of the rest of the family reflects the patient's distortion of his past, his tolerance of contradictory perceptions, which reflect an underlying mechanism of splitting? Or did the patient live in a bizarre, potentially chaotic family environment?

The mother's threatening to leave the father if he did not treat Peter better, symbolically repeating the patient's father's desertion by his own mother at age 3, suggests a potential for intense hostile tension between the patient's parents, probably fortified by the psychodynamic consequences of the patient's mother's history of sexual abuse. All these data speak to a potential for violence in the relationship between the parents, but we are given no information about how they actually got along with each other.

Peter's childhood history suggests a severe personality disorder from early childhood on, with significant inhibition of his socialization. Throughout adolescence, his efforts to omnipotently control his friends and his becoming vindictive when he felt betrayed suggest the consolidation of a narcissistic personality structure.

Peter's sexual impotence after marriage reflects severe unconscious conflicts in his relationships with women, an area of difficulty that seems to have continued to the time of follow-up. At that time, he was 37 years old and still single, and there is no indication that he was involved in-depth in any sexual relationship. One might ask whether his past history of intense rage with women who rejected him—to the extent that he had fantasies to seek them out and kill their children—had been resolved, and what the development of these sadistic urges had been in recent years.

Peter's demanding, controlling attitude with the therapist is described, but I missed an in-depth analysis of the transference implications of these demands. The statement that "by 6 months after admission, Peter had formed an idealized view of the therapist" seemed particularly unsatisfactory because it fails to include the dynamics of this idealization.

There are many types of idealization, from primitive idealization as counterpoint to split-off persecutory fears, to the narcissistic idealization derived from the projection onto the therapist of an idealized self-image, to the idealization expressing unconscious guilt as a reaction formation against aggression toward the therapist. To see an "idealizing transference" as an indirect confirmation of a narcissistic personality disorder is, in my view, too simple a way of dealing with the subject.

The statement that Peter was able "to talk about how getting better posed a problem if it meant the therapist would win his colleagues' admiration" may reflect conflicts around envy that are usually very prominent in narcissistic patients (but have not been highlighted in the two patients with this diagnosis). It is often the patient's unconscious envy of the therapist that determines a specific type of negative therapeutic reaction typical for narcissistic patients. The diminution of hypochondriacal symptoms as he developed an "idealized transference" would speak for the transformation of unconscious conflicts expressed in his hypochondriacal concerns into a transference constellation, but again, the case report furnishes no further information about this issue.

It is puzzling that this patient did not try to obtain further individual psychotherapy after completion of his treatment at the Austen Riggs Center. The information that Peter conveys about himself at follow-up—he was a social drinker, was somewhat dissatisfied with his personal life, but also found it interesting and felt sure of himself much of the time—together with his continuing concerns about his health, and the previously mentioned problems in his sexual adjustment, all raise questions about the stability of his present levels of adjustment.

Mary

Mary's history seems typical of a patient with narcissistic personality disorder functioning on an overt borderline level; that is, with nonspecific manifestations of ego weakness (lack of anxiety tolerance, lack of impulse control, and lack of sublimatory channeling) and with breakdown at school and in social functioning. That she was getting worse after having begun psychoanalysis a year and a half earlier raises the question of a possible negative therapeutic reaction at the time of admission, which may have persisted in one form or another throughout her Austen Riggs Center and subsequent treatment.

We are given considerable information about "objective" data regarding her background, and, indeed, it is strange that her parents should have taken into the family a 6-years-older female foster child when Mary was 5 "because of a crisis in her own family," and an 8-years-younger brother, adopted "because Mary's father wanted a male heir." But, because of the absence of the exploration of the corresponding unconscious elements of the transference, the dynamic implications of the past history remain elusive. The same questions I raised earlier apply to this case.

The history of her hospitalization is highly revealing: "She was subdued, defensive, shy, frightened, and self-conscious on the surface, concealing secret hatred and contempt for her peers. Psychological testing noted her superficially demure and unassuming manner superimposed over underlying contempt, mockery, and counterphobic denial, with envy of masculine strength, horror at her own sense of vulnerability as a woman, and strong competitive and hostile feelings toward other women." In other words, both clinically and on psychological testing, she seemed to be concealing hatred and contempt under a surface of shyness and an unassuming manner. Although there was concern about episodes of drinking, staff did not focus on this problem, and it emerges as her major, unresolved pathology only at the time of follow-up.

Mary, similarly to Peter, is described as having "initially manifested an idealizing transference." Here the inadequacy of this statement is illustrated even more strongly in the sharp contradiction between this supposed idealizing transference and the later erotic transference toward her therapist on the one hand, and her dishonesty in not revealing her ongoing alcoholism on the other. How can we talk about an idealizing transference in the case of a patient who is dishonest with her therapist? It is very important to differentiate a genuine idealization, whatever its dynamics and meanings, from seductive flattering, which may not have been properly diagnosed by her "relatively young male therapist."

As I said earlier, I have found the extent of antisocial features a prognostically crucial indicator with patients suffering from severe personality disorders, particularly narcissistic personality disorder. Mary's case may illustrate this issue. In any event, Mary's follow-up study shows her, at age 37, with chronic alcoholism, unmarried, childless, relatively socially isolated, not continuously employed, and with moderately unsatisfactory relations with men. It was at that point that she said, talking about her stay at the Austen Riggs Center: "It was the first place I had felt I belonged since childhood. The only great drawback was that I felt I was playing at living. I did nothing for 18 months but drink, party, attend therapy and meetings, and participate in activities."

I believe this case illustrates the danger of neglecting the analysis of the negative transference, particularly in patients with idealizing transferences typical of narcissistic pathology, that is, patients who are projecting onto the therapist their own idealized self-representation. Often an intense idealization in the transference is the counterpart of repression, projection, or dissociation of the negative transference. In Mary's case, of course, rather than any of these alternatives, it may have been simply a case of conscious suppression of the deceitfulness that marked her treatment at the hospital. It is a helpful principle of psychotherapy that in patients who are not fully honest with the therapist, this issue takes precedence over all other issues—with the important exception of acute danger to the patient's own life, to the lives of others, or to the very continuation of the treatment.

Susan

Susan's life history is fairly typical of the history of patients with severe borderline personality disorder who require hospitalization at some point. Once again, we are given a great deal of information about "objective" facts about her family and personal history, but it is hard to judge what her internal experience was of her relationship with her parents. There is important information regarding severe neurotic symptoms from early childhood on, such as head banging from ages 3 to 5, the "phobia" of seeing her brother's hands at the dinner table between the ages of 8 and 12, and the patterns of intense sexual relationships without birth control and of alcohol abuse. Susan's tendency to choose men who were sadistic with her seems to suggest the presence of masochistic needs; the sadistic elements predominate over the masochistic ones in the intense rages at her father.

We are given some indication that there may have been unconscious collusion from both parents in Susan's obtaining amphetamines and barbiturates from her father's supply of medications and the lack of an adequate reaction of her mother, who knew about this.

The initial diagnostic evaluation is satisfactory, except for the lack of careful evaluation of past antisocial tendencies. She was discovered to be concealing drugs in the hospital, and it is not clear to what extent that information and the discovery and confiscation of the drugs she had brought with her to the center was fully discussed and elaborated in the treatment situation. The availability of this information in the therapy, in any case, contrasts this patient's treatment favorably with the previous case of Mary. In general, the open and direct expression of her hostility in the therapy sessions may have facilitated working through the negative aspects of the transference and may have facilitated the integration of loving and hateful relationships that is so crucial in the long-term psychotherapy of borderline patients. In Susan's case, her development of sexual feelings for the therapist after a year of treatment would seem more genuine than the erotization of the transference in the case of Mary, who was concealing her alcoholism from him.

Again, it is surprising that Susan had no further therapy of any kind since terminating her treatment at the Austen Riggs Center. The failure to supply information about her relationship with her husband is unfortunate; to be married and to have a daughter are not, by themselves, evidence of a happy and satisfying life.

Larry

Larry conveys the impression of being the most severely disturbed of the four patients. His traumatic childhood included the accident involving his left foot, which apparently initiated his fixation on the fantasy of amputating his left leg below his knee. A second accident, a scalp cut requiring sutures, coincided with the unexpected learning of his sister's birth when he returned home, followed shortly by his mother's getting seriously burned while using gasoline as a cleaning fluid, and Larry's subsequently being sent away once more.

Severe personality disturbances show from early childhood on in Larry's being perceived as a "sissy" in various neighborhoods, his becoming a teacher's pet but being picked on by other children, and his development as a loner.

Larry's fascination with amputation developed throughout adolescence, as did his homosexual and heterosexual activities, both involving fantasies of amputation. The history of a severe masochistic perversion, Larry's unsettled, promiscuous homosexual life as an adult, and his 20 years of psychotherapy while changing therapists "every year or two" indicates, it seems to me, severe pathology of object relations. The same may be reflected in the annulment of his first marriage after 2 years. He was able to remain married for 10 years to his second wife before separating from her, but we are told very little about this second marriage except that he was unhappy and his marriage was "poor."

I am under the impression that this patient was inserting surgical needles into his leg and hammering them into the bone *in a secretive way*, similar to his efforts to spread the infection of his leg after surgical treatment for self-induced osteomyelitis in the hospital. The diagnosis of chronic factitious disorder in addition to an atypical paraphilia and hallucinogen abuse made retrospectively on Axis I would seem to confirm his deceptiveness about his physical symptoms, in addition to the deceptiveness about his drug intake discovered during the hospitalization.

In my experience, tendencies toward self-mutilation constitute a dire prognosis, particularly when they have chronic, bizarre, and life-threatening qualities. The fact that such severe self-mutilation may at the same time be an essential requirement for sexual gratification strengthens even further the ominous implications of such a symptom. This patient's pathology includes, in short, a life-threatening masochistic perversion, with grave prognostic implications. In addition, as mentioned before, Larry was deceptive not only in his relations with the medical profession in general, but with his psychotherapist in particular. Once again, the negatively prognostic implications of severe pathology of object relations and severe antisocial features seem illustrated in this case.

The diagnosis of a narcissistic in addition to a borderline personality disorder is well justified clinically and by psychological tests. Larry illustrates the combination of a borderline personality disorder and a narcissistic personality disorder, and illustrates well, in my view, a narcissistic personality disorder functioning on an overt borderline level. Whereas all patients with narcissistic personality disorder present what I have called a borderline personality organization, not all patients with a borderline personality organization present a narcissistic personality disorder, nor do all patients with a narcissistic personality disorder function on an overt borderline level. Most patients who fulfill the criteria for narcissistic personality disorder do not present a borderline personality disorder in a restricted sense, and these are patients who usually would not require hospitalization. Larry may also have presented the syndrome of malignant narcissism that I have described in earlier work (Kernberg 1984), characterized by the combination of a narcissistic personality disorder, ego-syntonic aggression, antisocial features, and paranoid trends.

It was only 3 months after admission that Larry revealed to his therapist that he was engaged in assaults on his leg. I would question the therapist's decision to make no intervention to thwart this self-destructive behavior. From the viewpoint of carrying out a psychotherapy in a hospital setting, I would think it important that the psychotherapist interpret to the patient the patient's efforts to divide staff by means of secrecy at the service of his self-destructive tendencies; it is not clear whether this was done here. The therapist discovered that Larry had been lying about the use of marijuana and threatened to discontinue the work if he were lied to again, "later feeling he had been excessively punitive in this response." I agree that the response was punitive, but the therapist's countertransference may have correctly alerted him to the patient's profound destructiveness against the treatment as well as against his own body, a theme that could then have been explored in nonpunitive ways in the treatment. In other words, it is important that the therapist elaborate very fully the transformation of self-destructive needs into the need to destroy the treatment. The transformation of a symptom into a transference reaction may facilitate symptom resolution by transference analysis. The possibility of carrying out such a difficult interpretation of primitive aggression in the transference in a consistent way may provide the key to a structural personality change for profoundly self-destructive personality structures. This approach is very important in the treatment of characterologically suicidal and self-mutilating borderline patients.

I found one aspect of the information about Larry difficult to understand. Toward the end of the "index hospitalization" section of Larry's case summary, it is stated: "After 2 or 3 months of outpatient treatment, Larry's doctor left the area. Larry's therapist's recommendation had been for Larry to stop therapy when the therapist left without resumption with anyone else. Larry reportedly disagreed with this plan but acquiesced." If I understood this passage correctly, I find it shocking. Given Larry's extremely severe psychopathology and his obvious risk for killing himself or destroying his life in other ways, it seems inconceivable that the therapist made such a recommendation. I wish we had been given the source of this information—whether it stems from the therapist or from Larry. If it stems from Larry, I think it fair to view it with suspicion—it might well have been a distortion related to his self-destructiveness. If it stems from the therapist, it suggests an unresolved countertransference problem which may, in part, explain Larry's poor outcome.

At follow-up, Larry was living alone in a private residence and had been married and divorced once more. He had attempted to obtain further education but had failed to complete a degree. He was unemployed. He had been in twice-weekly psychotherapy for the entire follow-up interval of 11 years and reported having made no suicide attempts and no further efforts to harm himself. It is difficult to assess how self-destructive Larry's patterns of daily living now were, and the final comment from him is dramatic: "Each day is spent in the crucible, yet one does well to remain alive."

Undoubtedly, Larry is one of those patients who are at the very boundary of what, with our present knowledge, is still approachable by intensive individual psychotherapy. The information that Larry had "a moderate problem with alcohol" indicates yet another self-destructive avenue in his life. Also, it is not clear whether all his recent psychotherapy had been with one therapist or, as was the case before his hospitalization, with numerous psychotherapists, treatment with whom always ended in failure.

Conclusion

I am compelled to return to a point I made at the beginning of this discussion. A frustrating aspect of the presentation of these four cases is the lack of available information about the treatment process itself, particularly about the transference developments. I find it difficult to critically discuss the treatment approach and to suggest alternative technical approaches—including my own version of ego psychology–object-relations theory—when the data provided preclude anything except speculations. We can only discuss clinical data when we have them and know their sources. What I have therefore offered are some reflections on these patients' lives, treatments, and outcomes from the available glimpses of the sort of data I view as most essential in understanding psychotherapeutic treatment.

Reference

Kernberg OF: Severe Personality Disorders: Psychotherapeutic Strategies. New Haven, CT, Yale University Press, 1984

Chapter 6

Case Discussion: The Self Psychology Perspective

PAUL H. ORNSTEIN, M.D.

Editor's Note

Dr. Ornstein is currently a leading spokesperson for the self psychology point of view originally described by the late Heinz Kohut and summarized by Dr. Sacksteder in Chapter 1, who includes the precursors of self psychology in earlier psychoanalytic theory and differences from the ego psychology–object-relations perspective of Dr. Kernberg. In Chapter 6, Dr. Ornstein provides a detailed clinical discussion of the four cases presented in Chapter 4. Because reconstruction of process material in a way that permits microscopic review of the vicissitudes of transference and countertransference has not been possible, Dr. Ornstein has allowed himself to make inferences liberally in the service of offering a thorough clinical illustration of his theoretical notions about narcissistic and borderline patients.

Chapter 6

Case Discussion: The Self Psychology Perspective

The four illustrative clinical examples of narcissistic and borderline personality disorders presented in Chapter 4 should serve as the basis for discussing the nature of the patients' psychopathology and the process of their treatment from the perspective of psychoanalytic self psychology.

One caution is immediately in order regarding the treatment samples and their descriptive diagnoses. As demonstrated in earlier chapters, such a clinical-empirical delineation of narcissistic and borderline conditions is useful and necessary for general psychiatry and psychotherapy. However, these diagnostic considerations originally emerged in psychoanalysis on the basis of specific transferences (the mirror transference and the idealizing transference in the narcissistic personality disorders) or the failure of such transferences to develop in a sustained and cohesive form (in the borderline personality disorders). In psychoanalysis, it is the nature of the transference that ultimately verifies the clinical diagnoses and guides the therapeutic efforts. This is so because the greatly variable, observable clinical phenomena may cover the specific narcissistic or borderline psychopathology, which then emerges in the course of the evolving and deepening transference. For instance, an apparent competitive attitude toward the father-therapist, with guilt over hostile destructive wishes (oedipal psychopathology) may hide an underlying structural deficit, with feelings of emptiness and low self-esteem (narcissistic personality disorder). The opposite may also occur: surface narcissistic disturbances may hide a well-structured neurotic disorder, protecting the self against the emergence of an oedipal struggle. The history and phenomenology often accurately hint at, but never clinch, the nature of the diagnosis in-depth and certainly never reveal those idiosyncratic pathogenetic details, which only the transference can reveal. The transference is also the foundation on which the treatment process rests, and it cannot be substituted for by even the most imaginative formulation of a character pathology that is not based on the pathognomonic transference itself.

The treatment samples in Chapter 4 were meant to offer an in-depth view of the lives of the four patients involved. Yet, they lack a consistent focus on the developing transferences, and the therapists did not use the transferences as their guide for the treatment of these patients. This is understandable, because the psychotherapies described (culled from the original notes by the researcher, without the subtle details of the therapists' own participation in the treatment process), were conducted in each instance before Kohut's contributions became widely known and successfully applied. This circumstance will put a limit, however, on how far we can illuminate the clinical examples presented from the perspective of self psychology. In these efforts, we shall guard against far-ranging speculations, but the latter may be forced on us where transference data, or at least interactional data from which the transference might be glimpsed, are scanty.

Our task is to show, always on the basis of actual data from the text, how we understand and explain, retrospectively, the nature of each patient's psychopathology. We shall try to gain this understanding by discerning it primarily from the patients' interaction with the hospital milieu on the one hand, and with the therapist in each treatment process on the other, and (wherever the data permit) on the basis of the available manifestations of the transference. What patients and therapists say to each other, the way they treat each other, and what this tells us about the way they experience each other is our key to the understanding of both the psychopathology and the treatment process. We shall use the available "life history" only to check our understanding against the patient's known life experiences, and to see how the "facts" and "events" now fit into a coherent narrative. Here is where a certain amount of speculation regarding the impact and meaning of the patient's early experiences may become inevitable.

Spelling out briefly the method of our approach should enable the clinician to follow the logic of our findings and therapeutic suggestions. It should be possible for the clinician to retrace (and reexperience) our effort at putting ourselves, imaginatively, at one moment in the patient's shoes and at another moment in the therapist's. It is through this "observation from within" or "vicarious introspection" (i.e., empathy), that we hope to enter each of the four treatment processes presented in Chapter 4 and derive understanding and treatment principles for each individual patient. Once we grasp how each treatment process was conducted, how each therapist listened and responded to the patient's communications, we may substitute ourselves (again imaginatively) for the therapist in each pair and describe how we would have listened, what we might have heard, and how we would have responded to the patient from the vantage point of psychoanalytic self psychology.

In the first step of this two-step approach, we position ourselves entirely within the described treatment process and do not engage in our review as "external observers." In the second step, we retain the necessary empathic vantage point vis-à-vis the patient, but substitute ourselves for the therapist—a move that thereby inevitably leads us to describe a hypothetical treatment process that is different from the one originally presented. The two steps will not be presented in a linear or sequential form, but will be intertwined throughout.

We shall discuss each clinical example separately and summarize our clinical findings and treatment principles in the concluding section of this chapter.

The Case of Peter

Peter's entry into a psychiatric hospital at the age of 29 occurred under the most dramatic circumstances of a massive regression, in which suicidal ideation, severe hypochondriasis, and an apparent "physical collapse" ("crawling around on the floor of his apartment terrified he would pass out if he were to stand up" and convinced that he had a serious physical illness) dominated the clinical picture. It attests to the severity of this regression that, although the suicidal ideas had abated, the hypochondriasis and the "physical collapse" (in fact an emotional collapse, since there were no physical findings) persisted even after 7 weeks of hospitalization and Peter "remained barely able to move." He was then taken by his parents to the Austen Riggs Center in a wheelchair for long-term inpatient treatment. Neither the immediate precipitating events nor the meaning of this regressive behavior at this particular time in Peter's life appears to have been elucidated, but evidence was presented of a slow and insidious deterioration in his overall functioning over a period of about 3 years.

Peter's ways of behaving toward and responding to the Austen Riggs Center's milieu and to his therapist are vividly and amply portrayed, but the milieu's responses and the therapist's interventions are barely (and then only globally) reported. The therapist's crucial verbal interventions are totally missing. This will require extensive extrapolations.

In various ways, Peter expressed his profound helplessness, easy vulnerability, and intense revengefulness in his behavior (e.g., "phobic fear of exertion" and "retreat to a wheelchair"; "vowing to seek out and kill [the] children [of the women at the center who rejected him] years hence"). Simultaneously, he gave evidence of an exalted view of himself ("brilliant, creative, and talented") and demanded that his specialness be recognized in the environment's responses to his every need, no matter how extravagant or contrary these were to the overall interests of the hospital community (e.g., to "be served lobster daily," to be permitted to disregard the rules of participation in community meetings). He engaged the dietary department in a protracted struggle by wanting a daily serving of lobster, but they steadfastly refused to comply with his demand. At the community meetings, however, he was free to express his withdrawal from and disinterest in the proceedings.

The self psychologically oriented psychotherapist would have used these opportunities to grasp and spell out what he or she understood as Peter's subjective experiences, expressed through his behavior. For example, he or she might have understood Peter's struggle with the dietary department as his desperate need to be recognized for his specialness in some concrete way, with additional meanings hidden in his fantasy about his need for daily lobsters. And he or she might have understood Peter's behavior at the community meetings as expressing his conviction of being above the hoi polloi of the hospital population and demanding that this be recognized by all. In fact, he said explicitly at one point that he prized only his individual therapy, presumably because there he had his therapist's exclusive attention and did not have to share the limelight with anyone. This understanding is buttressed by Peter's own recognition of "the pattern in his relationships of intense exclusivity with a constant expectation of rejection."

In the therapy sessions themselves, he continued to send his therapist the same messages. He was "angry, demanding, controlling, and complaining while also helpless, dependent, and passive"—as his therapist reported. I wonder if we may legitimately translate (through vicarious introspection) this simple juxtaposition of two sets of extrospective observations into a dynamic understanding of Peter's inner world, which could then be communicated to him at the appropriate moment. It would appear—as we put ourselves into his shoes—that it is Peter's subjective experience of his unresponded-to helplessness and neediness within the treatment process that provokes his anger and demandingness. Peter's way of appearing in the therapist's office at once bespeaks profound inner disorganization (referred to as "fragmentation") and an unmistakably loud dramatization of his emotional plight. But these two aspects of his behavior have to be connected with each other, i.e., understood and then communicated. It is important to find out to what extent he gets so disorganized in response to the fact that he does not feel heard. Here again, the meaning of it all could emerge convincingly only in response to the therapist's trial interventions and Peter's responses to them. Without a sample of those interventions, we are left in the dark. We do know, however, that his demandingness escalated within the therapeutic situation as much as in the hospital milieu (e.g., "asking for more than the four scheduled psychotherapy sessions weekly and feeling entitled to contact the therapist at any time"). We may thus assume that his outwardly bizarre behavior carried the message of his subjective feelings: "You haven't heard me yet! You are not in touch with my anguish! You don't know how much I need you!" so he had to continue to express his inner torment ever more loudly.

We may also assume that Peter's description of a recurrent pattern in his life was true of his experiences in therapy as well. "Inevitably, something would lead to a disappointment [in his relationships], perhaps something as trivial as another not laughing at one of Peter's jokes, and the relationship would fall apart in a storm of bitterness, cruelty, and vindictiveness"—in other words, in "narcissistic rage." Here the dynamic connection is implied, but we are not sure whether it was interpreted or not.

Peter's repeatedly expressed need "for something special from the therapist" apparently evoked a response from the therapist of "hold[ing] firm to his position but often [finding] the treatment difficult to endure." When the therapist would weather the ensuing "storms of complaint," Peter would praise him for having preserved the therapy. And then the cycle would begin again over some other issue. Calling Peter's praise of his therapist's management of the crisis in treatment a "flattery," which would soon give way to storms of complaints again, portrays this therapist as an "external observer." From that vantage point, the therapist can only see what Peter is doing to him, and not what Peter himself is feeling and what may motivate his behavior. For the self psychologically informed therapist, this is a crucial difference. Subjectively, Peter may be truly grateful that the therapist was steadfast and preserved for him the opportunity to continue treatment and at such moments he is ready to forgive the therapist, until the next inevitable "transgression," i.e., the therapist's unempathic intervention. Considering here Peter's praise of the therapist as "flattery" has untoward therapeutic implications. No matter how tactfully such a judgment of Peter's behavior would be communicated to him—even if only nonverbally—it would be experienced by him as a serious misunderstanding, a destruction of his good feelings about the therapist, and would further disrupt the precarious therapist-patient relationship. Even if Peter's praise for the therapist was "flattery" on the surface, this might well have expressed his need to maintain connectedness to the therapist. This could have been one of the crucial variables that aided the repair of disruptions in the transference, without this being achieved through "reconstructive interpretations"—interpretations through which the transference disruptions are placed into their genetic context.

There is no evidence in the report that the therapist's "salutary" stance was accompanied by an interpretive working through of these transference disruptions. It appears, however, that Peter's need for a strong, idealizable therapist was met at these moments of his noisy demand by the therapist's (at times at least) calm refusal. In any case, an overall atmosphere of nonjudgmental acceptance must have prevailed during some of these "battles," because Peter's preoccupation with death as well as his many hypochondriacal complaints decreased over the first 3 months of hospitalization—indications of a strengthening of the cohesiveness of his self, under the impact of a developing selfobject transference. His manner of approaching the therapy sessions also changed markedly over time, and "gradually, he was able to increase his ability to examine the process unfolding between him and his therapist," but again the details of these examinations and to what extent they were interpretively worked through remain unknown.

What is clearly stated at this point is that "by 6 months after admission, Peter had formed an idealized view of the therapist." This may have become a reasonably well consolidated and sustained view that allowed for the above changes and also for the entry of hitherto unmentioned topics into the therapeutic conversation (unfortunately, without samples of interpretive activity in relation to these topics).

One year after admission the therapist registered considerable improvement and documented it by stating that Peter could now discuss his hostile and murderous feelings. In connection with what? In relation to whom? And what did this mean within the therapeutic process? These questions illustrate the directions in which we would have had to explore Peter's subjective experiences at this juncture.

It was also a mark of progress that Peter could express the feeling that "getting better posed a problem [for him] if it meant the therapist would win his colleagues' admiration." This insight indicates that some important early experiences were remobilized in the treatment situation, for instance, that Peter felt he was treated as an extension of his parents and he mattered to them only to the degree that he fulfilled their needs. There is evidence for this in his background: his mother could have no more children, so Peter was an only child and "was to be the best" for his mother's satisfaction; his father's early brutal manner of upbringing, then his abrupt change from his son's "master to his servant"; "father and son [became] 'buddies' . . . did everything together in a way that made other playmates unnecessary." Thus we recognize here both mother's and father's "selfish" need for him—a frequent pathogenetic component in the later development of self-pathology (here narcissistic personality disorder) in the offspring. The parents' own serious personality problems, their sources, and their impact on Peter's development are those that are generally found in such self-disorders (A Ornstein and PH Ornstein 1985).

Peter was prone to acute as well as chronic narcissistic rage reactions already in his teens, and he experienced his parents' repeated change of habitat as highly traumatic. From early childhood on, Peter could neither easily separate from his parents nor tolerate the kind of suffocating closeness he felt they created by treating him as their appendage. From the time of his sophomore year in college, he distanced himself from his parents to the extent that he had little to do with them for the next 10 years. Interestingly enough, his remarkable success in the financial world occurred during this period. The fact that he gave up this success, along with the material advantages that went with it, is a phenomenon in Peter's life that would have deserved careful exploration. It was ultimately his completion of his doctorate (facilitated by his psychotherapy) and his employment as a college professor and director of a college dormitory that "helped turn his life around" and contributed to his increased well-being at the time of follow-up.

It is apparent that, in spite of early and ongoing traumata detailed in the report, Peter had many strengths. Besides his intelligence and capacity for initiative (especially during his very successful, albeit short-lived, career as an investment analyst), he was able at various times to extricate himself from parental domination and emotional subjugation (e.g., at one time he "refused to speak to his parents, and spent most of his time in his room," withdrawn and reclusive). These strengths, and his courage to make a drastic change in his career after hospitalization and after the completion of his doctorate, undoubtedly contributed to his considerable improvement noted at follow-up.

Although we heard nothing further about Peter's initially expressed "exalted view of himself" in the treatment process, we can only surmise that his (perhaps somewhat tamed) grandiose and exhibitionistic needs found appropriate expression and satisfaction in his teaching activities, whereas his idealizing needs were satisfied by belonging to a profession and institution he could value highly (more so than being an investment analyst and working for an investment firm?). His new profession and status appear to have allowed for a better regulation of his self-esteem and a return to his earlier (or increased?) capacity for the pursuit of his ambitions and the enjoyment of his work. This appears to have afforded him a modicum of health.

To conclude, we may now spell out the nature of Peter's self-pathology and offer our conjecture about his recovery. Initially, Peter's manifold demands for specialness, his exalted view of himself, his craving for unconditional acceptance and recognition, and his escalating these demands when not met indicated the remobilization of his archaic "grandiose exhibitionistic self." This appeared to coexist side by side with his viewing the Austen Riggs Center as the best place for his treatment and his therapist as a strong and powerful person, indicative of the remobilization of the archaic "idealized parent imago." According to his therapist, Peter ultimately settled into a more or less well consolidated and sustained idealizing transference. And this is plausible from the report. Did Peter have a more overriding "father-hunger" at the root of his problems than he had unresolved issues originating in his relationship with his mother?—Probably not. Peter's reaction to his mother's surgery ("short-lived affairs," "triangular relationship with two women simultaneously," and marrying the one with the "infantile, little-girl quality [which] he found irresistible") points in the other direction. So does, perhaps, his quickly failed marriage and his reestablished relationship with his former wife, in which they "enjoyed spending hours together baby talking and cuddling." As is frequently the case, initially both the mirroring and the idealizing aspects of the transference were in evidence. Usually one of them (perhaps the one mobilized by the more severe structural deficit) spontaneously recedes and the other becomes crystallized into the dominant one, in which the therapeutic work proceeds or is even completed. Or, after a sufficient period of working through in one transference configuration, the other moves into the foreground and presents itself for the working-through process, thus achieving a structural accretion in both poles of the bipolar self.

In Peter's case, the more fundamental "mirror transference" did not become mobilized—after its initial noisy appearance. Perhaps if it had been welcomed then and interpretively engaged (by not viewing it as a resistance?) this might have enabled its fuller emergence and presentation for working through. It might have developed later on, after sufficient work in the idealizing transference contributed to the cohesiveness of his self. The latter did, indeed, occur (although we were not given the relevant interpretations), as evidenced by a notable decrease in Peter's hypochondriasis and in his acute and chronic narcissistic rage. But Peter may not have been in treatment long enough for a secondary mirror transference to develop. The remaining deficits may have been compensated for by his capacity to perform successfully in his chosen profession. He seemed to be aware of this at follow-up.

The case report and our analysis of it leave us with the impression that Peter could have more profoundly benefited in both poles of his bipolar self in a self psychologically informed treatment process. The therapist, from such a vantage point, could have approached Peter's idealizing transference with acceptance, understanding, and explaining and would have been sensitive to any opening for the remobilization of the mirror transference—thus engaging the structural deficits in both poles of the self.

The Case of Mary

Mary's entry into the Austen Riggs Center at the age of 22 occurred a year and a half into her analysis. She began her analysis after she had dropped out of college because of her escalating social and academic failures (in spite of good intelligence).

Her initial diagnosis at the center of "mixed neurotic character disorder with depressive features in a postadolescent with an identity crisis" exemplifies what I said earlier regarding the unreliability of a phenomenological diagnosis without careful attention to the developing transference. But this diagnosis does indicate that she appeared to be reasonably well integrated so as to be considered "neurotic" by all observers. This went so far that at her first evaluation conference, "because of her superficially intact presentation," there was talk of discontinuing her hospitalization because she was considered treatable as an outpatient.

This preoccupation with the phenomenology (at the expense of the patient's subjective experiences and their meaning) shows up here as a serious handicap. The external observer's perception of Mary at the time of her hospitalization is contradictory: She "seemed to flee into health, actively involving herself in the community and activities programs," and at the same time, she is described as "subdued, defensive, shy, frightened, and self-conscious on the surface, concealing secret hatred and contempt for her peers." How could we reconcile this apparent contradiction and also identify the institutional climate within which her treatment was to take place? Could it be that when her efforts to put her best foot forward and gain acceptance (perhaps even admiration and validation) through her active participation in the center's programs were seen by the milieu as a "flight into health," she reacted to this response with an array of defensive reactions including hatred and contempt? As a descriptive phrase, "flight into health" may well be accurate but, without its subjective meaning and purpose, is worse than useless to the psychotherapist, because it is quite judgmental and it does not tell him or her how to respond to it. Traditionally, flight into health has either been accepted as the best outcome in patients with a bad prognosis—and then not explored as to its meaning and purpose—or it has been challenged as an evasion and a turning away from hidden pathogenic conflicts—and then not explored further as to its possible additional meanings and purposes. These responses to flight into health in patients with an enfeebled and fragmentation-prone self have often been unhelpful or outright disastrous, by derailing the treatment process.

Treating Mary's initial approach to her new environment as flight into health and not correlating her subsequent reaction to this reception may well have deprived the milieu of understanding what she was seeking through her behavior. This set the stage for a failure in meaningful therapeutic collaboration. Adding to this the fact that at the first evaluation conference her case was "baffling" to some staff members and hospitalization was thought to have been unnecessary, we may picture Mary as reacting adversely to the fact that her efforts to adjust to the center had not been received affirmatively. We know of her extreme sensitivity to even the slightest overt or assumed criticism—her "radars" must have picked this up from the milieu accurately.

Mary's four-times-weekly psychotherapy over a 20-month period is summarized in less than two pages, which, nevertheless, permit a glimpse into this treatment process and through it into Mary's psychopathology.

It is remarkable (though not unusual) in the light of the outcome of this treatment that Mary began her individual psychotherapy by communicating the same message to her therapist as she did to the milieu. "She was sweet, warm, and functioning at an apparently relatively high level"—was this also seen as flight into health or was it recognized as Mary's strength and her way of attempting to engage the therapist in being totally sold on her and expressing his joy in working with her? We cannot tell for sure from the protocol. But with this possibility in mind, we wonder about the initial manifestation of what is termed here "an idealizing transference" without its further characterization. We do not know what to make of the (possibly very meaningful) statement that "her colorful relationships with other patients were often the topic of discussion in her therapy sessions." What did she express through these topics? How were they interpreted? Should we assume that the word "colorful" indicates again Mary's way of making her stories interesting in order to capture the therapist's interest for her own person? Is what is called here an idealizing transference Mary's way of showing her enthusiasm for her therapist, as her way of saying to him, "I need this kind of enthusiastic response from you to get well—what do you say?" We are not told what he said, and this closes the first phase of this treatment process.

But the beginning of the second phase reveals the painful frustrations of the first phase for Mary. It "involved the emergence of an erotic transference toward the therapist, which was interpreted as a resistance to the psychotherapeutic work." With this statement the therapist takes us right inside the treatment process, which we may now examine from within. He appears to have taken Mary's "erotic" feelings toward him as an expression of progress, the emergence of an "erotic transference" and "interpreted [it] as a resistance to the psychotherapeutic work,"—right out of the old textbook, and not on the basis of his own, direct perceptions. According to his own perceptions the therapist was dealing with an idealizing transference (How?) and did not recognize that its breakdown (due to chronic frustration in the treatment setting) gave rise to an "erotized" transference. Such erotizations have long been recognized as emerging whenever idealizations break down, for whatever reason. The recognition of this erotization would have tipped us off as indicating Mary's continued (now perhaps more intensified) effort at winning over her therapist. This would have allowed us to interpret Mary's erotized feelings as a consequence of her failed efforts before (in the first phase of therapy) and as her response to the frustration of her need for unconditional love, admiration, and enthusiastic acceptance. In other words, we would have understood Mary's erotized feelings toward the therapist as her renewed effort to gain his attention and admiration, but now with different means. The idea that she resisted psychotherapeutic work could not have made any sense to Mary, because subjectively she was desperately trying to collaborate. The idea that she might have unconsciously resisted treatment is, of course, a possibility, but without evidence in the present context. Only the accurate interpretation of her subjective experiences could have led us to the discovery that "behind them" was an unconscious resistance and also of what that resistance was all about.

Without such a trial intervention the assumption of defense is merely a theory-based conjecture.

But Mary did not give up easily: in the third phase of her psychotherapy, she responded to continued frustrations with "neediness and proneness to rages and tantrums in her therapy and outside it." When we follow the process outlined for us in the text, we can make sense of these events and behaviors in light of the treatment Mary received (without discounting what she brought to it, which is amply detailed in her history).

While doing volunteer work at the Montessori nursery, Mary developed a "gratifying fantasy that [her] doctor's son was her own" and she "became overinvolved" with him. The therapist found it difficult to deal with this in the sessions. Why? We may assume that he did not discern the meaning of the fantasy (otherwise he would have told us about it) and perhaps interpreted it as the expression of a forbidden oedipal wish. The process, as we have reconstructed it so far, dictates a different possible meaning: If her therapist's little boy was her own in fantasy and she became overinvolved with him (translate this into "deeply caring for him and being totally absorbed with him") then this was Mary's way of portraying to her therapist again the very same message she had been trying to convey all along, in vain thus far: "Treat me as I treat my/your son—the child in me!" and "Do you still not understand my need for your caring!?" Of course, this fantasy must have had many additional meanings, some of which might have emerged in response to interpreting the one just proposed. It was wise not to stop her work at the nursery, but the experiences there and the manner in which they entered into the treatment process could apparently not be used by the therapist for a belated reorientation of his listening in order to hear Mary's urgent pleas.

No wonder this treatment failed. But not because of inherent characteristics in Mary that could not be transcended by the proper treatment approach. Far from it. It is retrospectively clear that communication between Mary and the milieu as well as between Mary and her therapist never quite got off the ground. It is also evident from the protocol that Mary tried her very best—she does come through loud and clear to us—but the meaning of whatever she brought into the treatment situation was not adequately grasped, hence it could not be translated into interpretive statements or made part of the therapeutic conversation by her therapist. In this connection it is retrospectively also clear—as it was to Mary on follow-up—that her drinking at the center may also have been a way to call the milieu's and the therapist's attention to her plight. The idea that her drinking was not a significant problem is again the external observer's judgment, without reference to the question: "What is Mary telling us with her sub-rosa drinking—of whatever proportion or severity?"

It is of note here that Mary's retreat into fantasy in connection with the therapist's inability to tune in on the wavelength of her communications came in the third phase of therapy, when her erotized transference was also misunderstood. This is all the more surprising, because she had had this particular way of dealing with painful frustrations available to her since early childhood, and she resorted to it in the form of her "Beethoven fantasy" in her teens, throughout college, and during her analysis. It appears as if she had given herself another chance in this therapy to obtain a cure through her transference to a flesh-and-blood therapist, but he failed to understand and respond to her "offer." The Beethoven fantasy appears to be complex and multilayered, especially with the idea that the romance was taking place the year before Beethoven's death. Although we cannot grasp the meaning or meanings of this fantasy in-depth without Mary's further associations, its context shows at least one element, namely that Mary retreated into this fantasy at times of painful failure (e.g., at music school) and that she used this for her secret self-aggrandizement and for secretly asserting that there were some things that others could not take away from her—her private fantasies. Thus, retreating into fantasy—but communicating it to the therapist during her treatment—signals her feeling threatened, which activates the fantasy, but the fact that she communicates it rather than keeps it secret indicates that she also reaches out with it for help. Of course, this is only a tentative understanding, not valid until we have Mary's confirmatory response to it. But the idea is formulated in such an immediate, experience-near fashion that it could be used as a trial interpretation to open up and explore this whole area of Mary's fantasy life.

Short of such an opportunity at this point, we may examine how our tentative understanding may illuminate and make sense of Mary's past experiences as well as her failure in her preceding psychoanalysis. Looking at Mary's life history, many of the details recounted in it begin to fall into place and to form a coherent, meaningful narrative and do not remain only an assemblage of facts and events.

Mary has had some significant strengths as well as blatant, chronic weaknesses. She is described as having been a "happy and healthy child" and she herself remembered the first 6 years of her life that way. She also recalled that she enjoyed nursery school and that she was "a special, spoiled, fussed-over child and an aggressive tomboy." Yet, the atmosphere at home, the parents' personalities, and their relationship to each other and to their only biological daughter are described as filled with problems almost from the beginning. Mary's mother lacked any self-assurance in dealing with her baby daughter. On top of that, Mary was soon made to feel she was not good enough. Her parents adopted an infant boy because the father wanted a male heir. It was at about the same time (age 8) that "Mary began to immerse herself in a fantasy world of dolls," which soon expanded into "fantasies of a comforting and loving relationship with a great man, especially with Beethoven during the last year of his life." From the abbreviated and highly condensed overview of Mary's life, it is plausible to assume that she not only used her fantasies successfully at times of loneliness, when she felt left out, rejected, shunned, or criticized, but later seemed to dwell in these fantasies as a way to avoid her increasingly intolerable reality. Perhaps we can now understand that her externally haughty, arrogant, or otherwise depreciatory attitudes toward others stemmed from her constant dread of rejection and criticism, which enfeebled her self and deprived it of its capacity to perform even her everyday school tasks: she "became self-conscious in classes, socially awkward, unable to complete her work, and isolated from her peers"—all signs of a crumbling self. Instead of being able to use these fantasies for temporary escape (which would have signaled strength), these became more lasting places of refuge for Mary (revealing weakness). Her discomfort with boys started in early puberty. She ended up dating very little, but was often infatuated from afar. She was able to pull herself together in her junior year of college, attempting "to turn her life around, earning good grades, dating three boys, but feeling she really had nothing to offer." With this effort to turn her life around, Mary again showed a distinct capacity, but she would have needed a supportive milieu to strengthen her enfeebled self in order to pull off this turnaround. Instead of a supportive milieu, she experienced only animosity around herself, especially from her roommate, which contributed to the collapse of her college life and led to her dropping out and seeking psychoanalysis. It is noteworthy that a further collapse of her life occurred even while in analysis, under circumstances similar to those at college. When in a new work situation as a secretary, "she felt disliked and left out," ushering in a pronounced withdrawal into a fantasy life, which now included "sadistic revenge fantasies when slighted," to the point of becoming fearful of hurting or killing someone without remorse. She was also frightened of her growing rage at her analyst, who became concerned about the collapse of Mary's life, especially after Mary quit her job just a few weeks before she recommended hospitalization.

There is only one comment by her analyst that offers us a glimpse as to why she might not have received the necessary support from her. Mary's analyst stated that the analysis "had been going relatively well," yet Mary was progressively falling apart and ended up at the Austen Riggs Center. We can only make sense of this retrospectively, by assuming that a selfobject transference was missed, remained uninterpreted, or was viewed—as it often happened before Kohut's work—as a defense, which undermined the support such a transference would have lent Mary for a more felicitous working through of some of her self-pathology. This particular hypothesis is buttressed by the fact that as soon as she entered the center, once again she was able to pull herself together vis-à-vis the hospital milieu and in her individual psychotherapy and she reached out for help, which (in our terms) she did not receive. There can, of course, be no certainty about the assumption that the necessary emotional support (through attention to the developing selfobject transference) would indeed have helped her turn around her life sufficiently at this time. But neither can we say, based on the available evidence, that she was offered through the milieu or in psychotherapy the required therapeutic responses to enable her to achieve a "new beginning."

The Case of Susan

Susan's entry into the Austen Riggs Center at the age of 19 occurred after she dropped out of college and struggled for a while with her manifold rebelliousness, serious drug taking, depression, suicidal thoughts (one prior attempt), and feelings of emptiness and boredom.

Her extremely chaotic and multiply injurious background (practically from birth to the time of her hospitalization) and its profound consequences are masterfully recorded in great detail and chronological sequence. We shall be able to use many of those details to round out our understanding of Susan's psychopathology and her treatment experience, after examining her less detailed hospital course and therapeutic process.

The externally observable manifestations of the way Susan presented herself at the center offer us a vivid portrait of this young woman, and we should use it as an entry point into her inner world. She was seen as a "potentially attractive, giggly, immature, and unkempt hippy who was noteworthy for her irritability, changeable moods, hyperalertness, and proneness to outbursts of anger." In addition, we are told that "she was shy, frequently self-depreciatory, and prone to see others as condemnatory of her." These descriptions sound at first as if the characteristics they encompass are fixed in Susan's personality and are not the sensitive barometers of her reaction to her environment—habitual patterns of reaction we might say, but patterns of reaction nevertheless. In other words, her irritability is not linked to what she might be irritated about or how this is triggered. We would also wish to know under what circumstances she becomes self-depreciatory and what leads her to see others as condemnatory of her. The observations are treated as if these questions did not matter—but for us they are central. All these questions aim at putting us in touch with Susan's self-experiences—a sine qua non for assessing the nature of her psychopathology for the conduct of psychotherapy. (Obviously, such an assessment is dispensable for a DSM-III diagnosis.)

Our first "meaningful" encounter with Susan in the hospital (in this abbreviated case report) is when she tells another patient of her secret supply of drugs. The nursing staff responded with proper firmness, and Susan complied by giving up her bounty, quite a contrast to how her mother handled a similar issue, when Susan took with her to college a supply of amphetamines and barbiturates and her mother lacked the strength to stop her. Could it be that she had to test the milieu for its strength, sincerity, and caring, or its weakness, corruptibility, and noncaring, early on? If so, the answer—in action—was helpful in that it communicated unambiguously: "We care and we are serious about this; we are concerned what these drugs would do to you," a very different response from what she was used to. Her father and mother did not speak to her about such important matters with one voice, leaving her confused and without inner guidelines of her own, as well as without much capacity for tension regulation.

Was it her "shy, giggly, girlish presentation" that was likable about her? And did this demeanor change into moodiness, irritability, and depression as well as into angry outbursts when her craving for enthusiastic reception met with no success?

Was it her sensitivity and quick response to what she experienced as rebuffs that made her interpersonal relationships unstable? We are searching here for a common central theme in her life, her hospital behavior, and her therapeutic experience in order to understand the nature of her personality and problems as well as the way in which she imagined her cure—her underlying "curative fantasy" (PH Ornstein and A Ornstein 1976).

Her presentation in the therapeutic situation sheds some light on these very questions: "Susan was *alternately* shy and pleasing and irritable and angry" [italics added]. Although the therapist does not explicitly make this connection, we see the irritability and anger emerging in response to the frustration of her efforts to please and entice, in order to be accepted and valued. If he did not make some such connection between Susan's "alternating" behavior, at first to himself and then (interpretively) to his patient, no wonder the therapist had to "struggle with feeling off balance with her for much of their work." The therapist needs to "know" (i.e., have a working hypothesis, which he can share with his patient) in order 1) to maintain his own inner balance and 2) to aid the patient in establishing hers.

Susan appeared to have been ready for serious collaboration, as indicated by her first reported dream. In it, she "extinguished a 'joint' when she realized smoking it was wrong." How much more directly could she have signaled that she was ready for therapy? We do not have the therapist's response to this "offer." But the fact that Susan later told another patient (in the earshot of nurses) that she had illegal drugs stashed away indicated that her earlier dream-message was not picked up on. The drugs were then promptly confiscated, and afterward Susan felt "singled out and condemned."

Susan quickly became attached (addicted?) to the therapist and as a result became highly sensitive to whatever transpired between them. For instance, "she experienced whatever the therapist said as an attack." Another area of her painful sensitivity was connected with "weekend and other separations and changed appointments." She reacted to these with angry outbursts. The intensity of her reaction is illustrated by the fact that she threatened to leave the center when her therapist announced his 1-month vacation (3 months after they began their work together).

We have to translate these observations into their possible meaning, otherwise we would have no therapeutic leverage—as apparently Susan's therapist struggled for a long time in vain to find one. Perhaps we can best enter more deeply into this treatment process if we survey the therapist's own remarks about the way he experienced working with Susan.

The therapist tells us how he reacted to Susan, and this permits us to conjure up the atmosphere that prevailed in this treatment situation. The therapist "realized he felt intimidated by [Susan's] constant angry outbursts and provocativeness toward him" and was under "much pressure to offer reassurance . . . feeling trapped by the position in which she put him." No wonder she felt that he "was disgusted with her," but this issue remained unexplored. Another significant reaction is contained in the therapist's description of Susan as "elusive and enigmatic as well as attacking in the hours." In plain English, this means that he did not understand Susan's experience and was baffled at having been constantly attacked—probably feeling that he did not deserve it, and he did not know how to put an end to it. We can sense the therapist's helplessness. We connect it with the fact that he could only think of *himself as the target* of these attacks and could not move to the empathic observational stance and picture what it must have been like for Susan to have felt the way she did. This helps us understand the therapist's predicament, and we may recognize its impact on the treatment process. But turning back to Susan, how should a person feel who has already experienced herself as "singled out" and "condemned" and now also "felt herself to be the most evil patient at the center"? Could it be that in feeling this way and in bringing it up incessantly to her therapist she wanted these feelings to be engaged and understood by him? And when he could not respond with understanding she became angry and attacking. (Our point is not on claiming validity for our reconstructions here, but on the need for some such formulation to determine whether the patient had, indeed, an adequate therapeutic trial, and to understand the outcome on the basis of the treatment as portrayed.)

The therapist helps us further when he recognizes that he "felt intellectualized and distant" in his work with Susan. We may wonder why he did not draw some conclusions from that self-reflective observation. He is telling us that he could not participate to his fullest capacity and satisfaction in this treatment endeavor, in part because of Susan's constant barrage of attacks and derisions of him as "ineffectual." He then gives us a telling sample interpretation which he is finally able to make in the 7th month of this treatment. He "made the interpretation that [Susan] was using him as someone to complain to and seek reassurance from that she was not wrong." How did Susan hear this interpretation as a response to what she had been bringing to him up to now? Susan's reaction was unambiguous: "She missed the next two sessions [and] then reported her sense that the doctor was tired of her complaints." We are entitled to surmise that Susan felt hurt, accused of doing the wrong thing by using the therapist to complain to him and by seeking reassurance from him. Even to us this sounds more like a criticism than an interpretation of Susan's experiences. It is more like "pointing out her behavior" without an explanation as to why she might have had to resort to doing it. Although phrased more tactfully, it still adds up to: "Why do you always complain to me and want reassurance from me? How are you ever going to get well this way?" There is a moralizing undertone, which made Susan stay away from the next two sessions. Should she not have felt attacked?

What follows is quite instructive. It appears that Susan desperately needed to get reconnected to her therapist and toward this end changed her tune. She now "began to speak more about a relatively stable relationship with a male patient who resisted entering an intense relationship with her because he insisted she was able to stand on her own." Susan—it seems to us—wished to adapt to her therapist's conditions for the relationship and took him off the hook by picturing that he kept his distance and rebuked her for her own good, a kind of adaptation that is a frequent camouflage for internal change in response to the type of intervention given to Susan. Add to this that she now spoke of her "'crush' on the doctor," and we should not be surprised if her efforts to idealize her therapist disintegrated into an erotized transference. When Susan's father began to press for her discharge for financial reasons, Susan dealt with this in a most revealing fashion. She herself asked for help in setting up discharge plans, but felt abandoned when the therapist would agree to proceed. What she may have wanted was to hear the therapist's explicit wish for her to stay longer (or forever)—a request to which he in fact responded by stalling her discharge. It would have been an important opportunity to deal with these issues of being wanted, interpretively.

During the last few months of her hospitalization, Susan's erotized transference escalated and brought out the connection of her frustrated erotized feelings with her "pattern of upsets." She was terrified of being alone and feeling empty and pictured having the therapist with her at all times as the remedy—her curative fantasy. Her dream before discharge, even without associations, discloses her fear of drowning without him around (and the protective shield of the hospital?). She tried to prevent this by holding her breath. We may wonder how this was understood and interpreted.

The final conference before discharge offers us a rare view: "a number of staff members commented that her doctor seemed afraid to engage with [Susan]." This collective insight was followed by what may seem a profound misunderstanding from our vantage point. The idea that "the growing intimacy between therapist and patient was seen as possibly threatening to both" appears to miss the main point. The therapist was, indeed, afraid of the growing intimacy, but the patient was not. She needed and wanted that "intimacy," but on her terms, of course, which was a mixture of wanting the therapist's acceptance and validation (perhaps even admiration) as well as wanting him to be on a pedestal for her. She was determined to keep him there in her memory even long after her treatment was over. But the therapist did not grasp this and could not participate interpretively in this intimacy. What some of the staff viewed as a therapeutic relationship that was growing more mature may well have only been the patient's adaptation spoken of earlier. The erotization may have been mistaken for an erotic transference. (The conference members may well have had more data to go on and therefore may have been more correct in their assessment, but we can only go by the text in Chapter 4.)

How is it then that this treatment turned out so much better than this analysis of it anticipated? Nine years after admission, Susan was married, had a daughter, and had had no further treatment, with her life in fact turned around. Her own response on follow-up holds the key: "Having an excellent therapist and a real desire to work with him and get better. Also having a wonderful husband and daughter," which "would not have been possible without Riggs." We may translate this statement as Susan's inner perception that maintaining an idealized image of her therapist was a part of what aided her getting better. This idealization allowed her "real desire to work with him" to continue (silently) even during the very trying periods of their relationship.

Could certain details of Susan's life history pinpoint some of her strengths and weaknesses and thereby enable us to understand better the nature of her psychopathology and the outcome of her treatment? Assessing Susan's prognosis on the basis of her life history *alone* might have led us to dire predictions—such stories as hers engender hopelessness in clinicians who put too much weight on the predictive value of history alone without additional observations from a therapeutic interaction. But data and assessment derived from a psychotherapeutic experience can illuminate the life history retrospectively.

Susan had serious problems with her mother from the outset—her mother was depressed when she was born. Her father was absent in the military overseas, and the move to Japan to join him was a serious disruption in their lives. Her relationship to her father is depicted as the stormier and more sustainedly pathological one. He apparently tried to break her rebellious spirit quite coercively by attempting to force her to conform to his wishes regarding social behavior, religious issues, and dating. He is reported to have disregarded Susan's individuality to the extreme, but—and this may have been Susan's strength—was unable to crush her. She resisted by defying him (e.g., in her dating patterns, by taking drugs) at the cost of a serious derailment in her own emotional development. Nevertheless, after her hospital stay and psychotherapy (and to some degree because of it), she could resume her further emotional growth as wife and mother.

On the basis of Susan's history alone and some features of her adolescent behavior, some might argue that she suffered from what could best be understood as a neurotic character disorder, with a defensive narcissistic overlay and that her defiant rebelliousness, drug taking, and promiscuity were manifestations of a structurally more intact (neurotic) personality. The treatment process as a whole, the nature of the transference (as far as discernible), and the outcome as described do not provide compelling data for this view.

Susan's recovery does not appear to have been the result of an interpretive psychotherapy and a process of working through according to the available data. Patients with Susan's endowment are able to extract from a psychotherapy relationship some of what they need for their "cure," that is, if they are not repeatedly and chronically stymied by the kinds of interventions that discourage them from hoping that in this relationship they will finally obtain what they have been searching for all their lives. The therapist, having been intimidated, offered his interpretations sparingly. Perhaps he succeeded thereby in staying out of Susan's way most of the time. Susan, on the other hand, was able to maintain him in her mind as an idealized, helpful figure, which appears to have played a significant part in her recovery. Perhaps none of this would have led to the remarkable (and unanticipated) positive findings at follow-up without her having "a wonderful husband and daughter," both of whose presences may indeed have contributed to Susan's further maturation.

The Case of Larry

Larry's entry into the Austen Riggs Center at the age of 44 was a culmination of "numerous failed outpatient psychotherapies" over a 20-year period. Indicative of his deep-seated and complex life problems was his preoccupation "with a fantasy of having an above-the-knee amputation of his left leg, a fantasy that had been essential for sexual gratification and that he had made efforts to implement." It is this core fantasy, its origins and vicissitudes, and his efforts to have his leg actually amputated that will be at the center of our discussion of Larry's psychopathology and psychotherapy.

It is noteworthy in Larry's history that simultaneously with his profound "masochistic" need (that is, to incur suffering as a prerequisite for heightened sexual pleasure) he also pursued a relentless search for help continuously for 20 years, in spite of apparently consistent disappointments in one therapist after another. After his most recent disillusionment, which led him to an increased use of hallucinogens, he went from one well-known expert to another around the country to seek advice regarding further treatment, while actively trying to provoke the amputation by injuring and infecting his left leg. He followed the recommendation of one of his consultants to enter the Austen Riggs Center for extended inpatient treatment.

Paradoxically, Larry's life history and the follow-up information are more richly textured than the report of his hospitalization and psychotherapy. Nevertheless, we shall have to enter Larry's inner experiences through the opening that the report of his hospitalization and psychotherapy permits and then extend our grasp of his psychopathology and treatment process by turning to the extratherapeutic data.

It is significant that the observers were impressed with

Larry's "external" presentation and saw him as an "energetic, sometimes grandiose, imposing man with charismatic, godlike qualities, who also appeared immature and dependent." In addition, they saw him as "an erudite and esoteric observer who had a dramatic presentation," and they noted that Larry "immediately challenged hospital rules and female authorities." However, the self psychologically oriented analytic observer would wish to know the inner experiences these phenomena expressed as well as their relation to each other. For instance, what might have led to a change from "godlike qualities" to "immature and dependent" presentation or vice versa? Or, when was he "energetic [and] grandiose" as opposed to "immature and dependent"? What inner feelings or treatment by staff led him to challenge "hospital rules and female authorities"? Without posing the questions in some such fashion and only offering a description of Larry's presentation without his inner experiences, we are left with the impression that the therapist may have considered his descriptions per se as having revealed universally agreed-on and generally known fixed meanings. Far from it. Our search, however, is for the contextual, idiosyncratic meaning, which emerges from the interaction with the milieu and, more importantly, from the therapeutic interchange.

In the same vein, Larry's angry outbursts and furniture smashing are mentioned without context, implying, perhaps, that as a clear and unambiguous expression of his aggressive drive, it needs no further elucidation. What should we make of the claims that Larry was "demanding and hostile and seemed to have a chip on his shoulder," without knowing in what situation such observations were made?

We learn from the few remarks about the treatment process that the therapy "gradually shifted its focus from the crippled leg to Larry as a crippled person." We are left with our own imagination regarding the meaning of this shift. On the surface, it sounds as if it were a necessary and desirable shift, and in some respects it may have been, but on further reflection, it appears as if the therapist did not fully grasp the meaning of the crippled leg in its close connection to the nature of Larry's crippled self. Otherwise, we would not read the next statement that "Larry responded angrily to the therapist's early interpretations of resistance" by warning him not to "fuck with my antisuicide kit." To us this means that the therapist may have considered Larry's obsessive focus on his crippled leg and his repeated trials to actually damage it as a resistance against recognizing and focusing on his crippled self. To Larry this was an infuriating therapeutic stance, because he may well have felt (however dimly he may have perceived it in awareness) that this fantasy was his only protection against outright suicide. This attitude of the therapist toward Larry's fantasy and concomitant efforts to harm his leg in order to have it amputated may well have resulted in Larry's renewed and escalating "assaults on his leg" and his reporting it to the therapist in his sessions.

This context offers us the evidence we seek that Larry's behavior and its communication reflected another desperate effort to reach out to his therapist. This moment in treatment presented another exquisite opportunity (most likely missed throughout the previous 20 years of treatment) to enter meaningfully into Larry's treatment experience. What I mean is this: Instead of no intervention to thwart Larry's efforts at assaulting his leg—which might well have been experienced by him as gross neglect—we would have interpreted (and thereby implicitly welcomed) his bringing it into the therapy as an expression of his frustration with the therapist's understanding and helpfulness thus far, but also as an expression of his unextinguished hope that it would now be taken seriously and finally explored and understood.

This intervention could have initiated a thorough and systematic consideration of the meanings of this long-standing, persistent, and complex fantasy and behavior, which repeatedly brought Larry to the brink of self-inflicted death. This exploration could easily have been undertaken, because the history reveals many of the precursors and determinants, perhaps to some degree also the evolution and vicissitudes, of this "masochistic" fantasy and behavior. (There is no indication in the report that the therapist ever used any of it to understand and explain the fantasy and the activity it engendered, although he faithfully recorded each known step in its evolution.) It was helpful that the "nursing staff independently confiscated Larry's implements." Why was this not a planned therapeutic move, conveying a caring attitude? Is this not a misapplied "abstinence" in relation to life-threatening behavior? Of course, without the additional requisite interpretations, this action could only evoke Larry's rage and his feeling intruded on and manipulated. No wonder he avoided seeing his therapist for a while. In our view, what followed is a frequent event. Larry now "spoke more of his identity as a sick, crippled, and deformed child"—but not as a felicitous therapeutic shift away from his preoccupation with his amputation fantasy, but as a way to try to gain his therapist's attention by adapting to what he may well have perceived as his therapist's preference. The adaptation drove the basic issues of Larry's transference to his therapist out of focus.

The same occurred in relation to the angry confrontation regarding Larry's "lying about marijuana use." The therapist recognized that he had been "excessively punitive" in threatening to discontinue treatment "if lied to." Larry, however, responded "by making apparently earnest efforts to turn over a new leaf"; he even went so far as to shave off his beard. Although he did make these "desirable" changes, Larry rightfully complained afterward "of feeling controlled and possessed by the therapist." A later dream may be of significance in this connection: in it his father's erection turns Larry into a girl, a telling metaphor about needing to (and perhaps wishing to) submit to the threatening and emotionally distant father-therapist in order to be accepted, loved, and cared about. Here also is a missed opportunity to explore and communicate some understanding about Larry's homosexual experiences and masturbatory fantasies and practices. Larry perceived the therapist as "forcing him toward health when what he really wanted was to be sick and helpless." What meaning should we attach to this statement? We have seen where Larry's feeling of being *forced* toward health may have come from. But the claim that he really wanted to be sick and helpless needs further decoding. Larry himself helps us by stating that he "consciously refused to relinquish his specialness by becoming like others." His wanting to be sick and helpless is clearly not a primary wish. Although we do not have his immediate associations, the evolution of his preoccupation with the amputation of his left leg and his efforts to actualize it appear to be inextricably connected with his perception that his otherwise distant and unexpressive father "had once shown rare compassion in his facial expression when Larry and his father passed an amputee on the street." Could this account (in part) for Larry's particular lifelong father-hunger, a (sexualized) longing for his affection, which was reawakened in the transference and presented itself for a therapeutic working through that never took place? Could it be that Larry's refusal to "relinquish his specialness by becoming like others" was (in part) in the service of extracting from the therapist-father that special kind of admiration and love that he hoped would cure him? Could it also be that Larry's seemingly bizarre effort to have his left leg amputated was a concretization of that wish, built on the memory of his father having been compassionate toward an amputee, along with Larry's own admiration of and fascination with a schoolmate amputee? These issues and memories did present themselves in this treatment. They appear to have been duly recorded but remained unexplored and uninterpreted. Hence, Larry did not really have, in our view, an adequate trial at psychotherapy.

The nature of Larry's transference was not clarified and it certainly did not serve as the guide for understanding and explaining, i.e., for the interpretive working through. Larry's was most likely a thwarted mirror transference. The therapist did not enable Larry to attain a more or less cohesive and sustained form of this mirror transference. He might have been able to do so through the proper recognition of Larry's efforts at eliciting from his therapist unconditional love, the needed admiration and affirmation for his specialness, etc., via the metaphoric language of his amputation fantasy and its various enactments. We can hear Larry scream: "I crave and need your love so desperately that I am even willing to cut off my leg to get it!" It is undoubtedly difficult for any therapist to be empathically in tune with the patient's transference wishes when they are expressed in such bizarre communications. The difficulty is further enhanced in light of the long-standing history of this fantasy and its repeated enactments, and 20 years of therapeutic failure.

The latter should not necessarily spell out a guarded prognosis. The fact that our reading of Larry's most recent therapy brought out some of the possible meanings of his core fantasy and its enactments with such clarity and vividness indicates that with our current understanding we would, indeed, be in a better position to offer him a chance for a more profound recovery. This optimistic assumption is buttressed by what happened to Larry after his hospitalization and psychotherapy ended.

How deeply the issues embodied in Larry's amputation fantasy and its enactments were connected to essential elements of his personality is highlighted by the fact that near the end of his treatment, he made plans to give up architecture and become a prosthetist, "as a sublimated partial solution to his preoccupation with amputation." He did in fact move to a city where he could pursue this goal, but we are not told whether he actually made this shift a permanent one.

Larry's life remained as unfulfilled and chaotic during the 11-year interval between discharge and follow-up as it had been before admission; a third marriage ended in divorce, another of his business ventures failed. He was in twice-weekly psychotherapy throughout, but needed no hospitalization and reported no suicide attempts and no further efforts to harm himself. If Larry could achieve all of this within the therapeutic atmosphere depicted, and with as little interpretive work as reported, we may perhaps be justified in our view that Larry could have achieved more in a therapeutic atmosphere and through an interpretive work guided by the recognition of Larry's efforts at mobilizing an archaic mirror transference. Its nonrecognition (perhaps even in his subsequent twice-weekly psychotherapy) may well consign Larry to needing a lifelong psychotherapeutic relationship.

On the Nature of Self-pathology and the Treatment Process

In the preceding sections of this chapter, we have discussed each clinical sample separately, indicating the nature of the psychopathology and the treatment process only as far as each instance permitted. In this concluding section, we shall endeavor to take a more comprehensive view and make some generalizations, still keeping the four index cases in mind as our clinical points of departure.

Broader and more encompassing descriptions and illustrations of the impact of self psychology on the conduct and process of psychotherapy in relation to the entire spectrum of psychopathology now abound in the literature (e.g., Basch 1980, 1981, 1988; Elson 1987; Muslin and Val 1987; A Ornstein 1974, 1983, 1984; A Ornstein and PH Ornstein 1985; PH Ornstein 1974, 1975, 1979, 1981, 1982, 1984, 1985; PH Ornstein and A Ornstein 1976, 1985, 1986; Stepansky and Goldberg 1984; Stolorow et al. 1987; White and Weiner 1986; Wolf 1988). This widely available literature—as well as the initial overview in this book—justifies restricting our focus here on what the four index patients teach us about the nature of self-pathology and their psychotherapy.

We have searched in all four clinical instances for the manifestations of the transference as our avenue toward understanding each patient and toward finding the appropriate treatment responses in each sample instant. We have followed in this approach established psychoanalytic principles that were systematically applied by Heinz Kohut, first in his extension of psychoanalysis to include the treatment of narcissistic personality and behavior disorders (Kohut 1966, 1968, 1971; Kohut and Wolf 1978) and later in his comprehensive reformulation of psychoanalytic theory, including the neuroses (Kohut 1977, 1984). From this point on, self psychology encompassed the entire spectrum of psychopathology and was no longer restricted in its understanding and treatment approach to the primary narcissistic disorders.

It was the approach of prolonged and persistent empathic immersion in the subjective experiences of his patients that led Kohut to his discovery of the selfobject transferences. A consistent interpretive focus on these transferences finally permitted their analytic working through (without the use of parameters), as well as their more effective interpretive use in psychotherapy. Thus, Kohut transformed psychoanalysis as a method, theory, and treatment process on the basis of the empirical data he derived from these systematically observed and painstakingly analyzed transference configurations. Others have translated his method and used his theories to formulate their psychotherapeutic approaches to the disorders of the self (e.g., Basch 1980; Muslin and Val 1987; A Ornstein 1984; A Ornstein and PH Ornstein 1984; PH Ornstein 1975, 1982, 1984, 1985; PH Ornstein and A Ornstein 1976).

Here we shall limit ourselves to 1) a few remarks on the method of empathy, 2) a brief survey of the nature of the transferences, 3) the self-pathology that activates them, and 4) the psychotherapeutic process that might lead to their substantive amelioration or cure.

On the Method of Empathy

Kohut (1959) defined the field of psychoanalysis (and by implication the field of psychoanalytic psychotherapy as well) as consisting of the complex inner life of humans, which is grasped—or potentially grasped—via empathy, or, as he preferred to put it, "vicarious introspection." By calling empathy vicarious introspection, Kohut lifted this ubiquitous human capacity out of its murky historical and conceptual past and brought it into the everyday affective-cognitive realm. Empathy in this sense is a capacity to feel ourselves and think ourselves into another person's inner experiences vicariously. Introspection (looking inward) is the most direct road to our own inner experiences and vicarious introspection is the most direct road we have to the subjective experiences of another, unsuitable for the direct examination of the outer world. In contrast, extrospection (looking outward) is the method of exploration of the external world, unsuitable for a direct exploration of the inner world. Empathy, therefore, is the method of psychology of complex mental states, and it delineates this field against biology on the one hand and against sociology on the other, where the extrospective mode of observation is the obligatory approach.

In surveying the four index cases, it is evident that none of the therapists have left behind records of the therapy that have systematically taken up the empathic observational vantage point. They have not presented us with examples of even a single intervention offered from an empathic perspective.

On the Nature of the Selfobject Transferences

Kohut observed his patients' transferences from the empathic vantage point (imaginatively placing himself at the center of his patients' experiences), and what he saw from "within" was, of course, very different from what he previously saw from "without." Traditionally, transference has been viewed as the displacement from and projection on the analyst (or therapist) of repressed infantile and childhood needs, wishes, fantasies, and conflicts, originally experienced in relation to the parental imagos. In this view, transferences were considered anachronistic distortions of reality, based on drive-related intrapsychic conflicts. They were, in the extreme, thought to emerge entirely from within, to unfold without significant external provocation, just as in dreams unconscious wishes and conflicts attach themselves to the "insignificant" day residue of the analyst. But, we may ask, "distortions of reality" from whose vantage point? And where is there room here for hope or a capacity for a "new beginning," without which psychoanalytic psychotherapy would be inconceivable.

The extrospective observer will undoubtedly see the distortions, and from that vantage point, he or she will consider confrontation with current reality as the proper therapeutic response—regardless of the patient's immediate response to it. But to the introspective (and vicariously introspective) observer, entirely different vistas open up. Transference, from the patient's subjective vantage point, will turn out to be the upsurge of hitherto thwarted (repressed or disavowed) infantile and childhood needs, wishes, and fantasies for the completion and/or the strengthening of the self—a completion or strengthening not attained before. Thus, these transferences—the selfobject transferences as Kohut later called them—become established on the basis of developmental deficits, derailments, or arrests (with secondary conflicts and defenses as ubiquitous complicating factors) and express the thwarted need for belated growth and maturation.

Kohut first delineated the archaic selfobject transferences, describing them as the mirror transference, the idealizing transference, and later the twinship transference as a separate category. Each of these transferences reflects specific infantile and childhood developmental needs that were not adequately met, leaving behind a void or "a gaping wound" (as patients frequently put it). This void, or deficit, serves as the constant trigger for the elaborate and often recalcitrant defensive operations, but also (and often hidden beneath the former) for the unextinguished hope for a "new beginning." Later, when Kohut included the neuroses in his study, he spoke of the "oedipal selfobject transferences," which reactivate mirroring, idealizations, and twinship experiences vis-à-vis the oedipal imagos for the consolidation of gender-specific developmental achievements.

The *mirror transference* (arising out of the archaic grandiose exhibitionistic self searching for its mirroring selfobject) represents the remobilization of specific infantile and childhood developmental needs. *Mirroring* is simply an evocative global term for a variety of subtle and complex emotional needs of the human infant, needs that never cease, only become transformed in the course of maturation and development into phase-appropriate adult forms (for example, expecting praise for work well done). These needs include unconditional love, being at the center of attention, recognition of the child's uniqueness, affirmation of its specialness, and admiration of its greatness. Those who were fortunate enough to experience "the gleam in their mother's eyes" (reflecting the availability of all of these responses) develop strong self-assertive ambitions (in one pole of the bipolar self) and acquire thereby the capacity for a relatively independent self-esteem regulation, for the enjoyment of mental and physical activities, for the free and unencumbered pursuit of ambitions and purposes, and for a healthy striving for power and success. During the oedipal phase, gender-specific developmental strivings emerge and require acceptance and affirmation (in the form of specific mirroring responses and the availability of idealizable oedipal selfobjects) for their internalization and consolidation. What is revived in the transference, however, is a noisy, intensified, and defensively exaggerated form of earlier phase-appropriate infantile or childhood needs, amalgamated with the various maladaptive solutions that have become the hallmark of the personality.

When the patient's mirroring needs and demands are not met with an empathic understanding of their meaning and sources, the mirror transference may become painfully disrupted, with the consequence of a transient enfeeblement or fragmentation of the self, leading to a variety of desperate efforts to stem the tide of further disorganization, including narcissistic rage.

Larry's transference appears to have been a "thwarted mirror transference" that manifested itself in such a bizarre fashion (via his masochistically elaborated amputation fantasies) that the therapist could not engage it interpretively. Frustrations in the treatment process provoked Larry's efforts at infecting or otherwise damaging his leg to force the amputation and thereby extract his therapist-father's love and compassion. But perhaps an added problem throughout the 20 years of prior psychotherapy was that Larry could not remobilize his earlier thwarted idealizations of his father, which together with his bizarrely revived mirroring needs might have given him a better chance at recovery.

Peter exemplified the episodic eruption of a narcissistic rage, especially during the initial period of his hospitalization, when he tried to establish a mirror transference, which remained interpretively unengaged. His behavior (and attire) expressed his intense longing for the recognition of his specialness, which then receded in favor of idealizing his therapist. Perhaps the remobilization of the latter helped him in his recovery.

Mary had similarly tried to elicit her environment's and her therapist's acceptance, love, and admiration. In her case, too, this was not adequately apprehended, leading to emergence of her erotized longings for the therapist. She too was struggling to establish a mirror transference in vain, and when her erotized efforts also failed, she retreated more and more into her fantasies. Thus, neither Peter nor Mary were able to revive what would have been the pathognomonic transference in their respective cases—the mirror transference that expressed their deepest self-pathology. But, as is true in all four index cases, the severity of their self-pathology was an expression of deficits in both poles of the bipolar self. Peter and Mary compensatorily shifted to the revival of their idealizing needs, hoping these would be engaged and fare better than their efforts at eliciting the mirroring responses from their therapists.

The *idealizing transference* (arising out of the archaic idealized parental imago searching for its idealized selfobject) also represents the remobilization of early infantile and childhood developmental needs, parallel to, but beginning later than, the mirroring needs. *Idealizing* is also an evocative, global term for a variety of subtle and complex emotional needs of the human infant, needs that never cease, only become transformed in the course of maturation and development into phase-appropriate adult forms (for example, the capacity for enthusiasm and to hold up ideals). Idealizations extend from the calming and soothing power of the mother in earliest infancy to the security that comes from attaching oneself to a powerful, omniscient, omnipotent, perfect other, in relation to whom one expects to acquire these same characteristics. When the parents are available to the growing infant and child as idealizable selfobjects, the functions these idealized selfobjects perform become internalized as self-soothing, self-calming, and drive-channeling capacities. In addition, their perceived power, omniscience, and omnipotence gradually become transformed into internalized values and ideals and form the second pole of the bipolar self.

When the patient's idealizations of the therapist are unempathically rebuffed or the patient's perception of a flaw in the therapist leads to a disappointment in the therapist's power and perfection, the idealizing transference is painfully disrupted. The consequences of such a disruption lead to the manifold failures in self-regulation and to depressions with suicidal ideas or attempts. Various emergency measures are then instituted (which fail in the long run) to reestablish the lost equilibrium (e.g., return to drug taking, overeating, alcoholism, perversions).

Both Peter and Mary exemplify the vicissitudes of a secondary idealizing transference (one that emerges after an effort at establishing a mirror transference fails or after a mirror transference that was sufficiently worked through).

Susan appears to have moved into an idealizing transference to begin with (after a cautious start). In her case, too, the idealizations disintegrated into erotizations and were punctuated by episodes of narcissistic rage, drug taking, verbal attacks on the therapist, and the like. But in the end, Susan retained an idealized image of her former therapist, and she was also able to idealize her husband and child in relation to whom she continued what appears to have been a significant emotional growth.

We have already remarked on the fact that Larry would

have greatly benefited had he been able to revive his massively disappointed idealizations of his father in his psychotherapy experiences. He searched incessantly for the best therapist.

The *twinship transference* is mobilized when innate talents and skills had been thwarted in their unfolding. Kohut suggested that it is in early twinship or alter-ego experiences that innate talents and skills thrive, as creativity often does later in life. Under felicitous developmental circumstances, these skills and talents serve one's ambitions in keeping with one's ideals. When they do so, when there is an unbroken continuum beneath ambitions, skills, and talents and ideals, we may speak of mental health. When the patient's twinship needs and fantasies are inadvertently disappointed, or deliberately frustrated (by pointing out their unrealistic nature), a disruption in the transference will interfere with all manner of performance.

None of the index patients showed this particular transference configuration. Whether Larry's difficulties in pursuing his work as an architect and Mary's inability to keep up with her studies in music would have, under appropriate circumstances, mobilized a twinship transference is a moot question.

On the Nature of Self-pathology

From this brief sketch of the selfobject transferences and the references to the index patients, it should be evident that these are the transferences that can disclose the nature of the self-pathology that gives rise to them.

Patients who develop a mirror transference are usually fixated on their infantile grandiosity. This means that they now expect and often demand, sometimes in rather bizarre ways, the affirming and admiring responses they should have obtained in their infancy and childhood, as the needed nutrients for their developing self. The unavailable or unreliably available mirroring responses lead to a faulty self-esteem regulation. Without an internalized and relatively independent self-esteem regulation, people are easily buffeted about in their daily lives and are prone to feel criticized, hurt, shamed, and humiliated and may even develop a "paranoid stance" vis-à-vis the external world. In addition, they may be unable to enjoy any of their physical or mental activities and complain of emptiness and despair. They are frequently unable to pursue their ambitions or to feel a purpose in life and complain of acting more like lifeless automatons. (Mary especially, but Peter and Larry also showed many of these characteristics.)

Patients who develop an idealizing transference are usually fixated on the idealized parent imago. This means that they now need to put the therapist on a pedestal and merge with his or her greatness and perfection. They feel whole and complete only if they are part of the idealized therapist and need his or her presence at all times. Separations are experienced as excruciatingly painful—"being ripped apart," "made to feel helpless and impotent," as patients frequently put it. Because they are without the capacity for self-calming and self-soothing, they need the therapist's presence as an external self-regulator. They often resort to drug taking to calm or to stimulate themselves and are prone to erotize their relations with things as well as with people, such as in various perversions and addictions. Because they are without internalized values and ideals, they also feel bereft of hope and value and experience their lives painfully as meaningless. (Susan especially, but Mary and Peter also showed many of these characteristics.)

Patients who develop a twinship transference usually show disturbances in the realm of their innate talents, skills, and creativity, which failed to unfold adequately or became seriously hampered because of the unavailability of needed mirroring responses. They are searching for the mirroring of their skills, talents, and thwarted creativity by a therapist they experience as resembling themselves, as their twin or alter ego. Whatever the therapist says or does that feels to them as his or her "insistence on being different," disrupts the transference and leads to transient failures in their performance in general, or in specific skills in particular—thus giving evidence of a "fragmentation" of the performing self. (Perhaps Larry showed the kind of inhibition of his skills and talents that might have given rise to a twinship transference under optimum circumstances.)

In addition to the manifestations of self-pathology indicated here, there are a myriad of phenomenological constellations to which these structural and functional deficits may give rise. Intertwined with the secondary conflicts and defenses these deficits engender, they present a multiplicity of clinical pictures. It is possible to have the major disorder involve only the functions of the pole of ambitions or it may include the functions of the pole of ideals as well, evoking thereby one or both transference constellations.

What these transferences and their working through teach us, among other things, is that "self development . . . is not a matter of taming the drives, but of whether or not the selfobjects respond optimally and phase-specifically to the unfolding, innate potentials and developmental needs. Only in such a climate of optimum responsiveness [or "optimum empathic responsiveness" (A Ornstein and PH Ornstein 1984)] will selfobject functions during development be progressively transformed, through transmuting internalizations, into permanent psychic structures" (PH Ornstein 1982). And only in a climate of optimum responsiveness will a psychoanalytic or psychotherapeutic restoration of the self become possible (Bacal 1985; Ornstein 1988).

We have emphasized thus far that the selfobject transferences reveal the nature of pathogenesis and psychopathology, but they have another fundamental function as well. Once these transferences develop, they offer transient safety, protection, and support to the enfeeblement- and fragmentation-prone self. Clinically, this translates into symptomatic improvement, increased cohesiveness, and vitality of the self, hence an improved overall functioning. The inevitable transference disruptions, however, will temporarily rob the patient of this safety, protection, support, and improvement. The significant therapeutic work will take place in connection with the repair of these disruptions. Stolorow and Lachmann (1984/1985) go even further and rightfully claim that "the transference bond in and of itself can directly promote a process of psychological growth and structure formation" (p. 33). Nevertheless, opportunities for interpretive work regarding the transference disruptions and their repair are considered to be central to the curative process from a self psychological perspective.

On the Psychotherapeutic Process

The following elements of the process of treatment are a requirement of every psychotherapeutic situation. They are so crucial for the treatment of narcissistic and borderline conditions that treatment quickly founders or becomes interminable without careful and ongoing attention to them. These were the principles that guided our scrutiny of the treatment of the index cases.

1. The creation of a climate of safety and the engagement of the patient in his or her treatment experience is a sine qua non for self psychologically informed psychoanalytic psychotherapy, and it is thus the first order of business in any therapeutic encounter. Safety is aimed at and progressively achieved by creating an unbiased, nonjudgmental, and noncondemning climate of acceptance of whatever the patient brings to the therapeutic situation. Engagement is aimed at and also progressively achieved by listening for the patient's subjective experiences from the empathic vantage point (i.e., putting oneself imaginatively in the center of the patient's inner world) and repeatedly reflecting back to him or her what one has heard and tentatively understood. "Making contact with these subjective experiences and continually reflecting back what the therapist tentatively understands, is the key to engaging the patient in the treatment process. As a result of such an engagement the patient's communications are 'enlivened'; [the patient] experiences what he/she reports as his/her own and not only talks about them, as if the experiences no longer had emotional signifi-

cance for him/her. Such an enlivened, affect-laden, account of experiences is thus both the result and indication of a [successful] therapeutic engagement" (A Ornstein and PH Ornstein 1984, p. 5). Safety and engagement remain central issues throughout the treatment process.

2. "From such an engagement, [once achieved and maintained] patient and therapist can then move toward an ever more comprehensive *understanding* of the patient's communications.... It is only from the platform of a solidly established understanding of the patient's subjective experiences that the therapist can move on further to *explaining* these experiences in terms of their dynamic interplay and genetic context. It is for these reasons that we speak of the two steps in the interpretive process—understanding and explaining" [italics added] (A Ornstein and PH Ornstein 1984, p. 6; see also PH Ornstein and A Ornstein 1985).

Understanding and explaining the patient's subjective experiences is an ongoing process throughout the therapy, but it is especially focused on the experiences of the disruption of the therapist-patient relationship, especially the transference. It is at times of such disruption that the patient's sensitivity to particular precipitating circumstances reveals the nature of the vulnerability of the self. Reconstructing what just happened in the treatment process goes a long way toward accomplishing the repair of the disruption. The work of reconstructing the immediate circumstances of the disruption usually leads the patient to recall earlier infantile or childhood antecedents of the specific traumata that created the chronic vulnerability the therapist inadvertently activated. The patient's reaction to the therapist's unempathic interventions thus repeats in the here and now the pathogenic traumata of infancy and childhood, offering patient and therapist an on-the-spot demonstration of the specific nature of the self-pathology involved as well as an opportunity for its experiential and interpretive repair.

It is thus the combination of safety and emotional engagement in the treatment process and the repair of the inevitable disruptions of the relationship (especially the transference) via the two steps of understanding and explaining that characterize the psychotherapy of self-pathology.

References

Bacal HA: Optimal responsiveness and the therapeutic process, in Progress in Self Psychology, Vol 1. Edited by Goldberg A. New York, Guilford, 1985, pp 202–227

Basch MF: Doing Psychotherapy. New York, Basic Books, 1980

Basch MF: Selfobject disorders and psychoanalytic theory: a historical perspective. Psychoanal Assoc 29:337–353, 1981

Basch MF: Understanding Psychotherapy: The Science Behind the Art. New York, Basic Books, 1988

Elson M (ed): The Kohut Seminars: On Self Psychology and Psychotherapy With Adolescents and Young Adults. New York, WW Norton, 1987

Kohut H: Introspection, empathy and psychoanalysis. J Am Psychoanal Assoc 7:459–483, 1959

Kohut H: Forms and transformations of narcissism. J Am Psychoanal Assoc 14:243–272, 1966

Kohut H: The psychoanalytic treatment of narcissistic personality disorders. Psychoanal Study Child 23:86–113, 1968

Kohut H: The Analysis of the Self: A Systematic Approach to the Psychoanalytic Treatment of Narcissistic Personality Disorders. New York, International Universities Press, 1971

Kohut H: The Restoration of the Self. New York, International Universities Press, 1977

Kohut H: How Does Analysis Cure? Chicago, IL, University of Chicago Press, 1984

Kohut H, Wolf ES: The disorders of the self and their treatment. Int J Psychoanal 59:413–425, 1978

Muslin HL, Val ER: The Psychotherapy of the Self. New York, Brunner/Mazel, 1987

Ornstein A: The dread to repeat and the new beginning: a contribution to the psychoanalytic treatment of narcissistic personality disorders, in The Annual of Psychoanalysis, Vol 2. New York, International Universities Press, 1974, pp 231–248

Ornstein A: An idealizing transference of the oedipal phase, in Reflections on Self Psychology. Edited by Lichtenberg J, Kaplan S. Hillsdale, NJ, Analytic Press, 1983, pp 135–161

Ornstein A: Psychoanalytic psychotherapy: a contemporary perspective, in Kohut's Legacy: Contributions to Self Psychology. Edited by Stepansky PE, Goldberg A. Hillsdale, NJ, Analytic Press, 1984, pp 171–181

Ornstein A, Ornstein PH: Empathy and the therapeutic dialogue. Paper presented at the 5th annual psychotherapy symposium on "Psychotherapy: The Therapeutic Dialogue," Harvard University, The Cambridge Hospital, Boston, MA, June 28–30, 1984

Ornstein A, Ornstein PH: Parenting as a function of the adult self: a psychoanalytic developmental perspective, in Parental Influences in Health and Disease. Edited by Anthony EJ, Pollock G. Boston MA, Little, Brown, 1985, pp 181–231

Ornstein PH: On narcissism beyond the introduction, highlights of Heinz Kohut's contributions to the psychoanalytic treatment of narcissistic personality disorders, in The Annual of Psychoanalysis, Vol 2. New York, International Universities Press, 1974, pp 127–149

Ornstein PH: Vitality and relevance of psychoanalytic psychotherapy. Compr Psychiatry 16:503–516, 1975

Ornstein PH: Remarks on the central position of empathy in psychoanalysis. Bulletin of The Association for Psychoanalytic Medicine 18:95–105, 1979

Ornstein PH: The bipolar self in the psychoanalytic treatment process. Psychoanal Assoc 29:353–375, 1981

Ornstein PH: On the psychoanalytic psychotherapy of primary self pathology, in Psychiatry 1982: The American Psychiatric Association Annual Review, Vol 1. Edited by

Grinspoon L. Washington, DC, American Psychiatric Press, 1982, pp 492–510

Ornstein PH: Some curative factors and processes in the psychoanalytic psychotherapies, in Cures by Psychotherapy: What Effects Change? Edited by Myers JM. Praeger, 1984, pp 55–65

Ornstein PH: The thwarted need to grow: clinical-theoretical issues in the selfobject transferences, in The Transference in Psychotherapy: Clinical Management. Edited by Schwaber EA. New York, International Universities Press, 1985, pp 33–49

Ornstein PH: Multiple curative factors and processes in the psychoanalytic psychotherapies, in How Does Treatment Help? On the Modes of Therapeutic Action of Psychoanalytic Psychotherapy (Monograph 4, Workshop Series of the American Psychoanalytic Association). Edited by Rothstein A. Madison, CT, International Universities Press, 1988

Ornstein PH, Ornstein A: On the continuing evolution of psychoanalytic psychotherapy: reflections and predictions, in The Annual of Psychoanalysis, Vol 5. New York, International Universities Press, 1976, pp 329–370

Ornstein PH, Ornstein A: Clinical understanding and explaining: the empathic vantage point, in Progress in Self Psychology, Vol 1. New York, Guilford, 1985, pp 43–61

Ornstein PH, Ornstein A: The functional integrity of the self: understanding its disintegration products. Psychiatric Annals 16:486–488, 1986

Stepansky PE, Goldberg A (eds): Kohut's Legacy: Contributions to Self Psychology. Hillsdale, NJ, Analytic Press, 1984

Stolorow RD, Lachmann FM: Transference: the future of an illusion, in The Annual of Psychoanalysis, Vol 12/13. New York, International Universities Press, 1984/1985, pp 19–37

Stolorow RD, Brandchaft B, Atwood GE: Psychoanalytic

Treatment: An Intersubjective Approach. Hillsdale, NJ, Analytic Press, 1987

White MT, Weiner MB: The Theory and Practice of Self Psychology. New York, Brunner/Mazel, 1986

Wolf ES: Treating the Self: Elements of Clinical Self Psychology. New York, Guilford, 1988